The Clock of Paradise
and Other Stories

Patrick M. Butler

ISBN: 978-1-941066-27-0

Book design
by Jo-Anne Rosen

Cover illustration
by Annette Matrisciano

Cover lettering
by Richard Olson

Wordrunner Press
Petaluma, California
www.wordrunner.com/publish

This book is dedicated to all the women in my life
who have made it such a great adventure
— most especially to my wife

Antoinette Lee Butler

and my daughter

Erin Marie Butler

Foreword

In my next life I'd like to be a writer. I've always admired those who are able to pull it off. Of course, I'll have to request the heart and voice for the profession prior to my return. In this current life I have occasionally taken pen in hand by way of practicing for my future career. A few short stories and songs are all I have to show for it. But with the encouragement of my wife Antoinette I have assembled a number of them in a book for friends and family. It has been a fun project, a project facilitated by a fortuitous reconnection with Jo-Anne Rosen, a friend I had not seen for nearly 40 years. She is a talented, published author in her own right; but also a publisher, editor, and book designer. Without her assistance these stories, for better or worse, would not have seen the light of day. In addition, I have included the lyrics of several songs. Sometime a story and a song have been drawn from the same well, though usually with very different results. When that has happened, the lyrics follow the story with which it shared the bucket.

Contents

Some of the stories in this collection were previously published or honored in the following journals:

"The Clock of Paradise," *Narrative* Story of the Week
(www.narrativemagazine.com/issues/stories-week-2015-2016/story-week/
clock-paradise-patrick-m-butler)

"River Women," *Witches & Pagans,* Issue 35, Winter 2018
http://pagansquare.tumblr.com/post/171111497386/
witchespagans-35-natural-paganism-this

"Pavane," finalist in *Narrative* Winter 2016 short story contest.

The Clock of Paradise
and Other Stories

The Clock of Paradise

There are, presumably, no clocks in paradise. But if there were, I should imagine they would least resemble the factory punch clock — that scourge of the working class. Yet Mademoiselle Conlin, who rented old Monsieur Pavot's place in the village last spring, was apparently of another mind.

Many of us found some excuse to pass by the cottage the day she moved in. Word had gotten out several weeks earlier that an American painter would be taking over the place. Crated canvases and other supplies had been arriving for some time from the United States and stacked for all to see in the single room that serves as the village post office. Betsy Conlin, the addressee, had instantly become the principal subject of café gossip. That an American artist, who some said enjoyed a considerable reputation, had chosen our village as a place to live and work was a source of pride, if not a little astonishment, to us all.

Those who caught a glimpse of her that first day reported that the new arrival was young, mid-twenties perhaps, and quite pretty. As we had no prior information concerning Mlle. Conlin she could as well have been young as old, attractive as plain. Yet her youth and good looks seemed to have caught most by surprise to judge from the talk in the café that afternoon.

I did not meet her until several days later. She was indeed pretty and I remember in particular her open manner and excellent French spoken with a touch of the Parisian accent. She had stopped by the second-hand shop I still keep open a few days a week to introduce herself and to admire a clock that she had seen through the window. It was something I had acquired for a few francs years earlier when the old foundry at Evreux was razed and the equipment sold off. The case was of plain, sturdy oak and about a meter in height. Just below the pendulum was a slot into which several generations of overall-clad workmen had slipped their time cards. When a lever was pulled the card was stamped with the day and hour. At the same time an alarm-like bell rang out from somewhere inside the mechanism, with a loud and piercing authority, as if to equate in gravity a worker's tardy arrival and a factory in flames. More than once a customer had used it to summon me from an afternoon's slumber in the back room. I had placed the clock at one end of the counter and, wound every three days, it kept good time for the next ten years. When it finally quit running, the day of my sixty-fifth birthday as it happened, I drove to Lisieux and bought my first wristwatch.

"Why, it's just like the one in that Charlie Chaplin film," she said, moving her hand across its face. "Does it still work?"

"No, not for a year now. I just never got around to carting it to the back room."

She hesitated a moment, never taking her eyes off the clock. "Would you sell it to me, Monsieur?"

She seemed somehow moved by the old relic. "But, Mademoiselle, it's of no use to anyone. It doesn't keep time. And there used to be a loud bell that would ring when a card was stamped. Even that doesn't work anymore."

She continued to gaze at the clock and replied softly, "Perhaps I could have it repaired." Then she turned to look at me and I could see that she was blushing. "Oh, I beg your pardon, Monsieur," she said. "I should not have insisted." I told her I'd be happy to give her the clock and she returned that afternoon in an old Citroen to pick it up.

Towards the middle of the next week, hearing an automobile on the loose gravel in front of the shop, I glanced up to see that the car had been completely transformed. She had painted flowers and ferns and thick, creeping vines over the entire body. The wild and limpid eyes of animals peered out from the dense foliage. I would have guessed it to be some kind of publicity vehicle for an itinerant circus had not Mlle. Conlin immediately alighted with a package under her arm. She wore a black cotton skirt fringed with embroidered flowers, a knitted sweater of a dozen colors, and shoes of red felt. With sparkling eyes and black beret she looked like a denizen of the jungle from which she had just emerged.

"Good morning, Monsieur Klein. I have something for you." She placed her package on the counter with a smile and her manner suggested that she would not be leaving until I had opened it.

A couple of tugs at the paper and I found myself looking at a most unusual painting. I remember feeling slightly uncomfortable, not really knowing what to make of it. The old clock was floating, Chagall-like, in a blue sky above gabled roofs and chimneys. Around it swirled dozens of time-cards, some painted in such detail that days and times were clearly visible. Looking carefully at the top of one of these cards I could just make out the small face of a clock encircled with the words *L'Horloge du Paradis*, The Clock of Paradise. If I missed the sense of the painting, I was nevertheless touched by this unexpected gesture and I thanked her for the gift, hoping that she had not detected my initial uneasiness.

I do not know whether Mlle. Conlin's painting is of any great merit. She was not the famous painter rumor had made of her nor did she pretend to be. Painting was simply an avocation, her *violon d'Ingres*, she said, and she had come to the French countryside to paint a little at the suggestion of her teacher. Her choice of our village for this purpose we put down to the eccentricity of the artist for which the evidence was abundant.

Nearly everything about her contrasted with the drab routine of rural life. In Paris she might have passed unnoticed, but here her style of dress, her car, her friendliness, all at first led to wide-eyed wonder among the very young, who were instantly drawn to her, and to the amusement of their parents. The old folks, most of whom have farmed here for fifty years or more, smiled shy, toothless grins but came around soon enough. Of course, as a painter and as an American she enjoyed a certain indulgence that would not have been so readily accorded to, say, a feed merchant from Nantes. She addressed everyone except the very old with the familiar *tu* after an acquaintance of five minutes. Yet, in the end, it was her exuberant good will that opened all doors of the village to her.

Her own door, quite literally, stood open to all comers as well. Indeed, she never closed it except at night or in inclement weather. From early morning until dark every door and window of the cottage remained wide open, even when she went to the university some fifty kilometers distant for a weekly painting class. Her neighbors were somewhat scandalized by this, as if it were a reproof of their own obsession with privacy. But I think the open cottage stood as a kind of metaphor for what she wanted out of life. She wished to capture each smell, the slightest breeze, the faintest sound. For her, the cost of privacy came too high.

༺

Two months after her arrival a young man began to visit the cottage quite regularly. He too was a painter and they could often be seen in the countryside with their easels perched in fields of sugar beets and ripening corn. That this new friendship could go unremarked in a small village like ours was, of course, not possible and the fact that his automobile often remained in front of the house throughout the night was the subject of good-natured conversation at the café. If the farmers, after their jug of new Beaujolais, were inclined to jocularity in the matter, they were nevertheless moved by a solicitous regard for Mlle. Conlin. Their concern might be expressed in mirthful conjecture as to whether the young man, whom we assumed to be from the university, had enough of the French earth still in him not to discredit the fatherland. But it was motivated by the sincere conviction that this American was entitled to the best we had to offer.

We are aware that times have changed. Though unprecedented in the village, Mlle. Conlin's relationship was accepted in the broader context of the modern world and its current generation. In fact, I think we rather liked the idea. Gently, even innocently, she made us feel less of an isolated backwater. She added a bit of spice, as they say.

This is not to say there were no problems. It was old Madame Noyon, a woman not known for her *delicatesse*, who first told me of the awkward situation. As it happened, Mlle. Conlin and her friend often made love on returning from their afternoon painting forays into the countryside. The sounds of their amorous play were neither constrained by any inhibitions of their own nor confined by shuttered windows or closed doors. Parents in the immediate vicinity of the cottage deemed it prudent, she said, to keep their children indoors at such times. Apparently no one was willing to take up the matter with Mlle. Conlin — I presume this included even the redoubtable Mme. Noyon — but something would have to be done, she continued, for it really was going too far. Then she told me the most extraordinary thing. It seems the signal that it was safe to allow the children out-of-doors again was the sound of a bell rung in the cottage. God only knew what it was about, she said, and she had taken to crossing herself at the sound.

It was with the greatest difficulty that I managed to conceal my amusement for I was fairly sure that God was not the sole guardian of this mystery. The old clock must have been repaired after all. And I was certain that Mme. Noyon would have held me guilty in the affair had she known my own small part in it. For my sake, then, as well as for that of Mlle. Conlin, I did not betray her secret.

Lienard, the postman, who bicycled to the cottage daily and often dropped off small packages from the United States, later told me that one wall of the entryway was decorated in what he thought a most original manner. A private man, not given to gossip, he would not otherwise have mentioned it. Small cards on which one could make out the face of a clock and a series of days and times — a card for every week, he said — were cleverly positioned along the wall. The arrangement was regularly altered as new cards were added. When, after many visits, he had finally inquired into their significance, Mlle. Conlin explained that the times recorded on each card represented the happiest moments of that week. She placed the cards where she would often see them so that she would never forget those joys no matter how many trivial annoyances crowded her day. Monsieur Lienard asked no further questions, quite satisfied with a response he found altogether charming.

When spring came again, Mlle. Conlin made the rounds of the village, embracing all and making her goodbyes. The clock and her other belongings were crated and taken to the station in Evreux. Mme. Noyon's little scandal never amounted to much for with the onset of the winter weather Mlle. Conlin had been forced to keep the doors and windows closed. She is missed here and we still call her cottage *La Sorciere*, the name she gave it.

I have not displayed her painting of the clock. It rests in an old armoire in the storeroom. Yet I like to search it out now and then. It takes me back many years to a time when I too found much joy in life's extravagance. It has me thinking a lot about those days. I would not wish to forget them either.

Field Officer of the Preobrazhensky Regiment

West 86ᵗʰ Street Time Machine

*T*wo days ago there were still those who went about saying that
Peter was a false Tsar, perhaps the Anti-Christ himself. But
then, just as the hour of three was being struck, two long, thin clouds
joined in the form of a cross above our village. It was a Friday according to the new reckoning. Marina, the serf girl, was the first to
see it. She fell to her knees and crossed herself, then ran to tell the
priest, my father. If he was drunk, as usual, he was nevertheless
quick to realize how he could use this "sign". Were the rumblings
of those who opposed the Tsar to go unchecked, the soldiers would
soon be set upon our village to leave behind the smoldering remains
of peasant huts and bodies swaying from scaffolds. So I was ordered
to toll the bell which summons the peasants to the village square
where my father put them on their knees in witness to this miracle.
Such a voice he had!

"Shall God waste this sign upon your ignorance? Let him who
has eyes in his head understand. The great Tsar has ordained a
new calendar and has not God in heaven put His seal upon it? Is
it not the day and hour of His son's sacrifice? Prostrate yourselves,
fools! Bloody your heads upon the stones and ask pardon of the
Little Father that he might spare us."

He was magnificent, my father. The peasants craned their necks
like silly geese and groaned their astonishment to the sky. And you
should have heard his sermon today!

"Is it not enough," he roared from the gate of the iconostasis,
"is it not enough for the great Tsar to lift his finger that the Lord

of the universe acknowledges him? Has not his sacred person been set over you by God himself? Who will question it now?"

Each of these interrogations flew like a great gust of wind against the faithful who shuffled nervously in their felt boots.

"Fall on your knees," my father bellowed with a force that sent his hat flying. "Bow your stupid heads and thank our father in heaven who has sent you this sign before visiting his wrath upon you." And, as one, the peasants fell to the floor and implored forgiveness for their great sin.

In truth, my father hates Peter. But he is no fool. And now he has saved our village.

"Rest now, Dedushka. We'll bring you your tea after you've had a little rest." Svetlana looked nervously at Michael rather than her grandfather who was nearly blind and lost to another world. Or to another century. At the sound of her voice, Nikolai Sergeyevich relaxed against the pillows. The excitement which had animated his features in the retelling of these events sunk back into his face. He was ninety now, and the ancient skin sagged from his cheekbones like canvas from a tent pole.

"That was amazing," Michael said when she shut the door behind them. "When he talks it's like Chekhov or something." Svetlana had tried to prepare him for this first meeting with her grandfather but he had not anticipated such a robust, such a convincing performance.

"He's not always like that," she said, putting on the kettle. "Sometimes he knows who I am and we'll talk about Mama and the old days. But ever since she died he's more and more like you just saw him. He lives in a history book and you never know what page you're going to find him on."

"You mean that little scene just now, it's not always...?"

"Oh, no. He's all over the place. Sometimes he's a monk, or one of Catherine's courtiers. You never know. Anything but a Bolshevik. He's consistent though. He keeps coming back to the same roles. Like in the one you saw, his father is a priest in some village up near where Peter is building the new capital. The Tsar has just imposed the new calendar and the peasants are scandalized and resisting the changed dates of their cherished holy days. And Marina, that's me, I was owned by a brute who nearly beat me to death for stealing a little bread from his kitchen. When the priest reported it to the magistrate I was taken away and sent to live in the priest's house. His son, well, Dedushka, has been making passes at me."

"I don't believe this!"

Svetlana laughed. "Don't worry. I can handle it. Actually it's one of my favorite roles. I'm also a princess, one of Catherine's ladies in waiting, but that one's boring. Then, under Nicholas the First he's a retired cavalry office and I'm his daughter. He even calls me by my real name. I like that one. When Alexander II is assassinated he's a Narodnik, a revolutionary, and I'm his girlfriend or wife. I'm never sure."

Michael was shocked at Svetlana's complicity in her grandfather's delusions. Shouldn't the old man be looked after professionally, a nursing home maybe? Yet he was fascinated, too, by the scene he had just witnessed. "It's incredible," he said. "And, you know, it's like he was talking to me back there."

"Well, he was," Svetlana replied. "Yours is the first male voice he's heard for months. He must have thought you were some stranger passing through his village. He was happy, couldn't you tell? Someone new to listen how his father saved everybody from the 'Tsar's wrath'! Do you know how many times I've heard that story?"

The two of them spoke English, but with Nikolai Sergeyevich it was Russian. Michael had been an exchange student in Russia and spoke the language fluently. He and Svetlana met at an Eisenstein film festival at Columbia where Michael was finishing up his PhD in chemistry. He was attracted by the delicate, Slavic whiteness of her skin, and by hair and eyes as black and glassy as obsidian. He liked her from the start, though he was determined not to let it go any further than that. He wasn't about to go crazy over a girl whose life belonged to a bed-ridden old man. After the film, when he'd invited Svetlana for a cup of coffee and then accompanied her as far as her flat on West 86th Street, she'd told him that she wasn't free to have a life of her own. Looking after her grandfather took up all of her time except for the one day a week when she could afford to have a nurse in to care for him. She said this matter-of-factly, without a trace of self-pity, as if giving Michael absolution if he never wanted to see her again. Yet he caught her studying his face for a hint that she might be wrong this time, that, with him, it might be different. He asked for her phone number. There was something special about this girl. And, in spite of his reservations, within a couple of months they had become lovers.

But even then there was always something held back. Michael was careful not to give the impression that this was anything more than a friendship "with benefits", as his friends would say. There was the occasional twinge of conscience but, at this point in his life, the only relationship he was ready for was one with an easy out.

"Michael," Svetlana wanted to know as she readied the tea tray, "how did they call you in Russia?"

"Misha, usually."

"That's nice. Misha. I like that. Could I, you know, with Dedushka, could I call you Misha?"

"Sure."

"Will you take tea with Dedushka and me?"

Michael felt compromised by this new intimacy. But he was gallant. "I should be honored to take tea with the lady who helps the Empress out of her garters."

Nikolai Sergeyevich's bed was one of those darkly finished things you see in second-hand furniture stores. Heavy, urn-like lamps flanking the headboard looked as if they had long ago sunk roots into the matching nightstands. This was the solid symmetry that framed the invalid in Michael's vision as his eyes adjusted to the dim light of the sickroom. Svetlana pulled up two straight backed chairs at her grandfather's side. He was still sitting up, and speaking now with a lucidity that took Michael by surprise. He was back in the 21st century, in his comfortable New York flat, and perfectly aware of their presence. What was Michael studying, he wanted to know. What were his plans for the future. He seemed to assume that Michael was something more than just a casual friend of his grand-daughter's.

Svetlana fidgeted with her teacup.

"Aren't you tired, Dedushka?" she asked after some twenty minutes of this. "You should sleep a little now." The fragile, tender features of the old man relaxed as he closed his eyes and leaned into the pillows. Svetlana took Michael's arm and led him to the door. But she had not yet stepped into the hall when suddenly an authoritative voice was summoning the two of them back into the room's dark interior. Michal froze.

"Just one more minute," Svetlana said softly. "Please, Michael. I'll know what to do."

"Young man, what is your family's name?"

Michael was stunned. What was this craziness? And who was his interrogator? A monk, a soldier, a Narodnik? But

Svetlana was behind him, whispering in his ear. "Don't be angry, Michael. Tell him Kerensky, anything. No, wait. Tell him Orlov."

Feeling foolish and trapped, Michael did as he was told.

"An honored name, sir! To which regiment are you posted?"

"The Semyonovsky," came the voice at Michael's ear.

"The Semyonovsky?" Michael said.

"Very good. Excellent. Excellent! I myself served with the Preobrazhensky in the Caucasus. Now I should like to ask you, sir, about the condition of your family's estate. How many souls have you?"

"Sir," Michael stumbled, "I don't know... how many what?"

"Father, please!" Svetlana strode quickly to her grandfather's bedside. "It is not proper that you should speak of these things in my presence, and as if Mikhail Maximilianovich had asked for my hand! I am deeply embarrassed and ask your permission to leave the room." Michael stared helplessly at the two of them. It was as if he had been dropped suddenly into the middle of a Russian play. The actors improvised around him, contriving his role. There was something close to panic in his eyes.

"Dearest one, my love." The voice was tender now. "Do not be offended. You shall break my heart. You are right. Kiss me. A ridiculous old man begs pardon of you both. Mikhail Maximilianovich, give me your hand. Forgive me. I know you are a gentleman and your intentions honorable. Good day to you. Come see me again soon. We shall talk of soldiering, you and I. Good day to you both."

Svetlana was on the verge of tears as she closed the door. Michael put his arm around her. They walked silently to the kitchen where she put on the kettle again. Then they sat and looked at one another across the plastic top of the kitchen table.

"Michael," Svetlana blurted, "I'm sorry. I can imagine what you're thinking. You can leave if you want. I wouldn't blame you."

Michael was certain, and relieved, that Svetlana could *not* know what he was thinking. He had been assessing, with some discomfort, the ethical slippage of the last two hundred years. He was not, most decidedly, the worthy gentleman of honorable intentions the old man had addressed as his potential son-in-law. And so he preferred to direct the conversation back to Nikolai Sergeyevich and away from the choice Svetlana's words implied. "Couldn't someone help him?" he asked. "I mean, he seemed so normal there for a while."

Svetlana hesitated for a moment. A thought vanished behind a long blink of her eyes. Then she answered. "But, why, Michael? He's happy whatever century he's in. Besides, I like him just as he is. It makes all this easier, somehow."

"But he's not in his right mind."

"Michael, he sees clouds in the sky instead of a dusty light fixture above his head."

"But..." Michael did not complete his sentence. He felt again like the odd man in the play. But he was moved, too, even shamed, by Svetlana's selfless, playful devotion to her grandfather.

Neither spoke. Both were miserable. Michael turned clumsily in his chair and knocked his half-full teacup to the floor. Almost with relief they scrambled for paper towels. Then, on their knees, under the table, Michael began to laugh.

"Mikhail *Petrovich*," he howled.

"How was I supposed to know your father's name?" She wadded up her wet towel and threw it at him. He ducked and it splattered against the wall.

"I can hardly pronounce Maximilianovich," he said.

Then they embraced on the kitchen floor as the tension dissipated in Svetlana's tears and Michael's laughter. Finally he caressed her cheek and said, "I just have one question. What are souls?"

"That's what they used to call the serfs," Svetlana sniffled. "Dedushka wanted to know how many serfs you owned."

"Serfs?" Michael said. "I don't even own a pair of socks without holes."

Svetlana smiled. Then she reached up to touch his face. "I love you, Misha," she said.

Until now these words had never been spoken. Svetlana, in her delicacy, and Michael, in his stubbornness, followed a convention which precluded the verbal intimacies. Now Michael heard the expression of Svetlana's love for the first time. And something strange happened. Not that he recognized in that instant his own love for Svetlana. He was not so obtuse. Reservations aside, he had probably loved her from the day they first met. What happened, simply, was that Michael suddenly wished to be worthy of Svetlana's love, given to him as generously as it was to her grandfather. And worthy too of the chivalrous standards of the old man who had addressed him, Michael, grad student of questionable principles, as an officer of the Tsar's own regiment and, yes, as a gentleman. "I love you, too" he heard himself say. He felt as if he had stepped across the chalk line of a children's game scratched on the sidewalk. And, like a child, he sensed the thrill of no longer being in control of the situation. Svetlana smiled again and held him tightly.

After that Michael had three names: he was Michael to his friends, Misha to Svetlana, and Mikhail Maximilianovich to her grandfather. The old man occasionally greeted him as Michael and inquired about his studies. But more often than not it was as Captain Mikhail Maximilianovich Orlov of the Semyonovsky Regiment, fellow soldier, and prospective son-in-law. Michael came every day to visit with him. The time they spent together became the high point of the old man's day. Svetlana had to brush his hair and put a little vodka on the nightstand before the arrival of his visitor.

For his part, Michael had gone to the library and checked out everything he could find on the reign of Nicholas I. He managed to put together a rather good picture of the life of a young, aristocratic Guards' officer. He got so thoroughly into the role that Svetlana teased him one afternoon saying she didn't know who was crazier, Michael or her grandfather.

His thesis was on the back burner now but it didn't matter much. The data had been collected and the analysis was far enough along to know that it was going to turn out all right. He could afford to ease off a bit. So he filled his days with playing soldier, reading history, helping Svetlana with the housework and shopping. He generally spent the night at the West 86th Street flat. He would sometimes joke with Svetlana and address her formally in Russian as if she really were a lady and he a dashing officer of the Guards. She'd laugh and tell him to take it easy. She had no intention of looking after two lunatics.

In time, Michael's presence in the house somewhat altered Svetlana's relationship with her grandfather. The change made her irritable, even resentful on occasion. Now, whenever the old man reverted to the past, he invariably assumed the identity of Colonel Kalinin of the Preobrazhensky, retired, whose daughter was courted by his fellow officer and friend, Captain Orlov. Svetlana was excluded, however gently, from the hearty male ambience the two men created in the sickroom. When she entered, sentences were cut short and she was greeted with an exaggerated, patronizing civility. She was a lady now, no longer the saucy serf girl or liberated daughter of the revolution. She said that if Michael kissed her hand once more she'd slap him with it.

One day Michael noticed that Nikolai Sergeyevich seemed to lose consciousness for several minutes and slurred his words when he was finally able to continue speaking. A week later it happened again and Svetlana summoned a doctor who had treated her grandfather several times before. He told them that the old man could go at any moment and, at best, probably had no more than six months yet to live. Svetlana took the news better than Michael. He wanted to get another opinion, to call in a specialist. "No," she said. "He would suffer in a hospital. Can't you see how happy he is here with us? With you?"

Svetlana said nothing to her grandfather but he knew well enough that he was dying, even if he now lived more or less permanently during the reign of Nicholas I. The day after the doctor's visit he was particularly anxious, he told his "daughter", that Captain Orlov come to see him at the regular hour. "You needn't worry, father. He always comes."

When Michael entered the room the old man struggled to sit up as straight as possible. "Captain Orlov," he asked, "may I address you with the familiar form, even as my own son?"

"Surely, sir. You honor me."

"Then I should like to speak with you on a very personal matter. With your permission, of course."

"Certainly, Nikolai Sergeyevich."

"Do you love my daughter?"

"You know that I do, sir."

"I once spoke indelicately on this subject, but now I open my heart to you. I am a dying man, Mikhail Maximilianovich.

Before my death I should like to see my daughter married to a gentleman who will love her as I always have, more than life itself. If that is your intention, will you grant your fellow officer his dying wish?"

Michael placed his hand on the old man's shoulder. "Colonel Kalinin, I shall be proud to call you father."

Nikolai Sergeyevich smiled broadly. "Then let us call the bride."

Michael found her mopping the kitchen floor.

"Come on," he said, "we're getting married."

Svetlana turned and glared at him. "You're crazy. Leave me alone."

Michael picked her up and carried her kicking to her grandfather's bedside.

"Father," he said, "the lady protests."

"I think not," said the old soldier. "Svetlana Nikolayevna, I have given your hand in marriage to Captain Orlov of the Semyonovsky. What say you?"

Svetlana blushed deeply and turned her eyes to the floor. "Dearest father," she replied, "as in all things, I obey you."

And so Michael and Svetlana were married. Except for a brief civil ceremony they never bothered to make it more formal than that. Nikolai Sergeyevich, as expected, died within the year. But the sadness that his passing brought to the West 86th Street flat was soon mitigated by the birth of Michael and Svetlana's first child. Little Nick, named after his great-grandfather, liked to play with dinosaurs and dreamed of flying in space ships.

Pavane

According to the owner's manual, the cutting drum of Hartley's joiner spins at 3,600 RPM. It's fitted with three razor sharp blades so something like 10,800 slivers per minute are shaved from a board passed across its surface. More to the point, during the approximately one-half second the index finger of his neighbor's right hand was pressed against it, the drum removed ninety fragments of bone, fingernail, and tissue from that appendage. In all, it added up to about an inch.

They had been working in different parts of the garage when the machine's whirring ended abruptly in a sickening thump. Though his neighbor made no sound, Hartley knew without looking what had happened — as if, unconsciously perhaps, he had been waiting for this. So he dashed into the house and grabbed a towel from the linen closet. By the time he got back, Bokelman appeared to be in shock. He just stood there looking at his mangled hand, his pale, flaccid face registering only mild surprise. The joiner was growling furiously again, like a tiger whose appetite has been whetted for human flesh. Hartley flipped the switch and wrapped Bokelman's hand in the towel. Then he led him to his car which was parked in the driveway.

On their way to Harbor View Emergency, Bokelman talked about how bad the traffic was getting and what he was going to fix for dinner that evening. He was shivering and his face was as white and grainy as a peeled potato. Hartley thought he was going to pass out. But he made it. There was that soft, passive strength of fat people in him.

At emergency they whisked him off to an operating room while Hartley gave a bored girl at the reception desk what little information he knew about the patient. The man's name was Eugene Bokelman, he said. Middle sixties, maybe. No, it wasn't a work-related accident. Bokelman had just come over to his place to plane some boards he was making into picture frames. Yes, Hartley did have liability insurance but he presumed that Bokelman was covered by Medicare or some kind of insurance of his own.

This done, Hartley took a seat in the waiting room. The place was filled with people exhausted from the effort of holding in pain or fear, or both. Most were alone, slouching low in their chairs, eyes shut against the bleakness of linoleum and fluorescent lighting. Only the throbbing of an ancient soft-drink machine broke the silence. Hartley flipped through the grimy pages of a hot rod magazine, then through a couple of old Sports Illustrated issues. After half an hour he walked to the reception desk and called his wife. She'd been out shopping when the accident happened. "My god!" she said, "we don't even know the poor man."

This was true, despite the fact that there was but a single house between their two residences. The Hartleys had come to Seattle the previous year when Mr. Hartley was hired as finance director for the Port. Bokelman's wife had died shortly before they moved in. He kept pretty much to himself. Sometimes he'd nod if they encountered him on the sidewalk but nearly six months went by before he said a word. Mrs. Hartley had taped a campaign poster in the front window for a female politician. Hartley was working in the yard when his taciturn neighbor happened to walk by. Bokelman stopped and just stood there, watching him work. Finally he pointed to the window. "What do you think *she* can do for the city?" he wanted to know.

Hartley was embarrassed. He suspected that his wife had hung the poster simply because the candidate was female. "I don't know," he said. "My wife put that up. I guess one politician's about the same as the next."

Bokelman smiled sardonically. "Only when you don't know what's going on," he said. "I'll be voting for her opponent. You really ought to look into the record." Then he continued on his way. Hartley bit his tongue and dug deeply into the soil with his spade. Several months passed before they spoke again.

On this next occasion Hartley's garage door was open to keep the sawdust down. He was cutting some cedar fencing when he was surprised to catch sight of Bokelman coming up the driveway. As always, he wore a white shirt, open at the collar, and black everything else: baggy black pants worn shiny at the pockets, black belt and shoes. He was nearly bald and his pink face gave him a babyish appearance.

"Nice shop you've got here," he shouted above the noise of the saw. Hartley cut the power and walked to where his neighbor stood at the doorway, hands in his pockets jingling change and keys. "Name's Bokelman," he said without removing his hands from his pockets. "I used to do a lot of woodworking myself."

Hartley thought his hands must be dirty and began wiping them on his shop apron. "Thanks," he said. "I've always had a shop wherever we've lived."

"Nice to have a shop. Used to have one myself."

Hartley introduced himself and Bokelman said "glad to meet you" but still kept his hands in his pockets. Hartley found this unsettling. Of course, he could have extended his own hand and Bokelman would have been forced to take it. But his neighbor hadn't offered to shake hands earlier and, in fact, Hartley was even relieved at not having to pump Bokelman's puffy palm. Yet he was aware that, in withholding his hand now, he was accepting the distance Bokelman chose to maintain as the condition of their acquaintance.

"Gotta go," Bokelman said. "Maybe I'll stop by sometime and you can show me around. Your shop, I mean."

"That'd be fine," Hartley replied. "And if there's anything I can do for you, just holler." It seemed like the neighborly thing to say.

"I'll do that," Bokelman said with his back turned.

He was at least 25 years older than himself and since Bokelman had given only his last name Hartley felt obliged to say "Goodbye, Mr. Bokelman."

"Goodbye," Bokelman replied giving a flip of his hand without turning around.

What little the Hartleys knew about Bokelman they'd learned from old Mrs. Sullivan who lived across the street. He'd been an optometrist, she said, before some kind of heart condition had forced him into retirement. Dr. Bokelman, she called him. "He was always kind of different, but you couldn't call him unfriendly. A little gruff maybe. He and his wife, oh, she was such a lovely woman, would usually walk around the block a few times after dinner. I liked her a lot. Just the opposite of him. She always had a smile for everyone. She even helped me around the house after Frank died. But then when *she* died, Dr. Bokelman just seemed sort of lost. I don't think men are good alone, do you? He almost never comes out of the house anymore. Never says hello to anyone when he does. Just walks past like he doesn't see you. And it seems like he always has dreary music on his Hi-Fi when I walk by the house. Like dirges or something."

Hartley had heard the music himself. And he knew it well. He owned recordings of most of the French composers of La Belle Epoque. And the piece he heard most frequently emanating from the Bokelman home was among his favorites: Ravel's *Pavane Pour Une Infante Defunte*. Pavane for a Dead Princess.

Not long after their brief conversation in the garage, Bokelman came by one Saturday afternoon while Hartley, garage door open again, was refinishing an old chest-of-drawers. He was accompanied by a young man whom he introduced as his nephew.

"Roger here is helping me frame some canvases. You wouldn't mind cutting a few boards for us, would you?"

Hartley had not previously noted the nasal, sing-song quality of Bokelman's voice. Now it added to the impertinence of his barging in and asking him to cut up the bundle of lumber his nephew was holding. Roger remained a couple of steps behind his uncle, looking rather uncomfortable and saying nothing. "Come on, Roger, give him your boards," said Bokelman, taking the boy's arm and dragging him forward. "This won't take long."

Roger handed over four lengths of one-by-four clear fir and a piece of paper with the required dimensions. "Do you want to pick these up later on today?" Hartley asked.

"Well, we'd really like them now if you've got the time," Bokelman answered for the two of them.

So, as they stood looking on, Hartley cut the fir into eight lengths according to their specifications. When he had finished, Bokelman was bending over a miter box which was permanently mounted on its own table against the wall. "This is a nice one," he said. "We were going to go out and buy a 'cheapie' weren't we, Roger?"

Hartley was annoyed but too naturally gracious to force Bokelman to ask. "I guess we could miter them too," he said. "You haven't got much."

"Oh, splendid," Bokelman replied. "Isn't it wonderful, Roger? It's our lucky day."

Hartley adjusted the saw and cut the sixteen angles. Bokelman then gathered up the finished pieces, nodded to Roger, and said, "Let's get going. We've got work to do." Then, to Hartley, "Thanks. You've got a nice shop here." The two of them walked out, Roger a step or two behind his uncle.

After that, Bokelman was over nearly every weekend with some job he needed done. He even began to operate a few of the tools on his own. Hartley had been taken aback when asked if he minded and had been reluctant to allow this. The tools could be dangerous if you didn't know what you were doing. But Bokelman went on in his sing-song way about how he used to use power tools all the time. Hartley, who in any case was tired of doing his work for him, grudgingly gave in. He let him use the radial saw and the drill press thinking he couldn't run into too much trouble there.

Then came the day Bokelman showed up with some boards he wanted to plane. Hartley, normally an accommodating man with a long fuse, was feeling genuinely irritated by then: with himself for being unable to say NO and with Bokelman for taking advantage of the fact.

"You know how to work a joiner?" he asked.

"Sure," said Bokelman. "Used them lots of times."

"Well, go ahead then," Hartley told him with a glance at the short lengths of wood in his neighbor's hand. Then he went back to his own work and waited. When he thought back on this moment, as he often did, Hartley became increasingly convinced that he actually *was* waiting. But he could never be sure for it had been a day of waiting. It was three hours before hearing anything at Harbor View, three hours in which to build up a pretty good head of guilt in the matter.

Finally a doctor came out and told him they'd saved what they could. They had hopes he'd retain feeling and some freedom of movement in what was left of the finger. But they wanted to keep him in the hospital a day or two for therapy and in case of infection setting in. Hartley should go home now. He could visit his friend the next day if he liked.

When Hartley got home his wife started dinner while he sat at the kitchen table and told her everything that had happened.

"I don't know why you let him use those tools," she said. "He certainly doesn't look like the type that knows anything about tools."

Mrs. Hartley rarely hesitated to speak her mind. And if that occasionally made Hartley uncomfortable he'd be the first to admit that she was only giving voice to thoughts he often shared but generally kept to himself.

"Do you think we're liable?" she asked.

"I don't know," Hartley replied, his voice now tired and short.

"Of course, it really was his own fault," his wife continued. "If he didn't know what he was doing he had no business using those things. The nerve of the man, anyway. He's always over here asking you to do things for him."

"Barb, he's probably just lonely. I've never seen him with anyone except his nephew. And I don't mind much. I could have planed those boards for him in five minutes. I should have."

"Sure you should," she shot back. "And what else? Why do you let him take advantage of you like that?"

The next day, Hartley did go visit Bokelman. He wondered if he should bring him a book or something. He nearly stopped by a news stand to pick up the day's papers for him but rejected the idea at the last minute. They were neighbors separated by one house and a mile's worth of convention.

Bokelman was in a room with three other patients. They all had visitors except for Bokelman who was seated next to his bed.

"I feel terrible about what happened," Hartley said, pulling up a chair.

"Well," Bokelman sighed, "it was my own fault. I guess the boards were too short."

Of course they were. Hartley had seen that right away. Any experienced woodworker would have used a pusher instead of his hand. When he had returned home the previous day and glanced warily at the blood-spattered joiner he found himself feeling uneasy. The pusher for handling such small pieces hung on the wall next to the machine. It was in plain sight. But couldn't he have pointed it out anyway?

Bokelman sighed again. "I guess it's just one of those things."

Soon he was home and walking around with his hand all bandaged up. No one came to see him. When several days had gone by without their meeting on the sidewalk, Hartley got to thinking he should stop by and say 'hello'. Bokelman answered the bell, his bulk filling the doorway.

"How's the hand?" Hartley asked.

"Well," his neighbor whined, "I don't think it's right. It still hurts, especially when it's cold. I can't get much use out of it. You want to come in?"

Hartley didn't know whether to interpret this as an actual invitation. Bokelman's tone suggested that it was all the same to him whether Hartley came in or not.

But it *was* cold and he could not be standing there like that with the door wide open. He had little desire to enter, but neither did he wish to appear unfriendly or indifferent to his neighbor's discomfort. "Well, just for a minute," he said.

As his eyes adjusted to the dim light of the living room, Hartley's attention was immediately drawn to the walls which seemed to glow with an amber-like luster. At eye level throughout the room hung dozens of paintings, each in an ornate gold-leaf frame and illuminated by a small bronze lamp mounted above it. It was the paintings themselves which seemed to glow and fill the room with a warmth and passion that seemed so at odds with the Bokelman he knew. A few upholstered chairs were arranged at the room's center to create the effect of a well-appointed gallery displaying its many treasures to best advantage. Photographs of a woman, who could only have been Bokelman's wife, rested on a table next to the several chairs where Bokelman clearly spent much of his time.

Hartley managed a feeble "Are you an art collector?"

"No, my wife was a painter. They're hers."

Hartley felt uncomfortable. This room was a shrine. "She was... very good," he heard himself saying.

"Yes," Bokelman said absently, sitting down. "I'm sorry I can't offer you anything, but..."

"Oh, I have to get going," Hartley interrupted. Then he added, "But may I just take a minute to look at your wife's paintings?" Despite his discomfort he felt it would have been rude to rush off without admiring them.

"Help yourself," his neighbor replied.

Hartley walked slowly, pausing in front of each canvas. It was only then that he heard, how could he have missed it before, Ravel's Pavane. He turned his gaze to the stereo.

Then, involuntarily, to Bokelman who quickly looked away as if to say I'd rather we not get into a conversation.

Hartley returned to the paintings. Though not a painter himself, and certainly no connoisseur of fine art, he could nevertheless appreciate how beautifully they were done. 'Painterly' as he once heard a museum docent describe the works of an artist being exhibited. Though pastiches of the great French Impressionists, they clearly stood well on their own merits. He felt himself drawn into them by Ravel's haunting music. And suddenly he was aware of a deep empathy for Bokelman who spent his days in this room, gazing at these paintings, listening to this music. And the pavane, this slow, elegant dance of a Spanish court constrained by rigid, deadening convention - was it not like the dance in which he found himself locked with the sad, overweight man sitting in this room?

"I need to be getting home. Sorry your finger's still bothering you. Have you been back to the hospital to have it checked?"

Bokelman stood and walked to the door. "Of course," he said. "They just tell me it's healing fine. *I* know something's wrong though. Maybe you shouldn't have taken me to Harbor View."

"But... I've always heard their emergency room was first rate." Hartley knew he was sounding defensive.

"Just the same, I'd like another opinion. How about your homeowner's insurance? Wouldn't they cover that?"

Hartley was stung. What was Bokelman up to? Claims? Lawsuits? "I guess I could call and check," he said.

"Yeah," Bokelman agreed. "Let me know what they say."

"Damn him," Hartley muttered when he was home again. Still, an inner voice insisted that, after all, Bokelman had made a perfectly reasonable request. If his manner was curt, verging on accusatorial, wasn't the poor fellow drowning in grief? Could he have coped any better were he to lose his own wife? He called the insurance company. The agent wanted all the details. Said he was a woodworker himself. "How come he didn't use a pusher?" he wanted to know.

"I don't know," Hartley had replied. "I guess he really didn't know how to operate a joiner."

"Well, then, you shouldn't have let him use it."

Hartley felt a cold fury rising up in him. Was it just the impertinence of the agent or was it also a sense of helplessness that was overwhelming him? "Look," he practically shouted, "the guy said he knew how to use a joiner. He said he knew what he was doing. He didn't cut off his finger on purpose for god's sake. And what difference does it make whose fault it was anyway? Am I covered or not? All the man wants is a second opinion."

"Maybe you're covered," the agent said sourly. "Send in your claim and we'll see."

As it happened, things turned out OK. Bokelman went to the UW where the doctors affirmed that the surgery and been performed with great skill. The insurance company picked up the tab without a peep. Probably relieved to get off so lightly. Only Bokelman was unhappy with the outcome. He grumbled about his finger every time they met. The complaining got to the point where Hartley started having trouble sleeping. He had always considered himself a decent sort of fellow. Always ready to help someone out. If asked, he knew his friends would describe him in just such terms. But this thing with Bokelman was causing him to question the Mr. Good Guy image. If he was honest with himself, and this was not easy, had he not allowed the accident to happen? Perhaps, out of some deep unconscious malevolence, even wanted it to happen? Thoughts like that can keep a man awake at night.

One day Hartley was working in his shop when he caught sight of Bokelman coming up the driveway again. "Christ," he thought to himself. "What's he want now?"

"I need to talk to you, Hartley." Here we go. Hartley felt the blood rising to his face. "I just want to say you've been a good neighbor."

Hartley was caught off guard. "Well," he stammered, "maybe I could have been a better one. I could have planed those boards for you and you'd still have ten fingers."

"Nonsense. That was no one's fault but mine. I did something stupid. And that's all there is to be said about it."

"Still, it happened in my shop and I feel terrible."

"Just forget it, OK? By the way, there's something I'd like your opinion on."

Hartley couldn't keep himself from saying "Anything I can help you with?" What's the matter with you, Barb's voice was shouting inside his head. Do you need to save Bokelman and the rest of the world with him? Don't be such a sap!

"It's like this," Bokelman went on, never missing a beat. "I'm going to be moving soon. I'm putting the house up for sale and moving to Florida to live with my sister. She's the only family I've got. That's Roger's mother. And the thing is, I've got to get all my wife's paintings back there somehow. There's more than you saw, probably a hundred. And some are just on their stretchers. Roger and I have been framing those and still have a few to go. And I wondered if you had any ideas about what kind of a crate I could use for shipping."

Hartley felt a wave of resignation come over him. He knew what his wife would say. But it was too late now for saying NO. "I suppose I could design some kind of crate with partitions so the paintings wouldn't be damaged. Maybe five to a crate. That'd be a lot of crates, though. I don't really have time..."

"Oh, I'm not asking for your help to build them or anything. Johnson's cabinet shop is going to do that. I've already talked to them about it. They just need some kind of drawing of what I want." Then he added: "The paintings are all I have left of my wife. I need to take them with me. I can't go without them."

"I understand," said Hartley. He meant it. And he was relieved. Designing a sturdy shipping crate would be child's play. And Barb could scarcely complain when he told her what it was for. Especially when she understood that this would be the extent of his contribution to the project. "I'll draw up something for you," he told his neighbor.

"Thanks, Hartley. You've been good to me." And he thrust out his hand for Hartley to shake.

That evening after dinner Barb saw her husband sitting at the computer doing something with his CAD program. "Whatcha up to?"

"Oh, just sketching something for Bokelman."

His wife drew in her breath audibly and deeply. Then let it out in a burst of exasperation. "So what's it this time, Mr. Nice Guy?"

God, did she have to call him *that*? Hartley explained about the paintings, that Bokelman was moving and needed to ship them off to Florida. All he needed was a drawing. Just a drawing. It was a small thing to ask. And he was glad he could help.

"Sure," said Barb. "And next he's going to ask you to build those damn crates for him."

"No, he won't. He just needs a sketch to take to Johnson's They're going to make them."

"Just you wait!" his wife scoffed. "When are you going to realize that you don't owe this guy anything?"

"Barbara, don't..." Hartley broke off. Then: "It's not that simple," he said.

Barbara came and stood behind her husband, and placed her hands gently on his shoulders. "I'm sorry, darling. I'm just thinking of you, that's all." Hartley bent his head to one side and touched his cheek to her hand. And he wondered if Bokelman was gazing at his gilt-framed memories from the darkened center of his living room.

Two days later Roger knocked on the door. Hartley thought he'd come for the drawing. But he just stood there with a blank look on his face for several seconds. "Uncle Eugene died yesterday," he finally managed to blurt out. "He just fell down in the parking lot at Walmart . When the medical guys got there he was dead. They said it was a heart attack."

Hartley felt like he'd been sucker-punched. "Oh, god," he said, "I am so sorry."

"Yeah, well it happened real fast. I don't think he suffered none."

Hartley went to the kitchen and poured himself a drink. He was sitting at the table, head in his hands, when his wife came in and wanted to know who'd been at the door. He told her. Her face was unbelieving so he repeated it. "Bokelman's dead."

There was a moment of silence. Then, "Well," she said, "that's one problem solved." Her husband looked at her, speechless.

At work the next day Hartley arranged to take five days of unused vacation time the following week. Before going home that night he stopped by Home Depot and ordered thirty sheets of three-quarter inch plywood and an equal number of quarter inch panels. That plus five boxes of #8 woodscrews brought the bill to a little over $900. Home delivery added another $50. Hartley put it on his Visa card.

When the lumber arrived on Saturday he had it stacked in the driveway. If Barb had any thoughts about what she knew he was going to do she felt it best to keep them to herself.

Sunday, after church, Hartley put on his shop apron and for the next six days he hardly left his garage except for meals. Sometimes Barb brought him a sandwich and a beer when he failed to show up for lunch. The atmosphere was thick with sawdust.

Hartley got it down to where he could make a crate in about two hours. The longest part of the job was dado-ing the end pieces to receive the quarter inch panels that would divide the crate into five compartments. Five partitions per crate, nearly 100 paintings, twenty crates in all. A good forty hours of work. He let Roger try to help on the first day. But the boy was useless so he sent him home and told him to return at the end of the week to help load the paintings.

By ten o'clock on Friday morning the completed twenty crates stood side by side in the garage. Hartley had attached handles to facilitate moving them. Roger came as requested and the two of them removed the paintings from Bokelman's house and loaded them carefully into the crates. While Hartley screwed down the tops Roger filled out the labels with his mother's address in Florida. By the late afternoon the job was done. Before leaving the garage Hartley took a damp rag and wiped down the joiner again. There were still a few spots of dried blood he'd missed the first time.

Barb was out with friends so the house was empty when he went in. He poured himself a glass of scotch. He was glad she was gone so that he wouldn't have to try to explain why he put Ravel's Pavane on the stereo. He wasn't quite sure himself. Then he sat in his favorite chair, listening to the music, letting the scotch warm his throat and clear the smell of sawdust from his sinuses. Images of the past few months came unbidden to his consciousness in no particular pattern. He thought of his neighbor, of how nice the weather had been all week, of the waiting room at Harbor View, of what would become of him if he ever lost Barb.

He heard the final notes of the pavane playing. The trucking firm would be coming to collect the crates first thing Monday morning. Hartley calculated that the paintings should arrive in Florida about the same time as Bokelman's ashes.

Lyrics to Kite String

A footfall on the walk when no one's there
The remembered sigh of a brush drawn through your hair
The last note of a song
A song that had no end
Is that your voice
Or a kite string in the wind

The last beat of a heart on a night forlorn
The cry of a book from which a chapter's torn
The sound of loneliness
In one without a friend
Is that your voice
Or a kite string in the wind

The peace of silence yet eludes me
Though my days your voice no longer fills
We once shared a life together
Now silence refuses to be still

The hush of rays of sunlight filled with dust
The sound of salt air turning ships to rust
The calling of a garden
No one's left to tend
Is that your voice
Or a kite string in the wind

The rush of air beneath a blackbird's wings
The tolling of a bell that never rings
Words that held a promise
Of things that might have been
Is that your voice I hear
Or the whisper of a kite string in the wind

The Time We're Given

I usually imagine that the Spain I know best was formed soon after the receding of the great flood. A child-like god smoothed and rounded its contours with muddy palms, then set the sun to dry it out. It was an afternoon's project in the sandbox. By the next day he'd forgotten all about it. Let devout Spanish Christians dispute this; yet who but the Moors will claim the hard, parched earth was ever part of Paradise?

There are, of course, exceptions to the general severity of the landscape — hilly, wooded estates where titled wealth and peasant sweat have coaxed a semblance of the Garden out of the hardscrabble terrain. And if they do not compare with the pleasure palaces which dot the handiwork of a more attentive god to the north, they are nevertheless distinguished by an ascetic character which gives scope to passion originating in the soul rather than the senses.

The extensive holdings of the de Ortiz family lie among these hills some five kilometers inland from the Costa Blanca, just north of the old Roman fortress town of Alicante. Here the harshness of the countryside is mitigated by trees and shrubs nourished by an abundance of natural spring water, long reputed for its healing properties. The latest descendant of this ancient family, the Marquis de Ortiz, comes here occasionally to hunt, but several generations have passed since the bustle of children and servants echoed in the great halls of the abandoned villa. Only a caretaker remains to hold at bay the stubby pines that long ago invaded the English gardens and ruptured the plumbing of its many fountains.

At the highest point of the property, about a kilometer from the old family compound, stands a sanatorium, now equally abandoned and overgrown, that once housed as many as two hundred tubercular patients. The large, handsome building commands an unobstructed view of the Mediterranean. Nearly a century ago the de Ortiz family granted five hectares to the Province for the construction of the facility. It had been beautifully laid out with well-tended gardens and a network of walking trails for the patients. Little of this elegance remains today, though a quiet, natural grace still rests upon the columns and stone benches of the old courtyard. Here, on a warm summer afternoon, one willingly mistakes the rustle of leaves on the paving stones for the hushed voices of patients long since dead. Employed as a military hospital during the Civil War, it was reopened for tubercular children at the war's end. Then, some twenty years later, it was closed permanently when the disease had finally been eradicated in Spain. Today an elderly couple remains in residence to shoo away trespassers and answer the questions of an occasional visitor.

It was Thomas Mann and a chance encounter with a retired Englishman along the Esplinada of Alicante which first led me to Aguas de Busot and its crumbling sanatorium. I had taken an apartment near the beach for the summer after throwing in the towel on an unpromising career as a concert guitarist. A European tour in small-time venues with second-rate orchestras had fizzled out in Strasbourg when my tendons began acting up again. My girlfriend had always maintained that there was only room enough in this world for about six classical guitarists to make a decent living. And I, she said, was not among these few. Having joined me with reluctance on the now aborted tour, she split for New York when we arrived in Madrid. Low on money, and without work, I couldn't face the prospect of going home just yet. I was at a dead end and needed time to think.

A stop at an outdoor table of the Delfin for a café con leche was part of my daily routine. Sitting there one afternoon, I had just begun Mann's *The Magic Mountain* for perhaps the sixth time, when I was startled by a hearty "I say!" from an adjacent table. "You've got one of my favorite books there, old chap."

"If I ever manage to get through it, it may become one of mine," I replied. "I bought it years ago but I never seem to get past the first few chapters."

"Ah! You're an American. How refreshing it is to hear your accent. This place is crawling with fat Englishmen in baggy shorts." Then, lowering his voice conspiratorially, "Mind if I join you? They get to be so tiresome."

He had gathered up his London Times and a pack of Players before I could answer. I liked him immediately on account of this bit of self-mockery for he possessed a considerable paunch of his own and, of course, wore baggy shorts. The English may be a reserved lot on their own home ground, but south of the 45th parallel, given a little sun, they can be as garrulous and outgoing as a Spanish horse trader. They are likely to talk the ear off of anyone who can understand them.

"I say, it's about time for tea, isn't it," he said, pulling up a chair. He motioned to the waiter: "Un te, por favor." Then, wagging his finger at the man, "con mucho calor!"

I was embarrassed at his atrocious Spanish but the waiter winked at me and repeated briskly, "Con mucho calor! Si, Senor!"

"Well now, this may interest you," said my new acquaintance, turning to me again. "By the way, the name's Brierly, Evan Brierly. Yours?"

"Michael Perry. Pleased to meet you."

"Ah! Perry. Now then, *The Magic Mountain*. Perhaps you'll finish it this time. Here's an idea for you. Have you heard of Aguas de Busot, old boy?"

"No." I smiled. It was rather pleasant being addressed like this.

"Well, here it is then," he went on. "There's an old abandoned sanatorium not far from here, no more than thirty kilometers from Alicante. You're far enough into the book so that I shan't spoil anything for you. You already know the whole thing takes place in a sanatorium. And I'm sure you've figured out by now that nothing is going to happen. Just a bunch of sick people sitting about talking to one another, that sort of thing. That's the charm of it, isn't it?"

"I suppose it is," I answered, evidently without much enthusiasm.

"Well, of course it is! Now here's what I'd do if I were your age and still had the legs for it. I'd take the old railway to Villa Joyosa. That's as close as you can get by train. From there it's just a couple of kilometers up in the hills. There's a sign, I think, but any of the locals can tell you which road to take. You'll probably get a lift. There are still a few old pensioners who live along the way."

The tea arrived and he wrapped a large, sun-blistered hand around the metal pot. "That's much better. Gracias." The waiter smiled at me again and hurried off.

"These blokes here don't drink tea. Don't know how to make it. Now where were we? Ah! So you walk to the sanatorium and ring the iron bell at the main gate. There's an old caretaker there, name's Don Antonio. Must be in his eighties. You just tell him you want to walk around and he'll let you in. He gets damned few visitors. And I must warn you, he loves to talk. One of those peasant-philosopher types with only his wife for company. Now, you take your book with you, you see? You walk those old paths and sit on those stone benches that look across the tops of the trees all the way to the sea, and you read your Thomas Mann. And pretty soon you won't just be reading about Hans Castorp and his cousin and all the others, you'll be right there with them. You'll get to know what it was all about soon enough. You do that. You go up there every day 'til you've finished that book. That's what I'd do, by Jove. That's what I'd do if I still had the legs for it."

He looked away from the sea, toward the hills, and I knew that he meant it. "I've been here just a week now," I told him, "and you're the second Englishman who's given me a bit of advice. The first fellow told me about a Spanish brandy called Magno. Said it's nearly as good as the best Cognac. I'm going to try it. Can I order one for you too, in return for a brilliant suggestion?"

"A jolly good brandy, I dare say. Thanks, old boy, I'd love one."

For the next few days my schedule never varied. Up at seven, I was at the station by 7:30 for a stand-up breakfast of chorizos, huevos, and hot chocolate fortified with a splash of Magno. By eight I was headed north in one of the boxy, motorized railcars which sway alarmingly down a roadbed flanked with giant granite boulders on one side and, on the other, by a precipitous drop of some fifty meters to the sea. Villa Joyosa was the third stop and getting to Aguas was simply a matter of taking the only road out of town except for the highway to Valencia. As the Englishman had predicted, someone usually stopped to offer a ride before I'd walked very far. Only once, as I recall, did I cover the whole two kilometers on foot.

He had been right, too, about Don Antonio, the voluble caretaker at the sanatorium. He was one of those wiry old Spaniards who wear Basque style berets and a frayed black cardigan sweater regardless of the day's heat. His eyes were clouded with cataracts but the thousand wrinkles of his face came to life simultaneously in a wide grin on finding an American at the gate. On that first day he had insisted on giving me a quick tour of the grounds followed by a glass of wine which we drank in the courtyard behind the main building. Thereafter we never met without taking a glass of wine together on his favorite bench under the shade of several orange trees. His taste ran to the cheap local stuff of which he consumed at least a liter most afternoons. But he grunted appreciatively when I brought along a bottle of the best Rioja I could find on the following day.

I told him what I proposed to do and he voiced no objections. But Don Antonio had never heard of *The Magic Mountain* and, when I told him what it was about, he couldn't see why I'd want to read about a bunch of sick people.

"Caballero!" he shouted at me when I waved to him from the gate on the second day. "Come and have a little wine before your paseo. Besides, it's getting too hot to walk. And if you have to read something I have a nice little French magazine with pretty girls in it instead of that mountain thing of yours."

Several trails led from the sanatorium into the surrounding countryside. The grades were gentle to avoid fatiguing the patients and, in any event, stone benches were located every hundred meters or so. Each day, after assuring Don Antonio that I'd be back after his siesta to share another glass with him, I took a different route. I walked slowly because of the heat, but also to adjust my steps, and my life, to the pace of *The Magic Mountain* and its inhabitants. If our separate existences are largely hidden from one another, it was not difficult to sense the rhythm of their lives here. They would not have abandoned hope, for few came here expecting to die, yet death's presence would have accelerated an inner, affective life even as it slowed what was visible to the unafflicted. Ordinary clocks could not have served to measure time here. That life ends is, finally, the only thing that makes any sense of it; but what we all understand abstractly, the dying live as a daily reality. An afternoon on these barren trails, for one whose lungs were marked like a tree for harvest, might contain the perceptions of five years of a healthy bank clerk's existence. Lives spent on the Magic Mountain were no less full for being brief and sequestered, where the entire range of human experience might be compressed into but a few short years — or less.

It was still early afternoon of the third day when I closed the first book of my two volume paperback edition and placed it on the bench beside me. I would no doubt have finished it had not Don Antonio managed to delay my setting out until the sun was nearly at its zenith. Now, gazing at the sea from a bench where the likes of Mann's characters spent their days, I experienced a pleasant feeling of disorientation, as if my life was slowing to the rhythm of the Magic Mountain itself.

With time on my hands, and unwilling to let the old man break the spell, I decided on a circuitous route back to the sanatorium — one which would pass near the de Ortiz villa whose tile roof I could just make out from my vantage point. What I could not see, until I had walked a ways, was a squat, narrow building perched on a slope about a hundred meters from the house. A well-worn trail led through the brush in its general direction and I followed out of idle curiosity. From a distance the construction seemed a solid, rectangular monolith but as I approached, I could see that its walls were pierced in three places: a barred window set high on each side, and a large opening in front, nearly as tall as the building itself, which served as the sole entrance. There was no door as such, only a double iron gate whose bars were set close enough to prevent larger animals - there was a cat sleeping in the cool shade of the interior - from entering. It was evidently the family's private chapel. I could still make out the faint blue and gold image of the Virgin which had been painted above the altar. No one had set foot here for many years. The few benches were deep in dust and the floor scarcely distinguishable from the ground cover outside. I pulled at the gate until the rattling echoed in the vaulted interior, but succeeded only in frightening the cat who darted behind the altar. It was then that I noticed the gate had been cemented shut, to keep out vandals, I supposed, now that the property was all but abandoned. As I was about to leave I was startled by something I had not seen at first. A vase of fresh flowers had been placed an arm's length inside the grate. Circling once around the building, I decided to ask Don Antonio about it on my return.

"Si, si," he said as he pulled the cork from a bottle of the Provincial red. "It was the family chapel. Closed a long time ago when the family stopped coming. My stupid woman takes the flowers. I should never have told her."

"Told her what?"

"Ah, Caballero, it's a long story."

The cagey old man was dying to tell me despite a shrug of feigned indifference. The Spanish love a good story, especially if it involves the Church. The papers constantly run stories of weeping Madonnas, and no custodian of a cathedral's reliquary is without his vial of dried blood that miraculously liquefies on the anniversary of some martyr's death. Beneath its precariously thin veneer of Catholicism, the Spanish Church has always been first cousin to naked superstition. Don Antonio would play this for all it was worth.

"But since you like stories, I'll tell you," he said as he poured us both a glass of wine. I made an effort not to smile and leaned back, anticipating an earful of solemn poppycock.

"I'll tell you what I know," he said, "and that's more than you could have read in the papers. But in the end it's a mystery, a great mystery. And it must always remain so."

I was amused at the serious air affected by Don Antonio, and I suspected that he might be mocking the gullibility of an American who had fallen into his clutches. So I smiled at this. Not enough of a smile to offend the old man, but enough to announce that I was no fool. He seemed to take no notice.

"After the war the sanatorium was reopened — but only for children, niños who were very ill with this terrible disease. The oldest were in their middle and late teens. There were never more than forty or fifty. I was the gardener here then and I knew all of them. They were like my own children. Some got better, but most did not. And none ever died that I did not cry like a woman. Death is a powerful demon, Señor. Niños like that? When is life ever stronger? Yet, full of desire, they would grow pale and die in silence.

Do you think death will have a hard time with an old man like me then?"

I was beginning to regret my calculated smile.

"Pilar de Ortiz and Miguel Samper." He looked at the ground and sighed, elbows on his knees. "She was fifteen and with but months to live. Her family owns Aguas. All of this land. Miguel, I didn't know much about him. He was maybe a year or two older than she, also very sick. No one ever came to visit him. Perhaps he was an orphan. Well, you who likes stories, do I need to tell you they were in love? Just like in all good stories, no?

"Now, in town niños that age fall in love too. They wait a few years and maybe they get married, and maybe they don't. But when you are dying you can't wait, can you? But your parents say you are too young. Do they think you will ever be old enough? Of course not. The doctors have told them. But they will never admit this to you, will they? And they think, anyway, that you cannot grow up without them. So they will never agree to let you get married. And the priest? This is Spain, Señor. The priest says God will call them before they can have children. You get married to bring children into this world, he says. The old fool! What does he know who never had a woman?"

"You didn't warn me, Don Antonio," I said, trying to lighten things up a bit. "I didn't know this was going to be a sad story."

"No, Señor," he replied vehemently, "no, Señor, this is not a sad story." Then, grinning, "My marriage, there's a sad story. But I do not speak of that. Now, listen, I will tell you what they did. But what I tell you must remain a secret. And I tell you only because you do not live here and will soon be returning to your own country. This secret must go with you."

I promised, though I was certain that anything to follow was a staple of local gossip.

"When Pilar's father came to visit he would sometimes take her to the ancestral home for an afternoon. They would sit in the garden and he would tell her about her family and the secrets of the old villa. Once he showed her a tunnel which had been dug from the grotto at the far end of the garden to the chapel on the hill above. It had been constructed over two hundred years earlier as an escape route should the main house come under attack. Barred by the statue of an angel, the entrance had been well concealed. The tunnel itself led to a crypt under the altar where family members were once interred. Whether she and her father visited the crypt on that occasion, I cannot say, though I believe they must have done so.

"One day Pilar asks me if I will help her and Miguel. When she tells me what they wish to do I am afraid for my job, and for my immortal soul as well. But how can I say no to these children? The next day I take some blankets and a pair of flashlights from the storeroom. As the sanatorium slips into the quiet of the siesta hour, I join the two of them and we walk to the villa's grotto. Pilar leads us to the tunnel's entrance and its guardian angel. They do not have the strength to move the heavy statue. I do this for them and go first into the tunnel. It is hard for me to walk all stooped over. None of us talk. When we reach the crypt I shine my light on the stone coffins. I tell myself that these are just old bones but I am glad to open an iron gate and climb the steps to the small area behind the chapel altar. The children follow me. I have not looked at them since we entered the tunnel, but when I now turn and see their faces, they are so beautiful, these niños. Miguel leads Pilar by the hand and the two stand in front of me. My heart is aching and I am overcome with such great love for this boy and this girl. I bless and kiss each of them. They smile and embrace, just as if they had been married by the priest. When I go, I leave the blankets and one of the lights behind me, and I do not push the statue all the way back over the entrance when I emerge from the tunnel.

"Was that not a great sacrilege, Señor, to consummate their love in a church? And in the light of day?" Don Antonio was smiling wistfully. "Even in our own bedroom, where my wife would never do it but half-dressed and in the dark, the woman always turned the Savior's picture to the wall before letting me touch her. But I tell you, Señor, if I were God, for those children I would have sprouted rabbit's fur from that stone floor for their marriage bed."

Who could not feel affection for this soft-hearted old Spaniard in his threadbare cardigan. "Were they discovered?" I asked.

"For the next two months, whenever the weather was warm, they returned to their nest. No, they were never found out, which was a good thing for me. But one day they disappeared, Señor. By God, there was not a trace of them. The Guardia came here, and men from the town, and a thousand times these hills were searched. Every paper in the Province had them on the front page. How do you account for that? They could not have boarded a ship or made it to France without being seen. They had no money. And, weak as they were, they could not even have walked very far. Of course, right away I think of the chapel. So one day, when the search teams had given up for the day, I let myself into the tunnel. Nothing.

"Ten years now, and still no one knows what happened to them. My stupid woman says they have been punished for their sacrilege. Why did I have to tell her? When I did she got down on her knees and crossed herself a hundred times and said we had to tell the priest. I threatened terrible things if she ever opened her mouth. So she keeps quiet. But for ten years now she puts flowers in the chapel. For atonement, she says. And she says that never again will she consent to sleep with the man who helped them. No importance. I am old now. And even before, if we did it once a year I counted myself lucky. But I was an idiot to tell her. If I die before she does she'll tell the priest and he'll go to the Marquis and make him tear the chapel down. That's the world we live in, Señor."

This was hardly the story I had expected. I was moved by the depth of Don Antonio's feeling in its re-telling. There was sadness in his eyes; but it was not for his young friends. "You know, Señor, death is the most ordinary of events. But in every life it plays a different role. For those two, it was an invitation to the fulfillment of love and desire. But me, now, what is death except deliverance from old age? Gladly would I have traded places with Miguel."

The Englishman knew the story, though not the intimate details Don Antonio had confided to me. When I ran into Brearly at the Delfin the next day it was almost as if he had been waiting for me. "I say, Perry, how are things on the Magic Mountain?" He was as English as old Spode.

"Well, you had a great idea." I nearly added 'old chap'. "Almost too good. I need a day off."

He laughed. "Feeling like one of the patients, are we?"

I found the interrogation somewhat annoying, but in a general way he was right about my state of mind. The novel and Don Antonio's story of Pilar and Miguel had merged in my imagination and were posing uncomfortable questions about my own life. The sick and dying of the Magic Mountain seemed to be doing a lot more living than I was.

Brearly had just retired to Alicante at the time of the mysterious disappearance. "It was in the papers for weeks," he said. "The doctors said that neither of them had more than a few days to live. Damnedest thing; the de Ortiz family offered two million pesetas for information. But not a word. If anything was to be learned, that kind of dinero would have turned it up."

"Could they have reached the Balearics, or Morocco, maybe," I asked.

"I can't see how. In their health? No money, no passports? Impossible. And, anyway, why would they want to?"

"I don't know," I fumbled. "They were in love. Who needs a reason? It's love, not reason, that's stronger than death." It occurred to me that I was starting to sound like Thomas Mann. But I was warming up to this now. "You know what it's like at that age. Put yourself in their position. You're 16, 17, whatever they were, and you know very well that you're dying. You're also in love in a way that one can only be at that age. How do you want to go? In a white, sterile room in one wing of a sanatorium while the one you love is dying in another room in another wing? Let's be a little romantic here. What would you do? How would you get the upper hand over the old demon, as Don Antonio calls death?"

"OK, ok, old chap. You've got the advantage of youth here. And I suppose you've got a point. I'll concede the motive. But how the deuce could they just disappear like that?"

"It makes for a great mystery," I said.

"Indeed it does, old boy. Indeed it does."

Afterwards I walked to the beach with yesterday's Le Monde under my arm. But I didn't read it. I just continued walking north alone along the rocks. Occasionally I stopped to massage the painful tendons that meant the end of my hoped-for career as a performing musician. And I was thinking about what we call time. What it meant to Pilar and Miguel. What it meant to me, the years that stretched so uncertainly before me. Time is a puzzle, I thought. There is something about it that is very hard to explain. Old platitudes came to mind, the ones about taking each day as it comes and living each moment for all it's worth. I supposed that on the Magic Mountain they must have made some sense. But when I looked at the sea, I saw only dark, ambiguous waves making their way slowly to shore.

The following day I stuffed the second volume of *The Magic Mountain*, a flashlight, and a bottle of Marquis de Riscal into my backpack and made it to the station in time for the 8 o'clock train. When I arrived at the sanatorium an hour and a half later I still wasn't sure if I'd go through with it.

Don Antonio opened the gate and greeted me, a little gruffly, I thought, as if he were out of sorts that I hadn't shown up the day before. He softened a bit when he saw the wine. "Yesterday," he said, I had a good Carta de Plata for you. But we'll drink this." He took the bottle from my hands as if it were a newborn babe. "I'll have it open and waiting when you return this afternoon." I tried to get him to talk about Pilar and Miguel before I set out but the subject seemed closed, almost as if he regretted telling me as much as he had. "An old story, Señor. Did you see the almond trees on the way up? Just starting to bloom. Soon it will be the best time of year."

Clearly it would not do to tell him. I had conceived of a visit to the abandoned chapel, entering by way of the hidden tunnel. If I could find it. A pilgrimage to the heart of the Magic Mountain of Aguas de Busot.

When I had read for an hour or two and eaten the bread and sausage I picked up in the village, I walked to the villa. It was the siesta hour and I had little concern that the caretaker would see me. I walked quietly nonetheless as I approached the overgrown garden. It was a complete maze of barely passable trails and crumbling fountains. There were still a few signs of more exotic plantings but the native scrub had returned with a vengeance to reclaim its birthright. The pathways were discernible by a few buckled paving stones and I followed one in the general direction of the chapel. Parting brush and tendrils with my elbows, hands protecting my face, I continued to an outer wall and discovered the grotto exactly as Don Antonio had described it. The angel's statue was nearly hidden by a mass of vines which had grown up around it. It was not so much the weight of the statue but the firm grip of nature, intent on protecting the secret, which took all of my strength to turn it from the wall. When it finally budged, lizards scattered in all directions for several seconds. But there, indeed, was the small opening of the tunnel, sealed since Don Antonio's last visit ten years earlier.

My heartbeat was audible, or so it seemed, in the damp interior, but not from any superstitious dread. Rather, I had the sensation of entering into the most intimate and hidden burrows of others' lives, as if I were slipping into the bed of lovers after their passion had subsided and they lay spent and silent in one another's arms.

When I could finally stand upright again I was in the crypt itself. Unlike Don Antonio I have always liked being among old tombs. I have knocked on any number of sarcophagi in the dark recesses of ancient cathedrals seeking contact with those I have known only through the pages of history books. "Can you hear me in there?" It is hard to believe, when you stand there alone with the dead, that they do not. I have conversed with the Empress Catherine of Russia and spent the better part of a quiet afternoon with Elinor of Acquitaine. I have shriven kings and listened to saints and princes as they told their side of the story. Now I shined my light on these stone coffins looking for inscriptions so that I could call the occupants of this room by name and feel myself in their presence.

One sarcophagus in particular drew my attention. Unlike the others, which stood apart, this one seemed almost sculpted into the wall. While examining its unique construction I was surprised to see what appeared to be old scrape marks on that part of the base which butted smoothly against the wall. When I got on my knees for a closer look, I became convinced that the tomb was not just standing closely against the wall but was actually a part of the wall itself. I sat for a moment considering what this might mean. If, indeed, one side of the coffin was formed by the wall, then nothing could account for the scrapings unless it could have been moved somehow. I was torn by a need to get out of there as quickly as I could and an overwhelming desire to see if I could possibly be right. Though the latter won out, it was with a sense of deep foreboding that I braced myself against a nearby sarcophagus and shoved with all the force I could muster in my trembling legs against this strange tomb. And there was movement. Slow, grinding movement. My skin prickled with the rush of adrenaline. A sharp inner voice cried out: STOP! FLEE! YOU DO NOT BELONG HERE! But there could be no stopping. For once forced, the tomb now continued to swing inward with no further encouragement from me. I lay flat on my back, tensed, as if expecting to be suffocated by some cold, infested wave of inky blackness. But there was only silence. And emptiness. When I could gain control of the arm which held the flashlight I was able to see into the opening. All that was revealed was an enormous cave. Many such caves are found in the hills along the Costa Blanca. Some, which served as hide-outs or munitions factories during the Civil War, are open to tourists today. Now, suddenly, it dawned on me that all of this had been very cleverly arranged by the builders of the escape tunnel. The tunnel itself, and the crypt to which it led, might have been discovered if the villa had come under attack. The besieged family would have sought safety, not in the crypt itself, which served merely as a decoy, but in this artfully concealed cavern.

I wondered if, in the couple hundred years since the escape route had been so carefully planned, the secret cave had ever served its purpose. Then my light shone on some scattered blankets, candles, and old food tins. And I understood immediately that it had, and did. I knew, without entering and searching for their remains, that Pilar and Miguel lay here. I swung the faux sarcophagus back into place and ground dust into the scrape marks until they disappeared.

I climbed the steps to the chapel where Don Antonio had married Pilar and Miguel. Overwhelmed by my discovery, I sat with my back to a wall in the dim light afforded by the small, high windows. And then the questions started to come. Who had known the secret of the cave? And how had these dying youngsters managed to move the heavy stone sarcophagus which concealed its entrance? They could not have done this without Don Antonio's help. Their disappearance was no mystery to the old man. And, until now, he had remained its sole guardian. He had forgone, what was to him, the enormous sum of two million pesetas rather than see the resting place of his children disturbed. How long had they lived on here as man and wife in their dark sanctuary, knowing that one of them would soon die in the other's arms? Don Antonio would have continued to bring food, candles, what little comfort he could until the end. But how many days passed before then? And those few days, would they not have been like Paradise, after the creation of Eve, when in wonder and innocence the first man and woman were alone in the universe?

When I finally left, I took extreme care in covering all traces of my presence and replaced the statue as I had found it. Walking slowly back to the sanatorium I was lost in the spirit of the Magic Mountain and an awareness of being alive, truly alive, that comes only from an intimate closeness to death.

"Caballero!" Don Antonio called out on catching sight of me. "Come and sit for a while before heading back. There's still some of your wine left. I couldn't wait."

"Buenas tardes, Don Antonio," I shouted back. "You old dissembler," I thought to myself, "You did not trust me with the whole story, did you."

I joined the old man on our usual bench in the court-yard. "You are later than usual this afternoon. Where have you been." Then, "Is there something wrong, amigo?"

I must have appeared shaken by what I had seen. Don Antonio had heretofore always addressed me formally as Senor, or Caballero. Never as Amigo. There was a note of real concern in his voice. But then, abruptly, I saw a startled look of recognition come over him. There were no further questions. He knew the direction I had come from. And he knew where I had been. Though I was certain he could not have guessed my discovery, I had nevertheless entered a sacred place where I had no right to go. "It is hot today. Have some wine, Senor." His voice was neither cold nor accusatorial but it was clear that I was never again to speak of Pilar and Miguel or return to the villa. I was sorry if I had hurt the old man. But I was not penitent.

The next day I came with my guitar. I went directly to my favorite bench and looked out over the barren hills to the sea. For a long time I just sat there. Then I picked up the guitar. I played softly, the music flowing easily from my fingers: some of the earliest etudes I had mastered by Fernando Sor and Mateo Carcassi, the ones every serious student learns but leaves behind before discovering how beautiful they are. And suddenly there was just this music, the sea, a cloudless sky, and an overwhelming sense of peace. I knew that I could pick up the thread of my life again. And I knew that, whatever came, my days would be filled with the passion for living I had discovered here. It was time to leave the Magic Mountain. It was time to go home.

I found Don Antonio waiting for me. He had seen the guitar. "Could you play for me, Senor? I want to sing." Surprised by his plaintive tone of voice, I removed my guitar from its case and began what little I knew of the intense, seductive strums of Andalucian flamenco. He started to clap, slowly at first. Then faster as his body began swaying to the music. His face, cracked as the bark of an ancient olive tree, became more animated than I had ever seen it. His eyes were closed. And then suddenly, in a soaring, rasping voice, he began to sing. And as he sang, every human emotion from deepest sorrow to joyous ecstasy was present in that voice. His wife, whom I had never seen until now, came and stood beside him. I judged, from the tears in her eyes, that many years had passed since she last heard her husband sing. And soon the sound of their joined and rhythmic clapping echoed throughout the deserted courtyard.

Lyrics to Santa Roma

In green, wooded hills
On the Spanish coast
Not far from Barcelona
Where my wife was sent
When her lungs were spent
To the hospice of Santa Roma

It was the time of discord
Of civil war
I fought in the cause not won
I died in those years
A thousand deaths
Elena, she died but one

I fought in the hills
With the partisans
In the Province of Tarragona
Once shot in that fight
I was carried by night
To the hospice of Santa Roma

A fortnight we spent
Above that white-capped sea
Each day more precious than diamonds
Or the cargos of gold
On the high seas of old
And the white-winged galleons that plied them

Like the white world we lived in
Like the walls of her room
The white robe than hung from her shoulders
The white light of grace
Elena's dear face
And the gauze 'round the head of her soldier

Blood stained the dressing
That bound up my wounds
And blood stained Elena's white pillow
But we walked hand in hand
On paths of white sand
Through orange groves and stands of white willow

We parted in tears
When my wounds had healed
But a life that was far past mending
Not a word was said
Of the road that led
To this life we both knew was ending

I've grown old, I'm tired
I sit by the fire
And think of my comrades who've fallen
And the wife I held dear
And a voice that I hear
I think it's my name she's calling

In green wooded hills
On the Spanish coast
Not far from Barcelona
Now abandoned to time
But for a memory of mine
Lies the hospice of Santa Roma

The Star

She disappeared just like that: no stop by the office, no official leave of absence, nothing. The postcard arrived a month later, written aboard the Alexander Pushkin in the Gulf of Finland.

> Loved your course. Thought I'd see the place for myself. We're supposed to be docking at Leningrad around 2 AM. I'll probably be up to see it since what passes for food on this rust-bucket has me spending most of my time in the can. Would you mind giving me an incomplete? Thanks for everything. Helen

The tone was familiar but in fact I barely remembered what she looked like. I don't think I even knew her by name until I noticed there was one less body in my Russian History class and consulted the roll sheet. Then I vaguely recalled a woman with an oval face and long black hair who sat on the right hand side, near the front.

I gave her the incomplete and had all but forgotten her when on the opening day of class the following semester there she was again, this time in the front row. Prettier than I remembered, a little older, 23, 24 maybe. There was no headband but she wore sandals and a loose fitting orange shift with the *de rigueur* beads of the sixties. The decade was over but the Haight Ashbury was still the arbiter of youthful fashion.

I had been teaching for three years at that time and had always maintained a certain distance where female students were concerned. Not that I was immune to the charms of a pretty face in the front row or the occasional pink triangle glimpsed through a tunnel formed of a taut mini-skirt and smooth, white thighs. No, it was the result of shyness rather than any professional scruple that I followed the advice given me early on by an older colleague: "Son, keep your cock out of the cash register." I was simply too lacking in self-confidence in those days to make the first move. So when the returned traveler stopped by my office the next day I fell easily into the friendly but rather formal manner I habitually assumed during conferences with attractive young women.

This time she was dressed in green cotton pants which tied at the waist and a white, form fitting tank top. Her bra, if in fact she owned one, had clearly been left in the lingerie drawer that morning. Her hair fell naturally about her shoulders, unconstrained by barrettes or hairpins. She wore no make-up and had made no effort to enhance her considerable physical attractiveness. Listening as she recounted her recent voyage I could not have imagined her otherwise. Her personality was equally simple, unadorned, and altogether charming.

"I don't know," she said, "suddenly I felt this urge to get out of the city for awhile. So I hitched to New York. I thought I'd just spend a few days there and come home. But then I saw a poster at the YWCA where I was staying for a student charter to Helsinki. And the next thing I know I'm on this boat to Leningrad. You remember those slides you showed us of the Hermitage? God, I spent three days there. It was fabulous."

She told me about the people she'd met, places she'd visited, and I found myself reliving my own experiences as a student at the University of Moscow. Once, when she paused to ask a question, I was embarrassed at having to ask her to repeat it. I had been thinking of Gorky Park and Nina and how we made love in her parent's apartment on Nevsky Prospect when they were away. It was my first time. I was 19.

"I'm sorry," I said. "Your stories have me daydreaming." She smiled and repeated the question.

We went on like this for perhaps half an hour and finally I began to rummage through a file drawer. I gave her a list of readings she'd be tested on to remove the incomplete and set a date three weeks hence for the exam. She was about to enter the date in an appointment calendar when she caught her breath, then laughed. "I don't know what kind of shape I'll be in. That's the morning after a production party for a film I've been working on."

"Something for a film class?" I asked.

"Noooooo," she replied, puckering her lips around the 'O'.

Suddenly I had a presentiment of what was coming. A lot of creative young people in the Haight were getting by like that. I wondered, too, if I had stumbled into a trap deliberately set for me, a ploy to breach the walls of professional propriety, or if we were both just stumbling ahead in a direction neither of us was entirely sure of.

"Actually," she said, blushing only slightly, "it's a porn flic."

My prescience had given me time to formulate a response to this expected announcement and to muster a show of outward calm. I cleared my throat significantly. "I hesitate to ask this, but.... is yours a starring role or are you in the production end of things?"

She was smiling again. "Both, really, a little of both. I wrote the script such as it is, did a lot of the camera work, and, well, yeah, a little acting too."

I can't remember if I laughed at that. I must have. But it was time to steer for safer ground. "Maybe I should find another time for your exam."

She reached for her bag. "Oh, that's OK. I'll manage. Can I stop by your office a time or two to go over this stuff?"

"Yeah, sure. I always have office hours on Wednesday afternoons," I added, feeling that the safer ground might be eluding me.

She stood to leave and I walked her to the door. "Um," she said hesitantly, "you could come you know. We're renting the New Follies Burlesque Theater at 16th and Mission. We get it after their ten o'clock show, around eleven I guess. You could ask for me at the door. We're going to screen the film and party it up afterwards."

No inner warning had prepared me this time. She clearly detected my discomfort. "Oh, I don't really expect you to come. I just invite everyone I know."

I doubted that, but in the few seconds it took her to say so I had recovered a degree of equanimity that surprised me. For with a strange, inner calm, I heard myself replying "I just might."

Well, of course I wouldn't really go I thought to myself as I closed the door behind her. But why had I so spontaneously suggested that I might, and with so light a heart? And what of that feckless reserve, long despised if never overcome, which had always served as the first line of my defense in similar situations?

I returned to my desk and sat down. I'd go. I was sure of it. Before the day was over I'd made practically an obligation out of it, homework, so to speak. And the ivory tower? In my case the foundation had been rotten all along.

The two meetings I had with Helen to go over the material only served to counter any backsliding. She did not repeat the invitation, nor did I tell her that I intended to go. But her knowledge of the subject matter was so good that I moved the day of her exam up a week, thus removing the one possible objection I could reasonably sustain. The night of the film party she would no longer be my student. Her final grade would already have been submitted.

On the day of the "event" a few doubts about the propriety of my going diminished somewhat the guilty pleasure of anticipation. Would anyone recognize me? Would I not appear ridiculous to the *demimonde* of the New Follies Burlesque Theater? And what do you say to a porn star after the film? "Nice tits" or "You were faking it, right?" Yet these concerns, instead of driving me back to the rarefied atmosphere of the tower, only served to strengthen my resolve. If I backed out now I'd hate myself for it. I was going.

I arrived promptly at eleven, and, with some effort of will, managed to avoid looking in both directions when I presented myself at the door. I was going all the way. Helen was summoned when I gave her name and then it was her turn to be flummoxed. "Oh, my god! I never thought... well, come on in then."

She was needed elsewhere and rushed off soon after I'd set foot in the lobby. An usher directed me to the balcony. The late show was still in progress and we'd have to wait for the patrons below to leave when it was over. At least fifty people were already there. The mood was festive, delirious actually, and it didn't seem to matter that no one knew who I was. A young woman passed me a bag of popcorn as I sat down to join the hooting crowd and watch as the show came to its finale. Miss Chantel Capri pranced on stage and lost no time jiggling out of her sequined gown. Her legs weren't bad but I judged her to be well past her prime. Even from where I sat I could see a little cauliflower starting to bloom on her thighs. But she had the moves and she could do amazing things with an ordinary straight-backed chair that provoked whistles and cheers and a shower of popcorn form my seat-mates. Miss Capri, so long accustomed to the leaden silence of her paying fans, was appreciative. We got the works. The girl next to me howled and buried her face against my shoulder. I was starting to have a good time.

When Miss Capri took her final bow and the heavy breathers filed out, we all returned to the lobby. If I was the stranger there I didn't feel it. Helen introduced me to a number of people by my first name and we all stood around drinking wine and talking shop. I learned that the movie was entitled **Deep Tango**, a none-too-subtle blending, I supposed, of the intrigues of **Deep Throat** and **Last Tango in Paris**. When I expressed my unfamiliarity with both of them, the popcorn girl, whose name was Sarah, said "Don't worry. You'll get it."

Helen whistled, held her hand above her head, and asked us to take our seats. The projectionist was ready and wanted to get home by two. So we shuffled noisily into the theater where the curtain had been parted to reveal a standard sized screen. The lights dimmed immediately and I settled in to watch the first pornographic film I'd ever seen except for some grainy Tijuana clips in a Stanford frat house.

The film was amusing enough. Actors and crew obviously had a good time making it. But nothing like the time they were having now, watching themselves or their friends on the screen for the first time. They cheered, whooped, booed, hissed, and rolled in their seats doubled up with laughter. And it was infectious. When Helen made her first appearance I joined a cheer which rocked the hall. She played herself, a member of the camera crew. During one scene she steps into the picture with her camera and begins to disrobe.

"Hey, this stuff's great," she says. "Let's get some close-ups." She zooms the lens out as far as it will go and aims it at her crotch. "Some extreme close-ups." The screen turns blurry, then black, and she's moaning, "Yeah, closer, closer!" The crowd hoots and I see Helen, two rows in front of me, pull her coat up over her head. And I'm chanting along with everyone else "Hel — en, Hel — en...." Finally she tosses off the coat, stands and turns to make a quick bow, then dives for her seat again. Laughter. Pandemonium. Then on to the next scene. When it's over, having never figured out what you say to a porn star after the film, I leave immediately, skipping the party. But I'd had a wonderful time.

The next day Helen opens my office door a crack and peeks in. "Hey, we missed you at the party last night."

"Oh, come on in. Frankly I wasn't sure I could face you after that." We were both smiling a little sheepishly.

"Yeah, it was kind of embarrassing, wasn't it? I can't believe you came." She was blushing now.

"I can hardly believe it myself. But I'm glad I did."

"Well, then... me too."

We talked about other things for awhile. Then I blurted out: "I thought you were the prettiest woman in that film."

"No kidding?"

"No kidding. Have you had lunch yet?"

"Not yet."

"Neither have I. Care to join me?"

"Love to."

I picked the furthest place from campus I could find.

Illustration by Tanya Stewart

River Women

We are all visited periodically by incidents of our youth, moments of dreamy substance, yet preserved in images that never seem to lose their clarity. It is as if a winding artery passes through every life's forgotten mass of trivial detail, porous only to that essential information which is the nourishment of personality, of the self, of the sense each must ultimately make of life. The significance of such incidents is often unperceived during the events themselves. For example, in the experience I tell of here, my only thought was of apple pie and ice cream as I walked into a room full of naked witches. Scarcely six years old at the time, a newly enrolled first grader at St. Edward's Catholic school, it was only much later that I knew I was bewitched in that moment. And so effectively was the spell laid that some fifty years later I am still held fast.

My parents were gone on holiday and I had been sent to stay with my Aunt Elisa, the most fascinating of all my relatives, in her yellow house on the Russian River. To me she was the most exquisite creature on earth. I am told that as a toddler I would point to a Rossetti-like image in a book of fairytales, laugh, and say ""'lisa". I loved her loose-fitting clothing, the embroidered flowers and bits of glass that were sewn into her flowing skirts, the strands of shells which adorned her neck, the enameled bracelets that encircled her wrists, her long shimmering earrings of translucent beads and silver. The tinkling music which accompanied her every move, her habit of passing a hand through her long black hair, these are my earliest memories of her visits to our house in the city. These, and an air of mystery that hovered about her like smoke among the redwoods.

I had been to her house once before, a year earlier, with a friend who pronounced it "spooky" and who was glad when we left that same afternoon. But it did not appear so the day my father left me there for a week's stay. Surrounded by trees, straight as sentinels, the house radiated warmth and welcome. Yet I soon enough recalled my friend's misgivings. For my aunt was a witch. She confided this astonishing fact to me after dinner the first night. We were sitting in a wicker swing on the front porch, rocking gently in the sultry night air. I was wide-eyed and utterly credulous as she explained that there really were witches, but only good ones, who lived in the forest along the river's banks.

"What do witches do," I asked, perhaps somewhat timorously. "Real ones, I mean. I mean good ones."

"That's the only kind there are," my aunt assured me. "Sometimes people who don't know any better make up stories about wicked witches. But they're not real. You're not frightened, are you, Michael?"

"I'm not scared of you, Aunt Elisa."

"Of course you're not." She took my hand between her own. And I knew I was safe. Perhaps there really were no wicked witches. Still, it couldn't hurt to have a good one on your side.

At the age of six my relationships with women had not been particularly happy. I do not mean to say that they were unhappy, not exactly. Rather, they were defined within authoritarian regimes that, however much I chafed under them, I nevertheless accepted as the natural order of things.

My mother's brow was generally dark and pinched from a resolute conception of motherhood reduced to feeding, clothing, and chastening her offspring. The measure of her devotion — and it was considerable — was to be found in laundry loads and grocery lists. Physical manifestations of affection were difficult for her and by the time I was five I think we were equally uncomfortable in one another's arms.

The other women in my life were the nuns at school: veiled Brides of Christ moving silently, quickly, menacingly, in sterile corridors of the school building that adjoined their convent. Fear of the Lord could best be instilled, they evidently believed, through fear of his brides and scores if little miscreants were punished in those halls, just outside of classroom doors, for the edification of petrified young Catholics within.

But now I leaned against the warmth of a woman under a blanket of stars and with a chorus of crickets pulsing in my ears. Perhaps I sensed in the slow rocking of our swing a tidal change in my small world, as yet indefinable, but certain as the pull of the moon above my head. It had never shone brighter. "Time for bed," my aunt was saying. And it was not the cool voice of female authority I heard but a promise of comfort, of sweetness, of a good-night kiss.

I awoke the next morning to the sound of my aunt building a fire in her wood burning stove. My room was on the second floor, in the attic really, its walls and pitched ceiling paneled in cedar. I descended the stairs to the kitchen, still in my pajamas. "Michael!" my aunt exclaimed, "I bet you're hungry. How about some toast with strawberry jam while we wait for the stove to heat up?" Thus began, simply and unremarkably, the day of my enchantment.

After breakfast I helped my aunt gather vegetables in her garden. There were green beans, I remember, and little peas that she called "pois-mange-tout." She told me what that meant in a different language and I delighted in repeating the name until I got it right.

At six I was thought old enough, at least by my aunt, to be allowed to venture off on my own for awhile. After we had rinsed the vegetables with the garden hose she told me that she would be spending several hours in her kitchen. And if I wanted I could do a little exploring on my own if I didn't wander too far off the trail that led to the river.

I had not gone far when I came to an outcropping of rock some ten feet above the water that offered a sweeping view of the river and the few houses on the opposite side. As it was already late in the season the water level had dropped considerably from the vegetation along the banks that marked the high point of the spring flood. The broader banks of the river below me added to the challenge of lofting pine cones into the water from my sunny perch. I carefully assembled a pile of them. A fisherman on the bank below, had there been one, might well have wondered at the source of these projectiles launched at regular intervals above his head. Perhaps half reached their target, splashing soundlessly into the slow moving current. I leaned out as far as I dared to follow their course downstream and out of sight.

I would like to remember what I daydreamed that afternoon, surrounded by the voluptuous summer softness of the forest and breathing in the odor of pitch on my sticky hands. I may have slept a little. The steady drone of insects circling in broken shafts of sunlight made me drowsy. I do remember that my pile of cones was only half depleted when I decided it was time to return. I hid them under some brush for another day and headed back to the house, not five minutes away.

When I arrived I found my aunt on the porch in conversation with a woman I had never seen before. She was taller than my aunt, and slimmer, but I was astounded to see that she was similarly dressed. I had come to associate the eccentricities of color, and the lavish use of bright bits and pieces of almost anything to adorn the body, uniquely with my aunt Elisa. Could this woman with the friendly smile and curly blond hair that fell to the broad band of cord and shells that girded her waist, could she also be a witch? My aunt had said that there were other witches who lived along the river. Was this how witches dressed then?

Aunt Elisa rose to greet me as I came up the pathway. She took one of my sticky hands and led me to the woman of the cascading golden hair. "Michael, this is Pamela," my aunt said as she placed my hand into one with rings on every finger. I felt myself blushing. "And do you know what she can do?"

"Is she... is she a witch?" I didn't know what else to say. The two women laughed. Were they laughing at me? I felt confused and on the verge of tears.

"Yes! A wonderful witch," my aunt said as she knelt and put her arms around me. Then in a hushed voice close to my ear, "But do you know what she can do? Pamela makes knives. The most beautiful knives in the world."

I looked up, dumbfounded, at this woman who made knives. It never occurred to me than anyone could actually make a knife. Knives were just... there, under glass at the hardware store to be admired and coveted by people like me. I found one once, in the dirt on a vacant lot near our house. It was a pocket knife, scarred and permanently rusted shut. I never told anyone for fear it might be claimed by its rightful owner. It was a prized possession, kept well concealed in my bedroom, though sometimes carried in my pocket when it seemed unlikely that I would be found out. Now I stood in front of a woman, as beautiful and fascinating as my aunt, who could make a knife. No further proof of witches' power was needed.

Aunt Elisa told me that Pamela had come to help prepare a big feast. Other witches would be coming, some from as far away as San Francisco and Ukiah. When my aunt went to attend to something in the kitchen Pamela asked if I would like to take a little walk with her. And soon we were strolling along the river's sandy banks.

"Why are other witches coming to Aunt Elisa's," I worked up the courage to ask.

"Well, Michael, today we celebrate the autumnal equinox. It's the day when summer turns to fall. And tonight there will be a full moon. It's an important time for us."

"Why?"

Pamela sighed happily, and smiled at me. "It's a time we give thanks to the Mother Goddess for the bounty of nature during the summer months, for the trees, for all the animals, for the river too".

"Can you do magic stuff?"

We sat down on a patch of grass that was still long and green in spite of the lateness of the season. "Yes, we can do magic." Her chin rested on her knees and the ends of her golden hair mingled with green blades of grass. "But people usually don't understand what magic is. It's kind of hard to explain. We can't make things happen that go against the laws of nature. It's like the river. We can't make the river flow in the opposite direction."

I told her about my pine cones.

"That's it!" she said, obviously pleased and putting her arm around me. "Your pine cones always go in the same direction because that's nature. The river flows from the mountains to the ocean. But when you understand nature then you know why the river flows the way it does. Like where it's narrow and shallow, the water goes faster. Where it's wide and deeper, it goes more slowly. The path your pine cones take depends on where they land. Things that happen in life are kind of like that, like your pine cones going down the river. We can't change their general direction. But if we try to understand life, like the river, then sometimes we can influence its little twists and turns. And that can make a big difference. And that big difference is magic. Does that make any sense?"

I had noticed that my pine cones didn't always follow the same course downstream. "I guess so." I may have sounded a little disappointed.

She laughed. "I think you will someday because you are a clever boy. Do you have a knife, Michael?"

I think I stopped breathing. I would not have dared to bring up the subject myself. "No," I lied.

"Would you like me to make one for you?"

I buried my face against my knees and put my arms around my head so that a smothered "uh huh" was my only reply. I was deeply ashamed. If Pamela were to see how red my face was she would surely know that I was lying. To have lied was bad enough but to profit so handsomely from it was more than I could bear.

"I could make you a leather sheath so you could wear it on your belt. Would you like that?"

I threw my head into Pamela's lap and struggled to keep my shame and happiness from spilling out in a flood of tears. She bent down and put a kiss on the back of my neck. Then we returned to the house, hand in hand as dusk began to fall.

By time time there were perhaps a dozen women preparing a long wooden table on the porch and helping my aunt in the kitchen. Even if I had not known that I was in the company of witches the scene would have had a magical quality about it. My aunt disdained electric lights, preferring instead the soft illumination of candles and oil lamps. Now there were several such lamps lighting the porch and transforming the weathered yellow siding into walls of honey. The interior of the house was bathed in the glow of countless candles that cast shadows of flickering intensity across the furnishings. A small table I had not previously noticed drew my attention as the light played upon an arrangement of leaves and fruit and numerous mysterious objects. I approached gingerly, on tiptoe, and made a quick inventory of these items, objects which are as clear to me today as they were then: a tall silver goblet or chalice, two knives, one with a black handle, the other white (could Pamela have made them?), a garden trowel, an old book stitched together with leather laces, and a statue of a woman like those I had seen in church but more beautiful. I stood there breathing in air suffused with the scent of incense and candles, the smell of cedar logs burning in the fireplace, and dinner being prepared in the kitchen. And all about me, touching my face, taking my hands, bending to speak their names close to my ear, were those smiling, laughing women whose long hair and swirling skirts were enclosing me fast at the center of their world. My presence represented something beyond the comprehension of a six year old. Pamela took my hand and led me to one of her sister witches, a cherub faced woman, somewhat older than the rest. She was robed all in white and wore a thin band of silver around her temples that was surmounted with a silver crescent moon at her forehead. She raised me in her arms and I remember a hush coming over the room. "Michael," she said, "we are happy you are here with us. Tonight you shall represent the male principle.

You will be our Mabon, son of the Earth Goddess." There was much merriment when I asked, sheepishly, if I would have to do anything.

At dinner I was seated at one end of the long narrow table while Rachel, the white witch with the silver crown, sat at the opposite end. Aunt Elisa and Pamela were at my right and left. We all joined hands while Rachel said a kind of prayer. Then the feast began. And I think I never ate so well — or drank so well. For the first time in my life I was allowed a little wine. Thanksgiving, Christmas, and Easter all rolled into one could not have compared. Yet here there is a gap in my memory of this sublime evening. For the male principle fell asleep in his chair long before dessert and was carried off to bed in the arms of a good witch.

It was not the cool light of the full moon which woke me several hours later, rather it was a rhythmic, shuffling sound accompanied by the low hypnotic chant of female voices. I sat up in bed, disoriented, and was about to call for my mother when I suddenly recognized my surroundings in the moon's soft light. My clothes were draped on the chair next to the bookcase but I could not recall putting them there, nor having gotten into my pajamas. Then I remembered the feast and realized, with considerable disappointment, that I must have fallen asleep and missed dessert. Assuring myself that my aunt would have saved me a piece of pie, I crawled to the window to investigate the sounds that had awakened me.

I am only certain that I did not dream the scene before me because at the age of six I would have been incapable of doing so. I had never seen a naked woman. I could not have dreamed the female body in the detail which only the experience of later years would confirm. Thirteen women — it had not been easy to count them — stood naked in a circle under the light of the full moon, their milky bodies casting long, thin shadows on the grass behind them like the spokes of a wheel. Rachel, for I recognized her by the crown she wore, stood motionless at the center, but the others, hands linked, danced first one way, then the other, around the outer perimeter of the circle which seemed to have been laid out with great exactness. Occasionally the dancers would surge inward until their bodies touched, hands joined high above their heads, but would then fall back and resume their circular movement. They danced in rhythm to the song they sang, a refrain whose words I did not understand, endlessly repeated.

I remained at the window for what must have been at least half an hour. The ritual continued essentially unchanged until suddenly Rachel knelt and raised her arms. This was a signal to the dancers who closed in around her and sat with their legs crossed, linking hands again to reform the circle. Rachel, still kneeling with outstretched arms now seemed the focus of all light which fell upon the earth. It was as if the moon were tethered by its own beams to the silver bracelets which coiled like serpents about her wrists. There was no movement, and no sound that I could hear, yet she appeared to be speaking. After several minutes she lowered her arms and grasped the base of the chalice, the one I had seen earlier, in both hands. As she raised it high above her head the witch who had been sitting opposite her stood and moved to the outer edge of the circle again. Facing now in my direction she picked up an object from the table that had been moved outdoors. I saw then that it was Pamela, her unbound hair transformed by the moonlight into white satin ribbons that fell about her breasts. Perhaps, at that moment, I fell in love for the first time. She returned to the center of the circle and stood in front of Rachel, arms held high, both hands around the inverted handle of one of the knives. She slowly lowered her arms until the tip of the blade entered the mouth of the cup. Then the witches began to speak with one voice, a soft, unhurried voice which rose to my window in a hushed and final benediction: "Bless us, Mother, who are your daughters...."

Rachel stood and kissed Pamela on the mouth. When this kiss had been passed to each of the women in turn the ceremony was complete and they returned to the house. As for me, the ambiguous stirring of unrecognized sexuality suddenly focused on apple pie and ice cream. I went downstairs to claim my portion.

And so I come now to that moment I spoke of earlier, one of those transformative moments that shape our lives and make us who we are. If it seems that I have gone on overlong about the events leading up to it, the only excuse I can offer is that, in looking back on these events, I see that each had a part to play in preparing me for the moment itself. No doubt every life contains many experiences that hold the potential to mould us in some fundamental way. But few there are for which we are willing, and unafraid, to make ourselves truly vulnerable. For me this had been a day of opening to receive, and to be shaped by, the grace I was accorded on that night.

I must have appeared somewhat comical, standing there sleepily in my pajamas. The women all smiled at me and made no move to cover their nakedness. Perspiring lightly from their exertions they sat in the dim light of the few candles still burning. I walked shyly to my aunt and placed a hand tentatively on her knee. As she bent her head to me I whispered that I would like my piece of pie. She laughed and took me into her arms. "Our male principle

has returned," she proclaimed, "and he would have his pie."
This announcement was met with cheers and applause. My
head was cradled against my aunt's breast and I could feel
the thin, cool film of her perspiration against my cheek.
She kissed my forehead. The feel of her skin, the taste of
salt on my lips, and the smell of her perfume banished all
thoughts of dessert.

Then, suddenly, the room began to turn and I was floating some distance above the floor as I was passed from the
embrace of my aunt to that of Pamela who sat next to her.
"And he shall have his knife," she whispered as she rocked
me gently in her hair. The world can stand still for six-year
olds as well as anyone. Part of me will rest forever in that
nest of golden hair like an undiscovered Moses among the
reeds. Then I was moving again, into the arms of Suzanne
who said that I would possess the wisdom of women. By now
I had abandoned myself completely to riding this wave of
womanly flesh and was beyond any sensation but the purely
tactile. My hands groped to steady myself as I was passed
from one embrace to the next and thus in innocence did I
discover the sweetness of a woman's touch. Each witch kissed
me and whispered her gift and when, at last, I was returned
to my aunt's arms I felt that I must truly be a prince like
those in books of fairytales.

Aunt Elisa carried me to the kitchen and I ate the piece
of pie she had saved for me . Then together we climbed the
steps to my room where she tucked me into bed again. I fell
immediately into the deep, untroubled sleep of a six-year
old, unaware that, for me, the source of sensuality, of all
things magical, had been permanently fixed.

Lyrics to Sisters of the River

How long have you been standing
Your nightly vigil by these waters
How many times has the light been passed
To the keeping of your daughters?

This river is as wide as dreams
As deep as love and sorrow
At every bend your beacons burn
'Til the coming of the morrow

Your fires guide the passage
Of the boats that journey on
And the embers when at last you sleep
Turn gray in the light of dawn

Sisters of the River
Keepers of the light
Sisters of the River
Daughters of the night

How few there are who know the way
Or recognize your names
Yet when the winds howl through at night
And the river's lashed with rain

I've heard their voices cry out to you
They beg of you a song
They beg of you a lullaby
And peace when the night is long

May their time of tribulation
Know the sweetness of that song
And may their journeys be kept safe
In the hours before the dawn

Sisters of the River
Keepers of the light
Sisters of the River
Daughters of the night

Jazz Hands

Mac was fat and short and black and had what my piano teacher used to call "jazz hands". She didn't mean it as a compliment. If a kid had delicate, fine boned fingers that splayed out like spoons at the tips and arched across the keys like a crab walking sideways, he had "classical hands". You were born with them. The consolation prize was "jazz hands". She'd tell that to some kid who didn't have "classical hands" like Van Cliburn's so his mother wouldn't give up hope and stop paying for lessons. But what she meant was: you'll never be a real pianist but you can always fool around and play a little jazz.

Except for Andre Watts, all the black players I knew back then had "jazz hands": stubby fat fingers that stuck straight out like Mac's. When he played, his fingers just padded around and smothered the keys like he was trying to round off their square edges. The notes that came out sounded like that too: fat and sweet and mellow. No edges. He was just about the best around but no jazzmen were getting any gigs in the early '70's. Jazz was out.

When I first met them Mac and Winifred were living in a run-down cottage just off Telegraph. Winifred couldn't stand Berkeley and it was a sore subject with them. She'd keep asking to move up north somewhere in the country and he'd say yeah, for sure they would someday. But they'd been in that house for three years already when I moved into the place next door. Without her it would probably have become a crash pad for spaced out musicians but she wouldn't put up with any of that shit and the inside was always neat as a pin. She was an Irish gypsy who still spoke with a brogue even though she'd been here for years. At 35 she was ten years older than Mac but you would have guessed them to be the same age. She was about his height and just a little plump, in a sexy way, not at all fat. I don't think I ever saw her hair because she always wore a scarf like gypsies do, pulled tightly across her forehead and tied behind the neck. It drew your attention to the sharpness of her freckled cheekbones and the quickness of her small, black eyes. She wore skirts too, never pants, full skirts of embroidered fabric to which she'd attach beads and bits of wood or glass. Usually she had a shawl around her shoulders, something she'd made, that fell below her waist in back. Her parents were Travelers, as the Irish Gypsies are called, and she was born in a caravan on the Ring of Dingle peninsula. Her father was a tinker and she grew up in that same horse drawn wagon moving from town to town until she was in her teens. She never talked much about her past but at some point she got hired as an *au pair* by the family of an American professor who was teaching at Trinity College in Dublin. At the end of the year she moved with them back to Berkeley where he was a specialist in linguistics or something like that. Later on she got a job working in a coffee house and that's where she met Mac. She just went over to the table where he was sitting and read his palm. Sometimes she'd do Tarot card readings for the customers but she couldn't resist taking one of Mac's fat hands into her own. Beats me what she read in that palm but it wasn't long before they were living together. Opposites attract, they say. And for sure they made a cute couple.

But apart from her job you had to wonder why Winifred was willing to continue on in Berkeley. She hated hippies, hippies and freaks and dead beat musicians and she could be a real witch when she thought Mac was being taken in by them. Nobody messed with her and that included Mac. He adored Winifred but I think he was a little in awe of her too. Or maybe respect would be a better way to put it. The kind of respect for a woman that wasn't all that common back in those days. When they horsed around and teased one another there was always a hint of shyness in his big, gentle grin. He really loved that girl and sometimes he'd start crying when he was drunk and go on about how he didn't deserve a chick who was so clean and smart as a whip and who took care of a slob like him who couldn't even buy her a decent pair of sheets.

I had an old "f" hole Gibson with a single pick-up and sometimes Mac and I would jam at the only bar on Telegraph that had a piano. We didn't get paid but the owner didn't mind if we passed a hat. On a good night we'd get maybe twenty bucks and a few joints. Afterwards we'd pick up a six-pack of Guiness and go back to Mac's to drink with Winifred, two each. She thought I was OK because I had a regular job teaching music at a junior college and never did hard stuff. Mac and I always split the grass before we got home but I'd let him keep whatever bread was left over after buying the beer. Winifred would take it as soon as we came in and put it down the front of her blouse like that was the normal place for it. I guess she must have worn a bra or that money would have just flopped around in there and I thought that was funny because none of the chicks I knew wore bras back then but they all wanted to be like Winifred. I mean what was funny is that Winifred took a bath every day, Mac said, and wore a bra and couldn't have been more different from the girls who wanted to be just like her. And something else Mac told me once when he was drunk. He said that Winifred was the best lay he ever had but right over their bed, like a foot above the headboard, she'd hung this crewel work thing she'd made that said "WASHED IN THE BLOOD OF THE LAMB". She could be hard to figure out but she was the best thing that ever happened to Mac and he was the first to say so.

What Mac wanted more than anything in those days was his own piano and Winifred was determined that he'd have one. The money she got from us went into a pot somewhere and she said she'd tell us when it added up to a hundred bucks. In the meantime we could just forget about that money and start looking for a piano. We didn't have to look far as it turned out. The music department where I was teaching decided to replace the old uprights in the practice rooms. They were all pretty scratched up but they'd been kept tuned and the felts were good and faculty members could pick them up for seventy-five bucks a pop. Winifred made me swear it was a good deal before she handed over the $87.50 in the pot. I knew a guy with a truck and the three of us brought one home. Mac was going out of his head trying to decide where to put it, but it finally occurred to him to keep it in the garage where he could jam with some of his more questionable pals without Winifred being up tight. Getting it into the garage was no problem because these pianos had big wheels attached to the cases to make them easy to move around. Mac grinned and walked all around it, patting its sides like a horse and wiping the keys with his shirtsleeve. Then, with Winifred sitting beside him, her eyes closed and her head resting on his shoulder, he played that thing for a solid hour, non-stop. Afterwards we toasted it with a bottle of French champagne we'd bought with the $12.50 we had left over.

Mac was able to pick up occasional session work at Bay Area recording studios and with Winifred's coffee shop money they managed to get by. But when she announced that she was pregnant Mac got to wondering how they could support a kid. Maybe he ought to get some kind of regular job he told me one afternoon as if he were the first person ever to conceive of working for a living. We'd been drinking beer and he was crying and laughing about how Winifred was going to have his kid. He said that if it was a boy he was going to call him "Big" because he'd always wanted to be big and besides it could stand for Black Irish Gypsy. Then he started saying how it was a real responsibility to be a father and how the word even scared him a little. He'd never had a father, not one that he knew anyway, so he didn't know too much about how to be one. But he supposed it meant bringing home enough money for food and diapers and things like that. The gist of it was that Big was going to have a real father so we started thinking what Mac could do to have a steady income. It wasn't hard to narrow down the possibilities. No education ruled out a lot of jobs. And as far as manual labor was concerned, he wasn't much interested. He didn't mind hard work, he wanted me to know, but he was a musician and had to think about his hands. He knew this bass player who lost three fingers to a Skill saw. I called him a lazy ass and he looked a little hurt. But when I glanced at those fat hands of his, soft as a woman's, I had to admit that manual labor really wasn't his thing. I just kept looking and thinking "jazz hands", and suddenly I had an idea.

When you got right down to it, all Mac could do was play piano. Maybe the clubs weren't paying for his kind of music but if we could just find a half dozen private students for weekly lessons he'd have enough to assure Big's immediate future and to make up the bed with new sheets for Winifred's return from the hospital. The trick would be finding the students and this was my idea: everywhere you looked back then there were bulletin boards — in supermarkets, coffee houses, health food stores, head shops, even on street corners. And probably half of the announcements that feathered the surface of these eyesores advertised free classes in anything from Tai Chi to how to strip for your lover. The idea seemed to be that if you had a minimum of expertise in anything at all, no matter how useless or uninteresting, you were duty bound to teach it to your fellow humans. If we could get up a class in basic theory or harmony, Mac might be able to get himself some regular students out of it. We'd run the thing in his garage and when I'd talk about something, Mac would demonstrate it on the piano. Then he'd jazz things up a bit as if to show what anyone could do after just a few lessons. With a little luck, he'd hook enough paying customers this way to put himself in business.

Mac thought it was a great idea, though I suspected his enthusiasm had something to do with the fact that he wouldn't have to leave the house or lift a finger. But Winifred wasn't convinced. People in Berkeley spent their money on grass, not piano lessons, she said. At best we'd get ourselves a garage full of free-loading freaks. If a regular job was what Mac really had in mind, why didn't he check out things like restaurants and supermarkets, or maybe a construction job. Mac looked at me with pain and panic in his eyes. Truth is, I had to half-way agree with Winifred but I could scarcely abandon him now. I told her she might be right but we'd know soon enough and there'd still be plenty of time for Mac to look for another line of work. He winced at that but Winifred said she guessed it wouldn't hurt to try. Still, she didn't like the idea of a bunch of pot heads hanging around the place, especially after the baby came. Not to worry, gypsy queen, I said, the class would be over in a month and by then Mac would have his hard-core half dozen.

So we put up our signs and I bought a big pad of newsprint and some felt pens to use in place of a blackboard. I found an old easel in a second-hand shop to prop it up. Then we sat back to wait for the first class, two weeks later. Mac was relieved. Winifred, on the other hand, never said a word about the class and became increasingly irritable as Mac just hung around talking about all the money that would be rolling in soon. I told him to cool it but he really believed now, far more than I, that it was all going to work out.

I thought he might be right when more than twenty people showed up the first night. A few were street people I recognized but the rest seemed like solid prospects. The big surprise was The Russian. I don't know if he really was Russian but that's what everyone called him on the street. It could have been on account of his looks. He was enormous and wore a beard so full that all you ever saw of him was eyes, a fat nose, and a little bit of forehead under a mass of wild, tangled hair. Or it could have been his politics. He usually hung out on Telegraph peddling pamphlets with a hammer and sickle on the front. He never spoke, just shoved them under your nose.

People sat on the floor and after introductions I started on standard notation and scales with Mac filling in on the piano. Everyone was mellow and some were actually taking notes and I thought it was going pretty well. Except for The Russian. He just sat there slowly shaking his massive head from side to side in apparent disagreement with everything I said. After awhile it got to be pretty disconcerting. There wasn't anything to disagree with. From C natural to E natural is a major third. But he'd just shake his head, almost sadly, as if I were the biggest fool he'd ever encountered.

At the break everyone sat around talking and lighting up reefers. The Russian kept to himself in one corner of the garage. I watched him unwrap a couple of soggy sardine sandwiches he'd brought with him. Pretty soon the place smelled like fish and dope but I was afraid to open the garage door. We didn't need any hassles from the fuzz or Winifred - especially on that first night.

The plan was that Mac would get more into it during the second half. I'd talk a little about chords and inversions and then Mac would go into long demonstrations of what can happen when you start moving things around the keyboard. The less I spoke and the more Mac played, the livelier The Russian got. His eyes squinted as he pulled out a fat joint and he would get to swaying crazily every time Mac took off. He must have had a colossal pair of lungs because he'd inhale for ten seconds straight. The joint burned down a good half inch with every puff. I never saw any smoke come out either.

Soon I wasn't talking anymore and Mac was "gone". He stood at the piano with his eyes closed in that blue marijuana haze and started improvising. His hands just lolled over the keyboard and his fingers scarcely seemed to move but everyone was really grooving on the music that was coming out of that old piano. I was choking on the smoke but I was happy. I'd let Mac keep it up for awhile — I was sure he'd keep playing until I stopped him — then I'd say "next week, same time, same place" and let it drop that Mac did occasionally accept private students if anyone was interested. I had no doubt that he'd have more than he could handle.

I still don't know what set The Russian off. Maybe he figured I was about to start talking again, or maybe he just freaked out. But he suddenly stood up and pulled a can of spray paint out of his bag. This was no doubt the explanation for much of the applied political science decorating the town's walks and buildings. I didn't want to think about what he had in mind for the garage. For awhile he just danced and bobbed around the piano shaking the can and the little metal ball inside in time with the music. No one paid him much attention. Stranger things could be seen on most Berkeley street corners. Mac, oblivious to everything around him, kept on playing.

But then The Russian started painting the piano — red. It was insane. He kept circling and dancing with that paint can going full blast. The piano, Mac, even the air was turning red. I was afraid the place would blow up the next time someone lit a match and I rushed to open the garage door. Maybe it was because Mac kept on playing, but everyone just sat there grinning and saying "Wow" and "Far out, man" almost reverentially as if we'd planned the whole thing. Anyway, there was sure as hell way no way I'd be able to stop The Russian alone.

There was paint everywhere. It speckled my newsprint, dusted the floor, and ran down between the keys of the piano. Mac finally had to quit playing when he couldn't breathe anymore and he just stood there staring at his paint spattered hands and clothes with a puzzled look on his face. The Russian kept it up until his paint ran out, then he let out a whoop and jumped on top of the piano. He landed so hard that it started rolling. Bodies scattered and The Russian rode it like a rodeo bull right out of the garage, down the driveway, and into the street. He was mashing the keys with his foot and belting out the Communist Internationale as he lumbered into the night on top of Mac's piano.

Everyone watched until he was out of sight, then they started shaking thumbs like they did back then and saying what a groovy class it had been and how for sure they'd be back next week.

When at last everyone was gone, Mac stood alone in the middle of the garage. The red paint had dried to a crust on his clothes and in his hair. He was still looking at his puffy hands, palms up in front of his belly, and he reminded me of one of those fat Buddhas you see in Chinese restaurants. "What happened, man?" was all he could say.

"I don't know, Mac, but we'd better go see."

I led him out of the garage and down the street the way The Russian had gone. He was pretty freaked out and just kept repeating "Shit, man, Winifred will kill us." I was a little annoyed that he included me in this double homicide but I knew we were both in for it. "How in hell are we gonna tell her about this," he wanted to know. For once I would like to have said "why don't you come up with something for a change?" But I didn't have the heart. The poor guy was suffering enough.

At the end of the block we saw it, run up on the parking strip and leaning against a tree. One of the legs had broken off and the top had popped open. It was a wreck. I thought it would have made a great album cover, this busted up, blood-rust piano leaning against a tree in the silver light of a halogen street lamp. I was trying to think up a good name for an album like that when I saw Winifred sitting on the curb. Her elbows were on her knees, her chin was resting in her hands, and she was looking straight at Mac. He had seen her too. He put his hands behind his back and shuffled his feet. "Hi, Winnie," he said.

Winifred didn't get up. She just sat there. Her skirt fell between bare thighs and lay bunched up on the pavement. Little mirrors sewn into the fabric caught what light there was in the street as she swayed slowly from side to side.

"Let's go, Mac," she said. Mac seemed relieved that there wasn't going to be a scene right there on the sidewalk. "I mean let's go away. I want to live in the country, you and me and the baby."

Mac was silent for a long time. Then he walked over and sat down next to Winifred. He scraped his heel along the pavement and looked at his hands. When he finally turned to look at her I saw the shy smile he got on his face when the two of them played around together. "Sure, Winnie," he said. Then he took one of her hands in his own and they got up and walked right past me like I wasn't there. When they had gone maybe twenty feet, Mac glanced at me over his shoulder and shrugged.

I helped them pack and gave Mac some money for the rental truck. They found a place on the Russian River and Winifred would be working at a café in Rio Nido until the baby came. Mac, true to form, was hoping to get a job pouring at a local winery's tasting room. One day I drove up with the last of the seventy-five dollar pianos as a belated going away present. Mac cried when he saw me pull in with it.

I went up to visit a few times after that but then we sort of lost touch. I got accepted in a PhD program at UCLA and had to move south. Our lives just went off in different directions. It's always sad when you lose track of old friends. Last I heard Mac and Winifred were living with their two kids near Santa Rosa where Mac was playing in a cocktail lounge with his own trio and doing real well. Jazz was back.

Damascening

Martin stands directly behind her in line at the bank: her narrow black heels planted in thick carpeting; full-length wool coat, blue, close-fitting around her boot-tops, less so at the hips, swelling in padded luxury about her shoulders; curls, deeply-hennaed curls, falling in lovely and profuse abandonment down her back.

"Next in line, please."

She steps quickly to the counter, vacating a column of perfumed air where he now takes up his place at the head of the line. She turns slightly, though not enough for him to see her face, and removes a small parcel from her handbag. Her hands are white, her fingers long and jeweled.

"Can I rent a safe deposit box for a month or two?" he hears her ask the teller. But things seem not to go her way.

"No, I don't have an account here."

"Sorry, regular clients only. But you might check down the block at Wells-Fargo."

"I see. Thank you. I'll give them a try."

The package falls to the floor as she backs from the counter. Martin's instinct is to reach for it but he checks his hand. The woman returns the package to her purse, then strides through the cordoned exit and out the door before he can catch even a glimpse of her face.

She would have been beautiful though, he thinks.

At dinner Martin considers relating this scene to his wife. The incident is trivial but the woman and her package intrigue him. What would Sarah say? It's one thing to look at a woman, another to install her in a gallery of romantic fantasies. Sarah has said this to him more than once, in gentle reproof, that he cultivates, he can't remember exactly how she puts it, a secret garden or something equally suggestive.

He thinks he is no different from other men — or women, for that matter with the possible exception of Sarah. He assumes we all occasionally imagine life in the company of another who once, if only in the space of a glance, sent through us something as delirious and full of possibilities as the sound of an orchestra tuning up.

But Sarah has gotten to him with this garden thing. Why give her the opportunity to bring it up again, unjustly too? For thirty years he has been faithful to this woman who prepares his dinner, who has been putting on weight these last years, whose skin has started drooping a little over the cheekbones and puckering under the eyes, this woman he has promised to have, hold, and so forth until death. Yet even as he opens his mouth to describe the day's events, he looks at Sarah and feels the sting of an old reproach. He will not mention the lady in the bank.

Martin steps from the streetcar at precisely seven fifty-five AM. So completely has he forgotten the incident of the previous day that he now walks directly past the bank's locked doors thinking only of the work he has planned for this morning. He is a lean man, with an energetic step, in clothes a size too large. His gray coat and rumpled slacks reveal neither vanity nor concern for style. A fringed, multi-colored scarf which Sarah has made for him lends an incongruously rakish quality to his tall, slightly stooped figure. The rounded shoulders are not uncommon in his profession, nor are the eyes. They seem to take in nothing which is not directly in front of them. They examine the sidewalk as if trying to decide the exact placement of his leading foot. Yet he walks briskly. As always, he will stop at Helen's for a cup of coffee before opening the shop. He will order "decaf" so that his hands won't shake.

Coffee is now served at Helen's in the kind of insulated foam cup which threatens to force scalding liquid up over the lip and onto your hands if you grip them too tightly. A paper napkin in one hand and such a cup in the other, Martin recalls a time ten years ago, or was it fifteen, when Helen's employed a good china cup, a reassuringly solid restaurant cup of pleasing dimensions, and a real saucer.

There are no vacant tables this morning. Each stands in a zone of studied privacy with its solitary reader, muncher, gazer at nothing in particular. He is looking about for a familiar face when he sees her for the second time, again from behind. It must be she — the same coat, the red curls. He circles the room affecting the slightly confused, indecisive attitude of the seat-less pariah until he can see her face. He is not surprised that she is beautiful; though she is older than he would have guessed, mid forties perhaps, not that much younger than himself.

"May I join you," he asks. He has to sit with someone, after all. He finds it easier and generally more pleasant to talk to women than men. And here he will know how to begin the conversation.

"Of course." She smiles easily, small crows' feet linking green eyes and high, cheekbones, a smudge of lipstick on perfect teeth.

He puts down his cup and before he has even settled into the chair asks, "Did you find a safe deposit box?"

She swallows hard on a gulp of coffee.

"I was behind you in the bank yesterday."

"Oh. Well, yes, I finally got one. Good thing there's lots of banks on this street."

"Good and bad," he says. "Any more and there won't be a place to get a cup of coffee."

Martin is almost comfortable sitting with this stranger. Another man, he thinks, might have been intimidated by her style of dress, her make-up. He is pleased with himself.

"Do you live near here?" he asks.

"No, I'm from Santa Rosa. I was raised in San Francisco, though, just a couple blocks from here."

"So you've come back to visit us."

"My father passed away last month. I'm down to put the house up for sale."

"I'm sorry…"

"It's been coming for a long time." She pauses briefly, acknowledging grief, then banishing it with a toss of her head. "It's depressing staying in the house and sorting through all the stuff so I walk over here to get out sometimes. I hope I don't sound too dreary."

"It must be hard for you."

"You're very nice. I'm just about done. I'm taking a few things back with me, the rest goes to Goodwill. What about you? What do you do?"

"I'm a jeweler, a watchmaker actually. I have a little shop down the street."

She places both hands on the edge of the table and there again is that gorgeous smile.

"You're kidding! Really?"

"Really what?"

"A watchmaker, I mean."

"The best," he says with a shy grin across the top of this coffee cup.

"Well, you're just the man I need to see. Dad had a lot of old pocket watches. He worked for the Southern Pacific and used to collect them. Some are gold, I think. That's what I was putting in the bank yesterday."

Martin winces, remembering the fall her package had taken.

"I thought maybe they're worth something so I should put them someplace safe for a while. Maybe you could look at them? It's not like I want to sell them or anything but I suppose I should have them appraised."

"I'd be happy to."

"I'd pay you, of course."

"No, no ... It would be a pleasure to look at them."

"See, I knew you were nice. Can I drop by today?"

He gives her his card. "Anytime. It's on the second floor. I'm Martin."

"Gillian," she says, extending her hand.

Martin climbs the flight of stairs to the neighborhood shop he has opened at exactly nine o'clock for nearly thirty years. Not once has his schedule varied — streetcar, Helen's, work — except for the switch to "decaf" in '81. At fifty-two his eyes are still good and his hands steady. "The best," he'd said. But isn't it true? The walls of his cramped quarters are lined with lathes, presses, and old oak cabinets of a hundred drawers crammed with still older and irreplaceable pinions, springs, wheels, and pallets. His workbench bristles with tools of surgical precision. He is not a jeweler who spends his time selling watchbands and replacing batteries. Only the occasional client sets foot here. Yet a stream of rare and antique timepieces flows through his skilled hands. They arrive from collectors, museums, and other jewelers across the country, drawn by his reputation as a master repairman and restorer of old watches. His new acquaintance cannot suspect how fortunate she is to have his services, and for nothing.

It is with satisfaction then that Martin opens a parcel from yesterday's mail and withdraws a Waltham Premier Maximus pocket watch. The exact layout of its movement is in his mind's eye: its harmony of twenty-three diamond, ruby, and sapphire jewels, gold jewel settings and train, so fitted and balanced that even today he can adjust it to within a few seconds a week.

He removes his jacket and scarf, then sits at the bench where so many years of his life have passed in quiet labor. There are no distractions here except for a travel poster of Geneva which Martin has taped above the bench. From long habit his eyes glance upwards. Couples are strolling at early evening beside the lake. In the distance a paddlewheel steamer is passing near a yellow and white building of rococo cornices and black iron balconies — the Hotel Bellevue. A soft light comes from a dormer cut into its slate roof. Martin has calculated that the view of someone standing there would be of the steamer, the opposite shore, of dusk settling on blue hills.

He turns the watch several times in his hand — and he is thinking of the lady in the blue coat. He is a nice man, she said. What would Sarah say?

Martin opens the case, the artist's eye beguiled by the exquisite damascening of the movement, fantasy etched in imitation of an extravagant god who hangs unseen rainbows in the shells of oysters. But the watchmaker's eye perceives the chaos. The mainspring has snapped in its necessary effort to escape an order of gears and pivots. He deftly removes the bridges to discover that three leaves of the center wheel pinion have been chipped and its lower pivot twisted beyond repair. Replacements are not available. They would have to be machined with difficult and time-consuming effort. And the watch has been abused. The once beautifully damascened bridges are discolored and deeply pitted with rust. Tomorrow he must return the timepiece to its owner for it is not restorable at reasonable cost.

There are footsteps in the hall. Martin glances up to see Gillian smiling and waving at him through the door's glass pane.

"I'm sorry," she says, sweeping in and flopping a huge, silvered handbag on the narrow counter which separates his work space from the entryway. "I just couldn't wait to hear what you'd tell me. Do you mind or should I come back later?"

"No," he says. "It's OK." He smiles. "You look... different."

She is wearing loose-fitting, black cashmere slacks, and an open jacket of white moiré silk. Her blouse is a print of enormous flowers in brilliant reds. On her head rests a black bowler, an amethyst-capped rabbit's foot pinned to its band.

"Oh, the day's so nice I thought I'd go back and put on something a little more cheerful before the bank opened. I like your poster." Her eyes take in the faded green walls. "I've got lots of them you can have," she says. "I'll bring some down next time I'm in town. This place could use a little color, don't you think?"

He laughs. "Maybe it could."

"You know, this is really nice of you." She removes the familiar package from her handbag and unwraps it on the counter. "Dad loved these things. He'd wear a different one every day. I think they all work OK."

The watches are well-packed. Martin is less concerned now about the fall in the bank. And they are magnificent. More than a dozen examples of the finest watches made to exacting railroad standards by American manufacturers: Waltham, Hamilton, Ball, Howard, Rockford, Elgin, and the rest. He takes them to his bench and opens each one. Then he astounds her with his assessment of their worth.

"Whey!" she says. "Glad I got to them before the tax man." Martin invites her to the bench and places a loupe in her hand. As she bends closely over his shoulder, he points out the characteristics of a railroad timepiece, the beauty and precision of its movement.

Her hand is on his shoulder now, a careless gesture perhaps. "Martin, this has been so good of you. Could I invite you for dinner tonight? Kind of a thank you. I'm going to try that new place where the drugstore used to be."

He is not prepared for this. "Well, I... that's very nice of you...."

"You'll come then?"

"I can't really. I mean, look at me!"

"Oh, come on. You're just fine. We'll have an early dinner and I'll drive you home afterwards. I'll make reservations for 5 o'clock." And she is out the door before he can make some further protest.

Did he just let this happen? She must know he is married. He wears a ring. So to her it doesn't matter. Why should it, after all? The invitation is perfectly proper. He's been out with clients and sales representatives in the past. And if Gillian had been rather flirtatious he'd certainly done nothing to encourage her. It's just the way she is.

He wishes he could speak with Sarah. He would like to tell her that his secret garden, if she must call it that, is a simple, uncluttered place. Most of its occupants come and go in a matter of days, hours, even minutes. Few have proven durable over the years, and even these are merely the subjects of innocent reminiscence. One is an angelic girl who scratched his name in her leg with her father's hunting knife when they were twelve. She moved shortly afterwards, "MARTY" still visible in the delicate traces of her dried blood, and he never saw her again. Another is a dancer who left for New York years ago but never fails to send a birthday card to the shop.

He picks up the phone. He'll be home late tonight. He is going to be appraising a consignment of old watches after closing. No, he'll just grab a bite at Helen's. He'll be home around eight.

Aisles of soap and toothpaste have given way to pink-draped tables and potted plants but Martin is pleased that the new proprietors have retained the black and white tile floor of the old drugstore. He and Gillian are seated at the exact spot where , for years, a scale told fortunes for a penny.

"You haven't told me what you do," he says when they have ordered.

"Oh, I have a travel agency in Santa Rosa. But it pretty much runs itself nowadays. Mainly just an excuse to travel."

"Ah, the posters."

"That's right." She smiles at him. "Do you like to travel?"

Martin is relieved to speak at last the words "my wife". He explains that she will neither fly nor take a ship and dislikes sleeping in any bed other than her own. This is not untrue, but he fails to add that it could apply equally to himself.

"But what about you, Martin?" Gillian insists. "Wouldn't you like to travel?"

"Well... perhaps I would. I have this notion of visiting Switzerland and seeing all those places I've ordered bits and pieces from over the years. I'd snoop around for old watches during the day and eat cheese fondue at night."

"Sounds great!"

"Maybe someday."

"What are you waiting for?"

"I don't know — a bridge, I guess."

Gillian orders wine with dinner, and a second bottle when the first is emptied midway through the main course. Biographical details are allowed to fall into place, the significant carefully set in a context of the irrelevant to avoid too obvious an acknowledgement of this sudden intimacy. That Gillian has been single for many years is revealed in reference to the demands of setting up her own business after a divorce, a love of life on the road, an inability to settle down. The quotidian of Martin's work and childless marriage is presented half-apologetically and without complaint.

Yet the concertmaster's 'A' has been bowed. By dessert, Martin, who is beginning to feel the effects of too much wine, scarcely hears his companion's voice. He is walking the streets of Geneva, Gillian's hand in his. A bell in the distance has just tolled seven. They turn onto a promenade which will take them along the shoreline. It is growing dark, and colder now. Gillian leans into him. The warmth of the Hotel Bellevue lies not two hundred yards ahead.

Gillian signals for the check. "Martin," she says, "did you and Sarah never want to have children?"

He takes a last sip of wine and begins to carefully refold his napkin. "We never... there was an understanding." Yet as he speaks he cannot recall the nature of that understanding. "Time went by," he says, "our lives fell into a routine." Was it really nothing more than this? The thought oppresses him.

"So you never really wanted kids?"

Martin places his napkin to one side and looks at her. "I think I would have liked.... yes," he says, "perhaps a son."

Ten minutes later they are standing at the door of Gillian's father's house. Martin is thinking of Gillian playing on these steps as a child, as a teenager returning from a date, and then she is inviting him in.

"How about some coffee?" she asks.

Martin glances at his watch. "It's getting late...."

"It's not even seven. Have a cup, then I'll drive you home."

Inside, their words echo faintly in the empty rooms. Martin leans against a wall, watching Gillian prepare the coffee.

"I think I'm a little tipsy," she says. She turns towards him, her hand to her mouth. "I don't normally.... It was fun though, wasn't it?"

In the living room there is but one place to sit, a large couch which has been covered with a protective sheet. Martin sits at one end, Gillian in the center. Her saucer is in her lap, her arm rests on a cushion between them. She looks about the empty room and says, almost to herself, "It's strange after your parents die, when you're not married, no kids." She sighs a self-mocking little sigh, and smiles at Martin. "It's lonely here," she says.

"When will you be leaving?"

"I'm listing the house with a realtor tomorrow. A few more days and I'll be on my way."

Neither speaks for a time. Then: "Martin," she asks, "are you happy?"

He replies slowly, not wanting to slur his words. "Such a question! I suppose so. I guess I never really think about it. Are you?"

"Sometimes I am."

"What makes you happy?"

"Oh, seeing a country for the first time, meeting people unexpectedly, people I like. Being here with you." She takes his hand and turns to face him. Her legs, bent at the knee, are drawn up and tucked under her thigh like a mermaid's tail. Head and curls incline to one side and rest lightly against the high back of the sofa.

Martin reaches out, hesitates for a moment, then touches his fingers lightly to her cheek. "You're so beautiful," he tells her.

Twenty minutes later Gillian is dropping Martin off a block from his house. "Tomorrow, if you like," she tells him. "I'll be at Helen's tomorrow morning."

The following morning, for the first time in many years, Martin skips Helen's and walks directly from the streetcar to his shop. He allows the door to lock behind him. The shades are still pulled and, from the hall, it appears that no one is inside.

He sits with his eyes closed, or staring occasionally at a row of tools or the poster which hangs above them. Perhaps the mainspring of Martin's life, measured out in an orderly repetition of unremarkable beats, is at this moment threatening to burst the mechanism of its restraint. What things are within his reach, one might ask: travel, laughter, absurdity, the fulfillment of many dreams? A child, perhaps? No, better now to grow in endless intellectual and erotic awakenings, unleashing devils in one another to be their children. Helen's is two minutes away.

Yet as Gillian, who still sits there, sees the clock's hands slide past nine o'clock, Martin reaches for the Premier

Maximus he had intended to return unrepaired. Within an hour, over two hundred of its parts lie before him. When they have been arranged in dishes for cleaning and polishing, he clears his bench except for the damascened bridges. These he measures to within one-thousandth of an inch and traces replacements on nickel shim stock of the same gauge. Two hours later the new pieces have been cut and shaped, pivots drilled, and the undamaged jewel settings remounted. Then he secures each bridge, in turn, to the workbench and with tools unused for years begins the damascening. For hours he remains bent over the work, inlaying in gold a fantasy of swirls folding endlessly in upon themselves. Like some medieval artisan laboring in the high vaulted darkness of a cathedral he carves beauty where none will see it. Noon passes without his noticing. He is undisturbed except for a faint knocking at the door around three. By five he has finished. Tomorrow he will make a new center wheel and fit a spring to the motor barrel. Still another day will be spent in cleaning and reassembling the watch. He will be unable to charge the worth of his labor.

He unlocks the last bridge and examines it under the loupe. It is perfect. In three days the watch will be fully restored. And so precisely will it be adjusted as to never vary by more than a second or two in a week's time. By five-fifteen he is on the streetcar, heading home.

Lyrics to A Road to Somewhere

I'm driving to work on a Monday morning
Radio's blaring something I don't hear
Forgot my turn at Fourth and Sunset
A turn I make a couple hundred times a year

And now I'm wondering what if I just keep going
I'm wondering where this road might end
It's gotta be a road to somewhere
Maybe somewhere that I have never been

I can't say that I'm unhappy
Things at home are OK I suppose
There's always bills and something needs fixing
'Round a house worth less than what I owe
But I won't say, I won't say I'm discontented
Got two kids, a home, and a loving wife
We usually go to church on Sunday
Just an average kind of life

I could stop and fill the tank down the road a spell
Watch those numbers fly by at the pump
Were you ever way up high and looking down
Fighting back a dizzy urge to jump

I don't know where this road would take me
I'd be travelling alone and travelling blind
The only thing I'd know for certain
Is the life that I would leave behind

And I can't say that I'm unhappy
Things at home are OK I suppose
There's always bills and something needs fixing
'Round a house worth less than what I owe
But I won't say, I won't say I'm discontented
Got two kids, a home, and a loving wife
We usually go to church on Sunday
Just an average kind of life

I'll be turning 'round at Ninth and Parkside
I'll be on the job by half past eight
I'll get myself put back together
And try to get my head on straight

Still I'm looking down this road to somewhere
Wondering what might lie beyond this light
It's just another Monday morning
In an average, an average kind of life

Pedro's Gift

Pedro awoke at seven to the pealing of the great bell, sounding this morning for the first time in ten years. The church had been rebuilt from the rubble in which it lay all those years and a new steeple constructed to receive the bell, the only part undamaged in the war. Now its steady tolling flowed in lava-like waves through narrow streets, lapped at doorways, and surged against stone walls still scarred with the pock-marks of gunfire. Today, ten years from the time those guns fell silent, was to be the day of healing, a day when the discord and hatreds left behind by civil war would be banished forever from the village of San Ramon del Rio. Pedro felt those sonorous waves course through him, bringing shivers of joy and excitement. If unclear as to the purpose of the day's events, he was nevertheless going to be a part of them. And he was ready. At long last he would present his gift to the village.

For over a year he had labored on its construction in a back room of the cottage where he was born. It was the house from which his mother and father were dragged and shot when he was twelve. From that day he never spoke again. Not that anyone was surprised for he had rarely talked anyway and was difficult to understand when he did. Now his silence was a source of relief for it eased the discomfort of those around him, especially the older residents who knew things about Pedro that from today must be consigned to the past and forgotten.

Though a mere postage stamp of a country on any map of Latin America, Chilapina had been brought from obscurity to international attention by the ferocity of its civil conflict. The blood spilling had gone on for nearly three years. Towns and cities lay in ruins, but nowhere was the conflict more bitter than in small villages like San Ramon del Rio where the residents were all known to one another. More or less evenly divided between those who supported the government and those who sympathized with the rebels, such villages were taken, lost, and re-taken again by the opposing sides. Villagers who had nursed long-standing grievances. unsettled scores, or simple envy found that a whispered word to the current occupiers could bring fulfillment of desires so dark that they could never be admitted by those who held them. If, as a result, neighbors were seized and summarily executed, as were Pedro's parents, that was certainly to be regretted. But political, even religious exigencies made it sadly necessary. Thus were quieted any pangs of conscience, much in the same way as the sound of the generator's engine rendered inaudible the cries of those being tortured by electric shock in the church's basement.

An orphaned, autistic child with significant intellectual disability, Pedro had grown to young adulthood living alone. But the village had seen to his needs. Mothers sent daughters bearing food, fathers sent sons to split wood for his stove, and all had been sternly lectured not to taunt or make fun of the boy. Over time these parental admonitions became unnecessary. For if Pedro was accorded the charity of the village adults, it was from the children that he came to draw affection, even love. His cottage frequently rang with their laughter. They found there a refuge from the dull routine of village life. Indeed, it was a place of magic. They brought him scraps of wood, shards of glass, twigs from the forest floor, discarded string, wire, scrap metal, rags, even match sticks. They vied with one another to coax smiles from Pedro's face as they handed over their scavenged booty. And they watched in fascination as he sorted it into the bins and boxes which crowded his workshop. Returning a few days later they would find detritus wondrously transformed into treasure. For the girls it might be a tiny bedstead or chair for their dollhouses. Perhaps a stove with a glass door that opened to reveal red paper cut to look like flames from a real fire. Boys might take home miniature wagons, tractors, baggage carts and train depots. No house in the village was without several of these beautifully detailed pieces. Seeing the delight in their children's eyes, parents sometimes had balsa wood, glue, paint, and other supplies sent to Pedro's cottage from the capital. If he never understood how the packages came to appear on his doorstep, he nevertheless knew how to put their contents to good use. Pedro's genius lay in his hands.

At noon on this much anticipated day of reconciliation and forgiveness, the great bell sounded once again summoning all to the village square. The dais that the men had erected two days earlier was now festooned with palm fronds and garlands of Bougainvillea. The school's band, smartly dressed in freshly pressed uniforms, led the procession of the mayor, the bishop, and other dignitaries to their assigned places.

At first all went splendidly. The mayor's speech, sounding the proper notes of comity and brotherhood, was received with vigorous applause and shouts of "Hear! Hear!" The bishop, with awe inspiring and elaborate ritual, reconsecrated the church and offered a solemn high mass in the open air. When the last hearty AMEN arose from the assembled villagers, the mayor directed everyone's attention to Pedro who stood at the center of the square. Since early morning he had been keeping vigil beside a four by four foot sheet of plywood, supported by makeshift legs, and carefully covered with a bed sheet. Secure of his place in the village, he glowed with pride at having been included in the day's events.

The villagers jostled for the best viewing places. Children, wide-eyed with curiosity, pressed closest to him. Then, with a flourish, Pedro swept away the sheet to revceal an exquisitely crafted diorama of the central village, all of its buildings and throughways. No detail, no matter how insignificant, had been left out. It was perfect. Pedro stood next to his creation, smiling broadly in anticipation of the approbation and praise of the assembled villagers. But there was only silence, a terrible silence that descended like a great weight upon him. Then he heard startled gasps and the anguished cries of mothers who hurriedly pulled their children from the display. Sounds of retching he heard too, and a low rumble of confused sound that might have been voices or something beating a tattoo inside his head. As those who had been nearest the diorama drew back in shock at what they had seen, others surged forward only to follow wave after retreating wave in stunned disbelief. In the attempt to avoid looking at one another, most found their eyes locked briefly with those of a neighbor. And in that instant, each perceived in the other frightening specters of the past.

There were some who found themselves frozen in place. They gazed with stupefaction at figures of men and women lined up against walls for execution. Firing squads with their weapons raised. Bodies crumpled in pools of blood where they fell. At the very center of this tableau, where the church should have been, there was only a depression and a model of the church basement where both sides had tortured their victims, extracting the names of those in the village who had sympathized with the enemy. There were crude tables and chairs fitted with leather restraints. Most gruesome was the metal bed frame that Pedro had fashioned in minute detail. On such a device men and women had been spread-eagled, stripped and shackled, electrodes clamped to frame and flesh. Parts from an old "dyno torch" flashlight had provided Pedro with all he needed to assemble a model of the generator itself. It was all so beautiful. How could the villagers not see it? He seized the tiny crank he had fitted to the generator and spun it frantically while looking with a hopeful, frightened smile at those who were still standing there. They would see the little lamps flicker and sparks arc across gaps in the bedsprings. Then they would know what a marvel he had created to help celebrate this wonderful day. Yet he saw only horror in those faces before they turned away. How, they must have wondered, could Pedro have known about this room and its terrible implements? To be sure, there were some among them who knew the answer. Some who knew that a simple, confused child had been taken there ten years ago by government forces. How easy it must have been to interpret his guttural cries as *Si!* when asked if his parents were allied with the rebels. Perhaps it even *was* a *Si!* that they extracted from the twisted mouth of this convulsing twelve year old body. *Si! Si!* and again *Si!* But it did not matter. The next day he was made an orphan and never spoke another word.

Now Pedro cowered as two men came forward with sledgehammers to smash his masterpiece, the product of over a year of painstaking labor, into bits. He was incapable of comprehending what went on before him. Was this not the day to commemorate the games the villagers had invented to play with one another when he was a child?

Games in which he himself had been allowed to participate even if he did not understand the complicated rules? He fell to the ground, hid his face and wept as the sledges did their work. A few men huddled nearby and made plans for the following morning. The boy would be transported to an asylum in the provincial capital. There he must remain for the rest of his life.

The villagers shuffled in tense and painful silence to their homes. Doors were closed and bolted, curtains pulled over windows. Some men cleaned their guns. For you never knew, did you. And what would you tell your children when they asked why Pedro no longer lived in the village? Why there could be no more visits to his cottage? Why there would be no more of the wonderful toys he made for them?

Night fell on the village of San Ramon del Rio. A sleepless night haunted by old and bitter memory. Ten years, it seems, had not been enough. How many more would it take?

Naked

The phone rings at 2 AM like an insect caught in my ear, one of those cheap phones, the kind without a real bell. Awake and strangely alert — perhaps I have not been sleeping long — my first reaction is surprise at having slept at all. I came to bed with a fever and chills which usually mean the flu and can't remember anything but tossing with a cramp in my belly and a hot, tight pain behind the eyes. Rising awkwardly on one elbow, I fumble for the phone. It will be Karen.

Who else calls at this hour — from a bar on Castro, half-drunk and shouting "I love you!" above the din; or at her apartment, sleepless, anxious, with a new poem she wants me to hear. "No, I'm not angry," I'll tell her. "Just tired, I was sleeping." But when I answer there is only a high, thin wail and the sound of cars passing. Then sobs and my name forced past clenched teeth.

"Karen, what's wrong? Where are you?"

A frightened moan from deep within her chest. "I don't know."

The restaurant closes at eleven. She usually goes to a bar with the other servers and drinks for an hour or two. Sometimes she sits in a corner writing poetry. Then she walks home, alone. How many times have I told her to call a cab?

"What happened?" She doesn't answer. "Are you hurt?"

There is only the sound of traffic outside what must be a phone booth. Then the words are thrown out on a sob like flotsam pitched ashore on a breaking wave. "Yes. Oh, god, yes. I'm so scared."

"Listen, Karen. Karen?"

"What?"

"Look at the street signs. What do they say?"

Silence again. Time to think. What should I do? Christ! How did I let myself...?

"It says Howard. I'm on 18th, I think."

"Good. Good. Now read me the number on the telephone. It takes her several tries but I finally get it down.

"OK, I've got it. I'm going to call the police."

She shrieks. "No! I don't want, don't, please, no. Don't call the police! Promise me. Just come get me."

I know. But I had to say it. I'm trying to be responsible. Besides, it's their business, not mine. Shit!

"OK, OK, I won't."

"Oh, Joseph, I'm so scared. Please hurry. They're looking at me."

"Who's looking at you?"

"People."

"People, what people?"

"I don't know. People."

"OK, now listen to me. I'm going to send a cab for you. That'll be quicker. I'll have them take you home. Is Amy there?"

"No!" she cries. "I don't want to go home. I want to come to your house."

There is no point in arguing. It's too late for that. Long ago she sensed the hold she has over me.

"OK, all right. I'll give them my address and tell them to bring you here. I'm going to call for a cab now. I'll hang up and call them. But then I'll call you right back and we'll talk until they get there. OK?"

I call Yellow Cab and tell them it's urgent. They're pretty good about it. But I'm feeling trapped again. I've been trying to pull away from this. I have told her so. But now she'll be here, needing me more than ever. What do you do for someone who's been raped? Maybe she hasn't been raped. Mugged, maybe. I'm jumping to conclusions.

I call her back and we talk until the cab gets there and I know she's safe. I put on my robe and take a twenty from my wallet. I turn on the blanket and the lamp in the guest room, turn down the covers, then go to the living room to wait for her.

Two months before all this Lisa, Karen and I are sitting here together. Lisa had called the day before from the social services office where she works. She'd been given the case of a homeless girl and needed time to find housing for her. Could I put her up for a couple of weeks? I've been alone for over a year now, ever since the divorce. And I've grown comfortable with my solitude. Just for a couple of weeks, maybe less, she says. Would that even be legal, I ask. No, it wouldn't. Of course it wouldn't. But don't worry, she says. It'll be OK. I don't like the idea but it's not easy saying NO to my big-hearted social worker sister.

So Karen moves in — nineteen, languid, beautiful, anemic — with a kitten she'd found on the street, a sack of clothes and a box full of notebooks. All she owns. Her clothes lay for days where she sheds them, towels are used extravagantly then tossed wet on the bathroom floor. Her cat claws drapes and upholstery. There are lipstick smudges on the spout of the milk carton and a cigarette burn in the varnished surface of my desk where she'd spent an entire afternoon writing poetry while I was at work. I'm ready to strangle my sister. Then one afternoon I notice the scars on Karen's arms and we talk for the first time, seriously. She ignores my questions about the scars. She asks if I would like to see some of her poems.

When the cab pulls up I go outside to pay and thank the driver. He is young and courteous. What is he thinking? That this pale girl reeking of booze and cigarette smoke and dressed in a spray painted fatigue jacket, that she is my daughter? He helps her out of the car. With my arm supporting her I help her up the front steps like a patient returning from the hospital. She needs a cigarette, of course. I ease her onto the sofa and go to look for an ashtray. After the cigarette burn I don't let her smoke in the house anymore but tonight will have to be different. When I come back she is sitting there bent at the waist, legs drawn up, closed in, as if protecting her breasts, her belly. She is whimpering softly. I want to make one more try to report this, at least get her to a hospital emergency room. I sit next to her and put my arm around her shoulders. She begins to rock.

"Karen, I know it's hard to talk. But tell me what happened? Were you raped?" At first, nothing. Then her head nods in rhythm with her rocking. "How did he look? I mean, was he tall? What color was he? Do you know who it was?" There is no response. She only pulls in tighter, head on her knees, knees gripped in her arms. Then, on a hunch, "Was there more than one?" Her head nods again. "How many then?" This time she shakes her head.. She doesn't know, she can't remember, or she doesn't want to talk about it. "Will you let me call the police?" Violent shaking. "Will you let me take you to a doctor?" More shaking. I take her in my arms and rock with her. I don't know what else to do. I have never felt so helpless. And now, so afraid for this child in my arms.

I tell her I'm going to run a bath. She does not resist when I take her hand and lead her to the bathroom. She undresses while I sit on the edge of the tub as it fills. I see her watching me, fearful, I think, that I will look at her differently now, that I might find her repulsive. One night, after she had lived with me for a week, she came to my room naked and crawled into bed with me. From the first day I had made a mental list of all the reasons why this could not be allowed to happen. I got up and took her back to her own bed. Hurt, she turned her head to the wall and would not look at me. When she did it again a few nights later the list had lost some of its clarity. And then, the third time, I let her stay. We made love often after that and still do, even now that she has her own place. I am despicable in my own eyes but I have been unable to pull away. She says she is in love with me but I know this is a child's infatuation with a man twice her age, a contemptible man who is using her, a man who wants to know where the poems come from.

I have turned up the heat but, naked now, she stands there shivering, still looking at me with all that fear in her eyes. Her hands are knotted in fists, pressed to her mouth, forearms cover her breasts. She is filthy but there are no marks on her body except for a large lump on the side of her face where she has evidently been struck. I tell her how beautiful she is but realize immediately that it is the wrong thing to say. She cringes and I understand. I turn off the water and give her my hand to help her into the tub. When she has settled I go get her a washcloth and three towels. She never used less. Then I scoop up her clothes and take them to the laundry room. I know they should be left un-washed and saved for the police. I look at her panties. They are stained darkly with blood and semen. These, at least, I place in a plastic bag and throw everything else into the washing machine.

I put on some water for tea and return to the bathroom. She has not begun to bathe, does not even turn to look at me as I enter. I roll up the sleeves of my bathrobe and soap the washcloth. At the first touch she cries out and turns violently in the tub. She is sobbing again, but gently I begin to wash her back and she does not try to stop me. When I have finished I return to the kitchen to make the tea.

Soon she is standing in the doorway in the robe I put out for her. "Where am I going to sleep?" she asks. It is her first full sentence since the cab dropped her off.

"In your old room," I answer. "In the guest room."

"But I want to sleep with you. I need you to hold me."

"You can't. I'm sick. I have the flu." By this time I am feeling it all again, the headache and the painful sensitivity of nerves at the surface of my skin. I know she will think I'm rejecting her but it can't be helped. "Come and have some tea, then I'll sit with you for awhile."

She steps dumbly to the table, takes a few sips of tea and smokes another cigarette. Then she stands as if to say she is ready for bed. When I have pulled the covers over her and kissed her cheek, I hear the washing machine come to the end of its cycle. Telling her I'll be right back I go to transfer her clothes to the dryer. Stopping by my room, I take a pair of shorts from the drawer, men's briefs, then return to her room.

"I'm washing your clothes but I threw out your panties. You can wear these." I dangle the briefs from one finger. She smiles, that smile a gift to me. I lie down next to her on the bed. For a long time we remain there without speaking. When she is breathing steadily I rise and turn out the light. I walk heavily to my room and my own bed, exhausted.

But I can't sleep. I am back at the beginning and the first time Karen showed me some of her poems. The earliest were dated 1980 when she was fourteen. They rose from the scrawled, smudged pages of her notebooks like vaporized genies from unstopped bottles until the room could scarcely contain them. I called Lisa. She knew about the poems.

"Yeah, I leafed through a few of those notebooks. Pretty weird."

"Weird? Do you know the girl's a genius?"

"What do you mean?"

"The poems, Lisa. The fucking poems."

"Well, you're the English prof. But poetry and me... I don't really get it. But I did try to get her to talk about them. Thought she might open up. I didn't get very far. But I read in her file that an English teacher, without her knowledge, once sent a few of her poems to some magazine. They paid her $500 so I guess she must have something. But she was pissed. Gave it all to the SPCA."

"For god's sake, Lisa. Do you know what a big deal that is? Twenty years I've been writing poetry. You wanna know what I got? One published poem in a journal no one's ever heard of, three bucks and a box full of rejection slips. What else do you know about this girl that you aren't telling me?"

"I'm sorry, Joseph. I didn't want to scare you off. She desperately needed a place to stay while I find something for her. She has no defenses against the street. She'd be easy prey. It would kill her. I mean that literally, Joseph. You're keeping her alive right now."

"That's a hell of a trip to lay on someone, Lisa. Can we have a little honesty please? And don't give me any BS about not being at liberty to discuss her case. You got me into this mess."

"You're right, Joseph. I'm violating policy here but I owe you that. Karen was a sexually abused child and she's been in and out of foster homes and mental institutions since she was ten. Mostly out since she turned 16. There's no money to keep them there anymore. They just dump them onto local social services. People like me. They usually end up homeless. This kid's been to the bottom — electroshock, rape by male patients and orderlies, you name it."

"Jesus, Lisa. What about her arms?"

"She's a cutter, Joseph."

I could never tell Lisa that I am sleeping with Karen. And what does that tell me about myself? That I have betrayed her trust in me. That I am a criminal — if not in the law's eyes, then at least in hers. And in my own. I desperately want to believe that this is not who I am. But there is no excuse for what I'm doing. Who would not condemn me?

Still, I think I have been seduced more by genius than by Karen's uninhibited sexuality. It's almost as if there are two different entities: a child who won't pick up her clothes and a poet of the rarest ability. When I ask her where the poems come from she says she doesn't know. But then, after thinking for a minute, she says that when people talk they leave much unsaid. That is what she hears. And her poems are those unspoken words. I don't know what to make of this. But the love poems that she writes to me, aren't these the things I feel but am unwilling or afraid to say out loud?

Karen cries out in her sleep and I wonder if I should go to her. But then it's quiet again. I know that tonight's assailants will merely have taken their place in the tribe of demons that haunts her. Perhaps that is what led to her frightened cry. But I have heard this same cry before. Is it some technician dressed in white who is terrifying her? Is it her father? Is it me?

She's been mad at me and hurt these past few days. She says that I am rejecting her love. I do love her and I tell her so but that I could never love her in the way she wants me to. Once I even told her that her presence in the house was driving me crazy. That she would have to leave. Finally, after three weeks, Lisa found an apartment where she could stay with another girl named Amy. The rent is subsidized but I had to co-sign as a guarantor on the rental agreement and put up the damage deposit and last month's rent. With luck and a little persuasion I found her a job as a server at a nearby restaurant managed by a friend in the Castro.

Not long after she starts work a florist's truck stops by my house to deliver an expensive bouquet of flowers, flowers from a 19 year old girl who can't afford them to a man closing in on 40. The envelope contains a love poem. She calls at least twice a week, sometimes from work, asking if she can spend the night at my place, just the night, because her roommate is having a party, or because the heat isn't working, or because she needs me. OK, OK, OK. I'm a fool. I love her and it's nice having her body next to me in bed. But in the morning I always tell her we should see one another less often now that she's on her own. I know how much it hurts her when I say this.

Two weeks after moving into her own place Karen invites me over for dinner with her roommate Amy, Lisa, and some of her friends from the new job. After we've eaten, when we're all sitting near the fireplace, I ask Karen if she would recite one of the poems that were published. She can't remember them but will try to improvise something for us. Almost instantly images of the fire and our coming together begin to circumscribe the room, sealing its doors, entombing us in a space so intimate that it is as if we are all sitting there naked in front of one another. When she finishes no one speaks. Karen lies there with the soft light of the fire in her hair, the stillness broken only by the whispery darting of the flames. I heard Yevtushenko do this once. He was in San Francisco and had given a talk earlier in the day at the college where I teach English and American lit. Our department arranged a private party for him that evening. Perhaps it is unfair to compare Karen's poem with what the Russian struggled to do in English. But in any language Karen would have won hands down. Her words that night still glow with the intensity of embers raked for a Hindu firewalker. It is a strange feeling, other worldly and almost frightening, to be in the presence of genius like that. Where does it come from? And why does it elude those like me who in darkness seek even its faintest glimmer?

This memory of Yevtushenko's visit gives me an idea. I give her a biography of Pushkin to read. And another of Edna St. Vincent Millay. Perhaps her fellow child prodigies will help her better understand her rare and ineffable gift, a gift she does not seem to recognize. Or, if she does, perceives to be of little consequence. I asked her once if I could put together a collection of her poems to submit to a publisher. She said she would burn them first.

There is a sound at my door.

"Joseph?"

"Huh?"

"I don't want to be alone."

"I'm really sick, Karen. I want to hold you. I just can't." I say this, and it's true. My head is splitting and every reserve of strength has been drained.

"Can I just sleep on the floor then?"

"I guess so."

She takes a pillow and a spare blanket from the bed and settles on the floor. I can see her curled up there, next to my bed. An hour or so later, when it is nearly light, I get up and carry her back to the guest room. She is cold. Her arm is around my neck but she does not resist when I lay her on the bed and cover her. Then I return to my own room and fall, at last, into a deep sleep.

When I wake up it is already ten o'clock. I'm feeling a little better. I look in on Karen. She is sprawled in sleep. I make coffee and slice a grapefruit but I'm not really hungry. I've got a class at one and work to do beforehand. I want to talk - no, need to talk - about genius and the creative imagination. My thoughts are a muddle. I try to make sense of them.

I'm at my desk when Karen comes in. She is wearing my blue shorts and nothing else. I get up and hug her.

"Do you want something to eat? Maybe some coffee?"

"No."

"Do you want to go home?"

She looks at me sadly, forgiveness in her eyes. "I just want to stay here. I won't bother you. I'll just watch you. Maybe I'll write."

I go to get her clothes out of the dryer while she smokes a cigarette. Then I clear off a table for her and find some paper. I like the idea, her writing here while I work.

"Do you have to teach today?"

"Yes."

"Can I stay here until you go? I won't bother you."

For once she keeps her word. I almost want her to throw herself on me, laughing like she used to do when I'd try to work. But she comes only to stand behind me from time to time. Silently. Mostly she sits at the table writing. When she goes out to smoke I glance at one of the pages. She is split open like the grapefruit I had for breakfast. I can't bear to read more than a few lines.

Time passes quickly but I manage to finish my lecture notes. I tell Karen I'll drive her home on my way to class. She doesn't respond. I go to take a shower. When I come out of the bathroom I am startled to see her there, looking at me. I am naked, and for the first time, ashamed. I reach for a towel.

"No," she says, "I want to look at you." For what seems like a full minute she continues to gaze at me, studying my body. Then she comes close, eyes closed, repeating this examination with her hands as if she is trying to recover something that has been taken from her. She is trembling. When I can't stand it anymore I break away and go to my room to dress.

I can hear her crying in the hallway. What's wrong with me, for Chrissakes? Why did I leave her like that? I am worse than that vermin in the alley. They raped her, laughed and tossed her body back into the street. But I have raped her mind and heart then kept her close, looking for genius, trying to capture a spark of it for myself. And I've done it in the dark too, embarrassed to be seen with her by friends and colleagues, afraid that they'd smirk when we were gone and say "What's Joseph got himself now?"

I go to her. How can I explain all this? She won't understand or, worse, she will and love me anyway. She is sitting on the floor. I kneel and take her in my arms and cry with her. But I know that I am weeping for myself.

"You can stay while I'm gone," I tell her.

"Couldn't you stay here with me?" she asks. "You could call in sick."

"No, I need to go," I answer, knowing she will hear the words I leave unsaid.

Lyrics to A Simple Girl

She'd sit with day's last sunlight in her hair
In a tattered dress her mother used to wear
A frightened look and longing in her eyes
And she believed what she was told
'Til someone told her otherwise
Her father left when she was five
Her mother died a suicide
She lived alone
And you could hear her on her back porch
Singing la la la la, la la

A simple girl, half crazy they'd all say
And mothers always kept the kids away
But when their men crept 'round to her back door
She'd hang her head and let them take
Whatever they'd come for
A rag doll in their hot embrace
Their sweat upon her breast
She'd make no sound
'Til they'd leave her on her back porch
Singing la la la la, la la

A simple girl, no ties of family
A lonely girl in the hills of Tennessee
Whose dream it was to see the sun
Rising from the sea

In purple shades of dusk her visions came
A rider on a horse without a name
His beauty unmindful of her rags
His voice was like the sound of pearls

In the folds of a velvet bag
"Come be a silver bird," he'd say
"In the waves of my cold black hair"
Then he'd be gone
And she'd sit there on her back porch
Singing la la la la, la la

She wrote her poems in the darkness of the night
Then from a bridge on morning they took flight
They shone with all the colors of the dawn
Falling softly like the leaves
Of autumn's farewell song
Secrets once locked in her heart
In morning's light revealed
Then she was gone
Though some evening you might hear her
Singing la la la la, la la

Her house sits barred and empty
Floor strewn with broken glass
And though she's gone
Some evening you might hear her
Singing la la la la, la la

Concealed Carrie

I've always hated my pictures. Look at the ones in my high school yearbooks. I'm kind of stoop-shouldered with my head down, as if I dread looking up at the camera. Princess Diana was like that too and she was beautiful. I'm not very pretty. Not even medium pretty.

But I really like the picture of me that's in the paper. It's the one they took at the police station after my arrest. Funny, isn't it? The best picture of me *ever* is a mug shot. I'm looking straight at the camera, my shoulders back. For once there's a look of confidence in my eyes and my chin isn't drooping towards my chest. My mouth has the firm set of a woman who knows what she wants and isn't afraid to go for it. It's not the old Carrie. Maybe it's the me that I've become. Or at least the me I want to be. My lawyer says she's not too happy about the picture. But I am.

My lawyer's name is Martha. She seems nice even though she doesn't like my picture. Next time she comes I'm going to ask her why. She has to come here to the jail because it looks like they're going to keep me here until the trial. I can have visitors though. I wish Alice would come. Alice is my best friend in the world. I love her so much. I suppose you could say she's the reason I'm here. I don't mean it's her fault. Far from it. Ray brought this on himself.

One day I see this big cop walking down the street with his

thumbs in his gun belt and there's Alice bouncing along beside him with both arms around one of his biceps. When our women's group met at her place the next Wednesday she told us she was in love and I knew he must be the guy. His name was Ray she said and he had a good head on his shoulders (what a laugh) and was saving up to go to law school. And he supported women's lib 100% (another laugh). First thing he gave her was a Smith and Wesson .38 special for self defense.

Someone asked wasn't she scared to keep it in the house but Alice said no, that Ray was teaching her how to shoot. Then she went and got it and we were all like "ooh-ing" and "oh, my god-ing" while she held it out for us to look at. It was black with a barrel about an inch long and it looked scary lying there in the palm of her hand like a dead toad.

"It's great for close-in use," she said, in words I knew were Ray's. She positioned the gun close to her hip and said "this way an attacker can't grab it out of your hand." I asked if that gun was a Saturday night special and Alice said she guessed it was. When I said lots of Democrats wanted to ban guns like that she said the trouble with some liberals is that they have their heads in the sand. Ray could prove that gun control wouldn't work. She was going to ask him to come to one of our meetings to talk about it.

After that she started painting two or three canvases a week. "I can't paint unless I'm in love ," she said. "When I'm in love I really start seeing the things around me. Like the way trees create patterns of light and dark on the side-walk. Or I'll see a rainbow and want to paint all those little rainbows hiding in shells underwater."

Talk like that makes me ache inside. "Lovers see the world through an artist's eye," she told me once. What would I know about that? I don't think I've ever really been in love. Not with a man anyway. I do love Alice. That doesn't mean I'm a lesbian. It's just the way I feel.

Sometimes I go through my old yearbooks and there she is on practically every page. She was always queen of something and dated all the best looking jocks. Even us girls liked her. She wasn't stuck-up or anything so it was hard to be jealous. She was like a movie star we all wanted to get close to, hoping something might rub off.

There's a picture on page ninety-nine of our senior yearbook. It's a cast and crew picture from when we did "Most Happy Fella". Alice had the lead and she's standing front row center. Underneath she wrote "Thanks, Carrie. Couldn't have done it without you. Good luck to a sweet kid." Then she drew an arrow over to me, second from left in the back row. I was on scenery and lighting. It's the only picture of me in the whole yearbook except for my graduation photo. I've already told you about that one.

Martha came today to work on my defense. I asked her why she didn't like the picture in the paper. She says when people see a mug shot like that they figure you must have done something because they see those kinds of pictures all the time in the post office. Wanted posters. She says I look too strong and self-assured. If she only knew. I guess she thinks it would be better for the jury to see me like I am in the yearbooks.

I used to wonder what the world would be like if everyone was like me. Once I read about a village in Egypt where almost everybody walks around tired all the time because they have a tape worm. The ones who don't, they have more energy and are real unpopular. I thought it would be like that. I wouldn't want to have a tape worm but it's no fun being unpopular. Anyway, if everybody *was* like me we'd probably still be in the Stone Age. I mean, I could never have invented electricity or aluminum or television, things like that. But Alice always got good grades and even went to college. Six years later I'm still waitressing and she's back here in Cascade teaching art *and* French. Talk about brains.

Being in here I've had to miss the last couple of meetings but Alice and I are in the same women's group. We're real good friends. She's the best friend I've got. I love her to death. I should explain about our women's group though. Idaho isn't exactly the heartland of women's lib. We're probably thirty years behind places like California. Most of the women who come are either married or have boyfriends. Like Alice. And they seem to be OK with men, in general anyway. I've had boyfriends. They only wanted one thing and dumped all over me. I get lonely. It really hurts sometimes. But I want someone who will make me feel like I'm special, not just some easy lay. If there are any guys like that, they're all taken. The rest are creeps.

You take Ray, for instance. One afternoon I'm over at Alice's while she's in the driveway with an ex-boyfriend, another art teacher from her school. He was helping her make canvas stretchers. Actually he was making them while she sat there doing her nails. Around four Ray pulls up in his cruiser. He just sits there revving his engine until he knows we've seen him. Then he squeals his tires and takes off fast. What a jerk. How can Alice, who's a hundred times smarter than Ray, even if he *was* going to law school, which was probably just a lie anyway, how can Alice put up with a creep like that? Not that I judge Alice by Ray. The thing with him was just one of those mistakes like we all make. She's so smart and beautiful. No man deserves a woman like Alice.

At our next women's group Alice said she told Ray off for acting so stupid but I could tell she was kind of excited by the whole thing. "That's why men get what they want," she said. "They're not afraid to go after it."

A few weeks after his big scene in front of Alice's Ray actually did come to one of our meetings. He'd just gotten off duty and was still in his uniform. I'm always startled at how good looking he is. His brown hair is brushed straight back from his temples and there's a little red mixed in with it. His cheek bones are big and high and round with shadowy little hollows underneath. And there's always a kind of half-smile in his eyes and the corner of his mouth. But it wasn't right, him sitting there and Alice obviously dying to jump in his lap. And I could have puked the way he talked to us, like he's gone to the grade school to talk about what side of the road you're supposed to walk on. Still, what he said made sense.

"Your muggers and rapists are going to be a lot stronger than you. And, ladies, unless you've got a gun or forty different kinds of black belts in I don't know what, he's going to do what he damn well pleases." Ray offered to take us all out to the police shooting range for practice. I said I'd go. We all did.

It was in the next few weeks that I really started hating Ray's guts. I couldn't stand the way Alice tuned to Jell-O whenever he was around, which was more than ever now that he was our self-appointed drill instructor. Ray ate it up. "Follow Ray," he'd say in a sing-songy voice when he'd take us from the arms room to the firing range. And Alice would fall right in behind him and say "Let's go, girls." I could just hear Ray's cop buddies laughing their damn heads off. We must have looked like a bunch of ducks waddling out there. It was just so humiliating. And it was killing me the way Alice went to pieces over this guy. If he was for women's lib so's the Pope. Not the one they've got now, the other one. And you could tell Ray only said that because he knew about our group and figured it was the surest way to get into Alice's pants. It was sickening.

He knew about guns though, I'll say that for him. And I'll admit that he was right about knowing how to handle one. After awhile the feel of that walnut grip in the shape of my hand started to change something inside of me. I don't know how to describe it except in a way I'm ashamed of, but here it is: I felt like a man. For years it was old mousey Carrie on page 99 of the senior yearbook, afraid of her own shadow, screwed over so many times she'd lost count. But now, that silky marvel of blue steel that clicked so precisely under my fingers was teaching me something. I was learning how it felt not to be afraid. It's like a field of new snow in the morning: quiet, unmarked, voluptuous. I'll give Ray credit for that.

At first I experienced this sensation only with the gun in my hand. But before long I discovered that I could bring it back merely by imagining the feel of its checkered grip. And then, just weeks after my first visit to the firing range, came the realization that I could achieve the same sense of control and inner peace with no reference to the gun at all. It was only necessary to recall the field of snow. I can't begin to tell you how liberating it was and it all happened so seamlessly. Maybe I will still buy a gun. Most of the women in our group are planning to. But I admit to having some doubts about it now. Maybe I don't need one. Maybe I shouldn't have one. I don't know.

I'm not proud of the fact that I lied to Martha the first time we talked. I told her that the gun went off accidentally. But Martha saw through that right away. "That'll never fly," she said. "You've had plenty of training on how to handle a gun. The jury won't buy it." So we're going with self-defense. That's not exactly true either but she says it's the best chance I've got.

Getting back to Ray and Alice. Cascade's not that big a town and pretty soon they were quite the item — good looking stud of a cop and heart-breaking art teacher at Cascade High. It was disgusting the way Ray would swagger around with her hanging all over him. But what really got me was the way she was selling out the rest of us for this guy. At first I figured he was just another one of her flings and in a month or two it'd be goodbye Ray. But then one day she shows up for group wearing an emerald ring with two diamonds. Ray had put five hundred dollars down on that thing, she said. He'd asked her to marry him and she'd said yes. Everyone was laughing and saying how happy they were for her but I think they were faking it. It was just so unreal. That night I looked at what Alice had written in my yearbook and there I was, crying all of a sudden.

It was a month or so later that I got the goods on old Ray. And I figured it would bring Alice to her senses. My sister was due and I had some vacation time coming so I drove up to Winchell to help out. It's only about a hundred miles north but it might as well be in another country. Nobody ever goes there from downstate unless they're passing through on their way to BC. One day I'm walking to the drugstore for my sister and here's Ray coming the other way with this woman hanging on him like Alice always did - only it wasn't Alice. My legs wouldn't budge but I managed to turn and look into a store window while they went by. When I looked again he had his hand on her butt. I couldn't think of anything else the next few days. Of course I knew all along that Ray was just another creep but now I could lay it all out for Alice without looking jealous. She'd drop the SOB like a hot potato.

I went straight to her as soon as I got back. She didn't want to believe me at first but deep down she knew it was true. "Maybe he's got a sister up there," she said. "He's got a sister, you know."

"It's me who's got a sister up there, Alice. Not Ray. And you don't walk down the street with your hand on your sister's butt." I didn't like hurting her but I knew the kindest thing would be to give it to her straight.

"We're supposed to go out tonight," she said. "What am I going to do?"

I told her to tell him it was quits and give his ring back. "Just make it a nice clean break. And don't say it was me who saw him." I didn't want to get mixed up in this.

She was crying by then. We both were. I put my arms around her. It was like we were sisters. And when I reached up to pull away the strands of hair that were clinging to her damp cheeks I knew I could never love anyone like I loved Alice.

Thank god, it's over, I thought to myself when I finally got back to my place. Then I did something I almost never do. I poured some bourbon into a glass and sat on the living room floor drinking. I looked around and thought of all the ways I could make the apartment nicer. I'd ask Alice if I could have one of her paintings for over the couch. I'd make new curtains. I'd make some big poufy pillows and have Alice over and we'd sit on the floor together drinking wine and talking.

Next day guess who walks into the restaurant looking like his dog just died. Maybe I was gloating a little. But who could blame me.

"How's it going, Ray?" I asked.

"Come off it, Carrie. Alice tells you everything."

"Not everything," I said. The place was practically empty so I pulled up a chair like I really felt sorry for him.

"Hell, it didn't mean anything. Just an old flame. Didn't mean jack-shit."

"Sure."

"Hey, it's true. But Alice was really pissed. Says she doesn't want to see me for two weeks. Then we'll talk about it. I guess I can't blame her for being pissed but two weeks! I might as well go back up to Winchell for Christ's sake."

I couldn't believe my ears. Alice wasn't going to dump this creep or she would have told him to get out of her sight for good. I was shaking when I got up.

"You wanna order now, Ray?" I managed to say. I fumbled so much with the pad that I had to re-write the order so the cook could read it.

I went to the ladies' room and sat down for awhile. I was furious at Alice and I felt so helpless. I tried to think like a man. I tried to think what it feels like to do things and not be afraid. I thought of that field of snow.

I had myself under better control when I brought Ray his coffee and berry pie a-la-mode for dessert. A plan had been taking shape in my mind while he'd been eating dinner and I'd been behind the counter refilling ketchup bottles. "Listen, Ray," I said, sitting next to him again, but closer this time, "you got a minute after work tonight?" I put my hand on his arm. "You could probably use somebody to talk to after everything that's happened. And, anyway, I'm thinking of getting me a gun and maybe you could give me a few suggestions."

Ray looked a little surprised but there was a grin on his stupid face as he put his hand on top of mine. "Yeah, sure, Carrie. Sure I can. What time you get off?"

"I'm just working the afternoon shift. I'm off at five-thirty."

"Same as me," he said. "See you out back." He'd be sure nobody saw him this time, the jerk.

The days are short in January. By five-thirty it's so dark it might as well be midnight. I changed back into my street clothes and put my bra in my purse. I didn't look half bad in the restroom mirror. I'm no beauty queen but my figure gets plenty of attention in this greasy spoon. And I knew Ray wouldn't be able to keep his hands off me if I gave him the opportunity. I'd let him go pretty far but not all the way. And then when I'd give Alice the details the next day Ray's goose would be cooked, for good this time. Like that George Jones song that's always playing on the juke box: *when you're caught cheating twice it's twenty to life in a place where the sun never shines.* I'd tell her I only wanted to ask him about getting a gun but he jumped my bones like the asshole that he is. It was a good plan and Ray was too stupid to see what was coming. He pulled up behind the restaurant at five-thirty in a blue Camaro.

"Nice car, Ray."

"1969 Z28 Camaro. If I told you what this baby's worth you wouldn't believe it."

Still in uniform, he sure looked pleased with himself when he opened the car door for me. A real gent.

He drove us out to the lake to the old parking lot that never gets used anymore except for making out. I could see old Ray was hot to trot. When we rolled to a stop he took off his tie and loosened a few buttons of his shirt. "You know, Carrie, you kind of took me by surprise. I didn't know... well, what I mean is...."

"It's OK, Ray. I could see how down you were. I thought maybe I could make things a little better."

Ray put his hand on my thigh. "Carrie, you're some kind of girl." He hunched lower in the seat. He was going to have himself a good time. "Lemme get a little more comfortable here," he said. Unhitching his gun belt reminded him of something. "Hey, Carrie, what kind of gun you thinking of getting?"

"I don't know, Ray. You're the expert. What do you think?"

"Well, there's a lot out there. So it's kind of a personal decision. But if it's for concealed carry, like I'm recommending for you ladies, lemme show you what I just picked out for Alice's birthday." Ray popped open the glove compartment. "Get a load of this little beauty. It's a Ruger LCR .38 special. Weighs less than a pound. And what I really like about it is that it's got a non-stacking trigger with a real light pull for a double action revolver. I don't think you could do any better than one of these babies." He put it in my hand. "Careful, it's still loaded. I was trying it out on the range this morning."

"It's a beauty," I said and I meant it. It was cold out and our breath was already condensing on the windshield. I thought of a field of snow stretching white as far as the eye could see.

"You like that, don't you, baby," Ray said and moved over closer and put an arm around me.

"It's beautiful," I said again. I set the gun back on the open shelf of the glove compartment and pressed my body against his. I know what I was doing was really shitty but Alice needed to know what kind of a guy she'd got herself engaged to. And I even liked kissing Ray. It felt dangerous and kind of exciting. Like a female spy behind enemy lines. The trick would be getting out without being fucked. Dead in the case of the spy. Literally in mine.

Soon Ray's hand was up under my shirt. When he didn't feel a bra strap his other one lost no time in proceeding to further explorations. That was OK for now. I was playing along. But Ray wasn't about to stop there and when I felt his hand slipping under the elastic band of my panties it was time to let him know this had gone far enough. "I need to stop, Ray." Not that it slowed him down any. "I mean it. Alice is my best friend."

"Aw, come on, Carrie. It's just this once and she'll never know." His fingers were moving between my legs.

"Please, Ray. I can't do this." I started to struggle but Ray just gripped me tighter. Things weren't going like I'd planned. I had counted on him stopping when I mentioned Alice's name. Like that would shame him somehow. But it didn't work. With Ray's face buried against my neck, I reached for the gun with my free hand. The grip felt cool and reassuring. I aimed at the floorboard and fired. Like Ray said, it didn't take much pressure on the trigger.

"Jesus Christ! What the fuck?"

At the firing range we always used ear plugs. Now I couldn't believe the noise when that that gun went off. In the closed car the sound was deafening. My left ear is still ringing a little.

I threw open the car door, grabbed my purse and ran like hell. I kept off the road for fear that Ray would run me down. I knew the trails and it was only a couple of miles to my place. It was starting to snow. If my heart was racing, still everything seemed so peaceful and quiet around me. It was like I was drifting through one of those Christmas scenes sealed inside a crystal ball. And you know what was really amazing? Was I crying and scared? No! I was laughing. I couldn't believe what I'd just done. I must have been crazy. But it was a good crazy. I felt nothing but exhilaration. I wasn't worried. Ray would be too embarrassed to ever tell anyone what had happened. And I hoped it would cost a ton to get the hole in his Camaro fixed. Old scaredy-cat Carrie had just shot a hole in a cop's car. Now she was running through the woods. It was dark. It was snowing. And she was laughing!

I was a soggy mess by the time I got home. I stripped as soon as the door was shut and locked. Then I ran a bath. I filled the tub with crystals and bubble bath until the suds were thick as the head on a glass of champagne. I settled in and felt the tension drain away. The pink tiles glowed like garnets in the light of the heat lamp in the ceiling fan. Little rainbows arched across the tops of a million bubbles reflecting a million me's. Steam rising from the bath made a soft, lacey cocoon around me. And I realized Alice was right. A lover sees the world through an artist's eye. That's just how she put it.

You'd think I wouldn't be able to sleep after all that had happened. But I collapsed into a dreamless sleep the second my head hit the pillow. I might have slept 'til noon if it hadn't been for loud knocking at the door a little after eight. "Oh god, don't let that be Ray," I thought. I slipped on my robe and peeked through the little lens in the door. There were two cops standing there. And for the first time I panicked. I couldn't believe Ray would do anything. But when I opened the door the sergeant read me my rights and arrested me for attempted murder.

The lady cop watched me as I got dressed, her hand near her weapon the whole time. Then she put the cuffs on and led me to their cruiser parked in front of the building. I'm sure some of the other tenants had to be looking out their windows when I got put into the back seat. You know how it goes. The cop puts his hand on the top of the perp's head and ducks him in. It's kind of like when preachers baptize people in those born-again churches. They put a hand on someone's head and bend them backwards under the water. I have always wondered what they feel when they come up. Do they feel like the guilt of sin has been washed away? I won't say it was a religious experience being shoved into a cop car. But I did feel something. And it wasn't panic anymore. I'd done something crazy, unbelievable even, but I wasn't going to be afraid. I'd done what I had to do. To protect Alice, to protect myself. And everyone would see that.

But attempted murder? Only a jury of classic Camaro nut-cases would consider shooting a hole in one to be attempted murder. "So where's Ray?" I asked tentatively as we drove to the station.

"Better you keep your trap shut, lady," the sergeant said.

But the woman cop said "He's in the hospital." I detected anger in her voice and what seemed like excessive concern for Ray's well-being. Was he fooling around with her too? I kept quiet after that and watched the snow falling outside. But what the hell? Had the bullet hit Ray, maybe ricocheted off something? God knows I wasn't aiming at him. Firing that gun was like the referee at a football game blowing his whistle to stop the action in the middle of a play. It meant STOP. And that's just what Martha is going to tell the jury. If Ray got hit that was an accident.

I met Martha for the first time that same day, just after my arraignment. She took my hand and asked if I was nervous. I said I was, a little anyway. But I said that only because I thought it's what she expected me to say. I had never been arrested, never stood in front of a judge where it's like the whole damned government looking down at you. Shouldn't

I be nervous? But I wasn't really. I was thinking of that field of snow. Just like when they took my picture

Martha told me that Ray had been hit in the leg. It wasn't too serious. And she says I have every reason to be optimistic. The prosecution has already dropped the attempted murder charge. They couldn't come up with a motive for that one. Now they want me to cop a plea to reckless discharge of a weapon. They'll ask for a reduced sentence if I do. Martha has advised me against it. It would mean a felony conviction since Ray was injured and I could be looking at a year in the can. She doesn't trust the prosecutor. She thinks it's better to go to trial with a claim of self-defense against a rape attempt. Of course Ray will say that's bogus. He'll say I asked him for a few pointers on buying a gun. And when he showed me the one he'd bought for Alice I started coming on to him, like I was turned on by it or something. He pushed me away and nothing happened. He had no idea why I fired that gun. He'll say I must be crazy. The prosecution does have a witness, a customer in the restaurant when Ray came in, who will testify he saw me hitting on Ray, or at least flirting with him. And one of his cop buddies is going to say he'd seen me schmoozing Ray at the firing range. That's a lie but nothing new about a cop lying for another cop.

I'd been leading Ray on all right, though of course I'll deny it. But even if the jury thinks I did, NO still means NO, right? Even if there'd been some heavy necking going on before. They teach that to college kids nowadays, don't they? And I did tell Ray to stop — more than once. And when he didn't it became attempted rape. I blew the only whistle I could. It just happened to be Alice's birthday present. I wasn't aiming at him. I didn't want to hurt him. I just wanted him to stop. That's going to be my defense.

Martha says there's a good chance I'll be acquitted. Or at least get a hung jury. And the prosecution will know their case is weak and won't go to the expense of a retrial. I'll walk out free. And when I do life is going to be so different. Alice might be pissed at me for awhile. But she'll soon get over it. In the end she'll be grateful for what I've done and Ray will be history. She'll see that I saved her from making a terrible mistake. And when that happens I'll switch permanent to the morning shift so I can spend every evening with her until she gets her life back together again. I'll have dinner ready for her when she gets home from work. Maybe I'll even move in with her and we can be roommates. I'll sign up for classes at Cascade JC. Maybe a writing class. My high school English teacher told me I had a gift for it. I can write while Alice paints. We'll be artists together. I love her so much.

Baptismal Rites

We're in some crummy motel off I-5 near Medford and I'm almost asleep. But Steve won't shut up. He's yammering on about the attractive waitress where we'd stopped for dinner. "How about those knockers? Hey, did you know most boobs go through life without being baptized?" LA is fourteen hours behind us and I'm exhausted. I try to sound like I've been sleeping so maybe he'll shut up.

"Mmm... huh?"

"Unbaptized flesh."

"What the hell are you talking about?" I'd tell him to stuff it but he's been great about coming along for moral support and to help if there are any legal issues about Richie to sort out.

"I had this French girlfriend once who had the most fantastic tits. When I told her so she laughed and said 'unbaptized flesh'. See, in France they call women's breasts unbaptized flesh because they aren't there when baby girls get baptized."

"Interesting. If I weren't beat out of my mind I'd ask you how come a nice Jewish boy was fooling around with Catholic girls."

"How did you know she was Catholic? Anyway, like I told you she had these fantastic..."

"Yeah, I know. Go to sleep, will you?"

"G'night, Tony."

"G'night, Steve. Can't thank you enough for coming along."

Now I can't sleep. This thing about unbaptized flesh reminds me of something that happened back when Richie and I were teenagers. We'd heard the crash while we were still on the trail. We dropped our fishing gear and ran. I saw the body first, just a few feet from the water and at least fifty feet from the car that was crumpled sideways against a tree. "Jesus, Mary, Joseph," Richie whispered as he came up behind me. He ripped off his shirt and soaked it in the lake. It was a Richie I'd never seen before. In a second he was bending over the woman's face, tenderly wiping away dirt and blood and probing her mouth with his finger. She was pretty. And she reeked of alcohol. We hadn't heard any tires squealing so she must have left the road at sixty miles an hour.

Not to be outdone by a younger brother I felt for a pulse. "She's dead," I said.

"Maybe not. We can't be sure. And we don't know when the soul leaves the body. Maybe she was never baptized."

"Come on, Richie." I was going to be a junior at Stanford and had left my Catholic upbringing behind. Richie never did. He lived it. Wore it painfully, it seemed to me: a non-stop examination of conscience. He'd been in a seminary studying for the priesthood since he was thirteen.

"We can still baptize her. Lady, can you hear me? Do you believe in God? Are you sorry for your sins?"

Richie scrambled back to the lake and cupped his hands in the water. He was shaking as he leaned over the body again. "Lady, give me a sign if you can hear me. Do you believe in God?"

"Richie, she's dead."

"I baptize you in the name of the Father, and of the Son, and of the Holy Ghost." The water that spilled from Richie's hands mixed with the blood on the woman's face and streamed rust brown to the earth. He bent close to her. I thought he was going to kiss her. Finally I pulled him away and we ran to get help. Though I'd always been the faster runner, Richie now raced ahead of me, seemingly fired by a faith which mocked the loss of my own.

I think about telling Steve all this but his breathing is already slow and regular. So I just go on thinking about Richie. I do it all the time. Ever since mom's call. Anything can set me off. Like right away, while she was still on the phone, I remembered how once, when we were little boys, Richie woke up screaming in the middle of the night. He thought he'd seen monsters in the shade of the lamp he always wanted kept lit on the nightstand between our beds. She came and sat with him for a while. He didn't tell her about the monsters but he asked her to turn out the light when she left. Next morning she said it was a sign that he was getting to be a big boy, not being afraid of the dark anymore. So after that he never cried out again. He thought that at seven you were too old to be calling for your mother. But I knew how frightened he really was so I'd make scary noises in the dark.

I feel so strange now. It's almost like back then. It's dark in this room. I no longer hear the highway sounds. I listen to Steve's breathing. He's lying in a twin bed, parallel to mine, separated by a nightstand with its single lamp. "Richie, I'm sorry. See, it's silly, I'm crying... Richie?"

By eight o'clock we've had breakfast and are on the road again. Seattle is another long day's drive. Steve is driving first. He wants to know more about Richie.

"When did he... you know... when did he start having problems?"

"It didn't happen all at once. Not like he just flipped out or anything. He'd spent ten years at St. Edward's Seminary preparing for the priesthood. Two more to go. But then he just left. Maybe he was asked to leave. I don't know. He would have been 24 at the time. I hardly knew him anymore. Christ, I'd only seen him a few months in all those years he was in the seminary. But that's my own damn fault."

"Don't beat yourself up over it, Tony. Not much you could have done. So what did he do when he left?"

"But maybe I *could* have done something. I should have tried. I'm his brother. I loved him. Anyway, he moved in with my parents. He had a hard time finding a job. What can you do with Greek and Latin? He finally ended up with the Catholic Youth Organization, a counselor, something like that. But he got canned six months later. I suppose that's when it all started."

"Canned?"

"I never got the whole story. I was living in California by then. It was a big family scandal. My parents clammed up. But apparently Richie tried to kiss a 14 year old girl in his office. At least that's what she told his supervisor. All hell broke loose. But the Church is pretty good at hushing things up too. There was no publicity, no charges filed. Next day he was given fifteen minutes to clear out."

"Lucky for him," Steve says. "Indecent liberties with a minor can get you three to four years in most states."

" Steve, he never had a chance to grow up. At least where sex was concerned. He was so... stupid. I suppose immature would be a better way to put it. If he did try to kiss that girl there was something almost innocent about it, know what I mean? Like he was fourteen too. A child, really."

"Jeez, Tony...."

"He couldn't get another job. When the unemployment ran out he got by somehow on welfare and handouts. My parents probably gave him something too. But they didn't want him living at home anymore. He got a room in one of the seedier Seattle neighborhoods. Mom thinks that's when he started drinking. And there were some run-ins with the law, I found out later."

"Like what?"

"Oh, god,,,,,,, this is hard. My poor screwed up little brother. Shoplifting. A Walmart security guard caught him with a pocketful of women's underwear. Later the cops came to his room with a warrant and found a drawer full of the stuff. He copped a plea in return for 90 days at Western State Hospital in Steilacoom. That really seemed to change him. I don't know if they gave him drugs or anything but it was kind of like that, you know? He looked so bewildered, so out of it when they released him. After that I was flying up nearly every other month to get him out of some kind of scrape — there were more shoplifting incidents — or to give him money. My parents were always calling me. They didn't know what else to do."

"Heavy stuff, Tony. Hey, did he ever have a girlfriend? I mean, jeez, didn't he ever make it even once with a woman?"

"Not as far as I know. No, he never did."

"A prostitute, maybe?"

"No way. No matter how screwed up sex was in Richie's head it was always something holy and reserved for marriage."

Steve just shakes his head. But I know what he's thinking. The news is full of stories about sexually abusive priests. Good thing they caught this "almost" priest early on. Maybe I've thought that too. We drive on in silence, our way of acknowledging this to one another. There's not much traffic. With a little luck we should be in Seattle before dark.

I'm tired. It would be nice to get a little sleep before my stint behind the wheel. But I'm thinking of the stone lady. I guess you could say Richie did have a girlfriend once. She was his tender goddess, his grace, the recipient of a frightening outpouring of devotion when the dam finally burst. Maybe Richie did "flip out". Maybe there was a point in time, a day on a calendar, when Richie crossed from a world in which he couldn't function to one of his own making. Three years ago it started. It was Thursday. It was a Thursday afternoon because the museum is free then, from two until it closes at six. Richie had gone in to get out of the rain. He must have walked through the exhibit rooms until he found a bench. After sitting down he would have carefully removed his hat and mittens and placed them in his lap. Perhaps, to avoid being evicted by the guard, he looked up as if studying some work of art. And then he saw her. She stared at him through half-closed eyes sculpted in marble who knows how many hundreds of years ago. Her lips were thin but smiling faintly and her expression was soft, full of warmth and comprehension. So he sat there in front of this bust of a Madonna, or saint, or noble lady, sat there in the glow of her polished cheeks until it was time for the doors to be closed. But when they spoke to him he didn't seem to hear. They couldn't get him to leave. So they called the cops. This one officer knew Richie, knew he was harmless and had mental issues. I was visiting at my parents when the call came. I picked him up at the station and took him to his room. It was a barren, high-ceilinged place cluttered with empty bottles and flakes of paint. There was a crucifix on the wall with palm fronds tucked behind it. I cleaned him up and put him to bed.

He went back to the museum every Thursday after that, and other days too if he had the price of admission. But he knew now to leave when they told him it was time and nobody made any trouble for him. Whenever I was in Seattle I'd go there and put some money in his pocket. And I'd always slip the guard twenty bucks too.

I guess I should tell Steve all this. It explains a lot. When the museum sold the bust to another museum in New York Richie would come and sit on the bench as if his lady were still there. The administrators got in touch with my parents who finally had Richie committed. I drove him to Steilacoom myself. He just stood there uncomprehendingly, staring at the walls. It was the last time I saw him.

"Hey, Tony! You sleeping or what?"

"No, no, I'm awake. Let's stop to eat in Eugene and I'll drive."

"OK. You know, I've been thinking about your brother and the Catholic church. How they've been fucking people up about sex for centuries. You know how they like to say 'hate the sin, love the sinner?' That's just bullshit. The Church *loves* sin. That and guilt. It's the business they're in. Where would they be without sin? Think about it. And their all-time favorite sin? Sex, man, sex. It's been their number one money maker for hundreds of years. If Richie bought into all that shit no wonder he was so screwed up. Oh, hey Tony, I'm sorry..."

"It's OK." I tell him. Then, "Your favorite sin too, buddy. You still screwing around on Gayle?"

"Nah. I'm burned out. Women, sex... what's the big deal? Know what I mean?"

"Not really. Let's stop for lunch. We need gas too."

Steve is still going on about women as we order beer and hamburgers.

"How's it with you, Tony? You gonna get married again?"

"Married? Yeah, probably. I envy you and Gayle."

"Don't."

"I mean it. Sometimes I think Ellen and I should have hung in there, maybe got some counseling."

"Listen, Tony. Take your time. Play around. You got it made."

"No, you've got it made, Steve. You just don't know it and could we please talk about something else?"

Our burgers arrive and we eat in silence for a while. I'm going to be driving so Steve orders himself another beer.

"Remember last night?" he asks.'

"What about it?"

"You know. Unbaptized flesh."

"You're crazy."

"Yeah," he says with a stupid grin on his face. "I got this great idea though. Wanna hear it."

"I'd rather not." I know he just wants to lighten things up but I don't want to go there. It doesn't feel right.

"No, listen. I start this new church, see. I mean LA's ready for it. Think of all the good looking babes back there. Multiply that by two and we're talking billions of unbaptized boobs."

I don't want to encourage this but I can't help laughing. The guy says he's burned out on sex but it's all he thinks about.

"So I build a temple in Garden Grove and dedicate it to Aphrodite. How cool is that? And inside, right in the middle, under a dome, there's this big round sunken pool in pink and blue tile. There's steps leading into the water around the whole perimeter and light streaming in past hanging plants and stained glass windows. New Age music coming from surround sound speakers high up in the dome. And every day there's this circle of good-looking women in white baptismal gowns standing around the edge of the pool. Me, high priest and boob baptizer, I'm in the water, right up to my ass. When I give a signal the women step into the pool in their flowing white gowns until they're all standing around me. Then I give another sign and slowly they let the robes slip from their shoulders, past their breasts and the peach fuzz on their bellies, until the fabric lies floating around their hips like lily pads. It's pure poetry, man. I go up to a woman and cradle one of her breasts in my hand while I dip a silver cup into the water. I pour it over each tit and say this little prayer I've written. I don't suppose you'd like to hear it? Yeah, I thought not. Anyway, then I kiss her on the mouth and start working my way around the circle. Every day, and twice on Sundays. There's a lot of work to be done, buddy. So what do you think?"

We're both laughing now. "I think you are one sorry sacrilegious son of a bitch. By the way, where does this new career leave time for your law practice?"

"You're just jealous. But you can be my assistant. Let's pay and get out of here. You're driving."

I just keep it at 60 in the slow lane. Steve's given up on trying to jolly me out of my funk and I'm not talking either. At least not to Steve. But it's like Richie is right here in the car with me and I'm talking to him.

"I should have understood, Richie. Maybe I could have done something to help, like dragging you to LA and introducing you to some nice Catholic girls. How about that, Richie boy? You were always so shy around girls when we were kids. I think you had a respect for them that the rest of us had yet to learn, or maybe never did. But it was like you put them on some kind of, I don't know, altar or something. I'll never forget what you said to me years later when El and I got married. I mean it really got to me. You said that marriage was a sacrament and undressing your bride on her wedding night was like a priest removing the cloth from the chalice just before he consecrates the wine. That was weird, let me tell you. It's not like that, Richie. They're just like we are. I mean they like to screw too and get sweaty in bed, and ... hell, Richie, there's nothing holy about it. Just two people holding on to one another. So they won't be afraid of the dark. But what you said... that was ... that was really beautiful."

Steve takes over again as we cross the Columbia into Washington. The skies are dark and it's starting to rain. We drive on into it, windshield wipers slapping away. The dense forests on either side of the highway have that melancholy look I remember so well from days like this after school when Richie and I would bundle up for our evening paper route. The clouds get darker and the rain heavier as we continue north. When we finally pull off the highway near my old neighborhood it's six o'clock and the rain is falling so hard we can barely hear one another when we talk.

My parents both come to the door. They look tired. And old. I worry about them, what they must be going through. But they try to act cheerful when I introduce Steve and tell them he's here to help if there are any legal problems to clear up. They show us to my old room, as if I needed directions, so we can put our bags away and freshen up. Steve will have Richie's bed.

My mother says she's sorry. She didn't expect us until the next day, such a long drive, so she doesn't have dinner for us. I say it's OK and Steve and I go off to a restaurant I know. We don't talk much. We're exhausted. Thank god there won't be a funeral to get through. The body was cremated three days after a nurse found Richie hanging in his room at Steilacoom. We can take care of the papers and legal stuff over the next couple days. I thank Steve again for coming along and pick up the check.

Back home now, and in bed. Steve's already sleeping. I reach up and turn out the lamp. Nothing's changed in this room. It's dark. Can you hear me, Richie? We used to be pretty close, huh? Before the seminary? The rain is falling heavily on the roof. I lie on my back in cool, fresh sheets and listen. I hear the water cascading over the gutters and spilling onto the walk below the window. I think about Richie baptizing the woman at the lake. I think about Steve and how, without knowing it, he's making something sacred out of sex. Like Richie. Maybe I'm starting to understand that.

Nothing's changed in this room. It's as if Richie and I are still kids, in our old beds. I remember our last night here together, Richie, the night before you left for the seminary. You gave me the hunting knife you'd won at scout camp one summer. It was a prized possession. And you knew how much I coveted it. You said that as a priest you wouldn't be needing it. But I knew better. We both did. Our lives, until that night, so closely linked, would now take different paths. The knife, the most precious thing you owned, was both gift and sacrifice, a way of marking the end of our shared life while leaving something of yourself behind. I knew then that I was losing you. The full pain of that loss would come later.

I still have your knife, Richie. Let me have also your generosity, your innocence, your gentleness of spirit. The rain drums in torrents on the roof. It descends in cataracts to the first flicker of a dream. A pool somewhere. Immersing me.

Lyrics to Pagan Baby Love

When I was a lad I was a Catholic schooler
Learned about God and Sister Mary's ruler
Studied 'bout hell and the wages of sin
And the terrible fix pagan babies were in

If there's no one to baptize
A pagan baby 'fore a pagan baby dies
The poor little soul to heaven can't go
Gets sent down the road to old limbo

Pagan babies dancin' on moonlit nights
Drums beatin' rhythm to pagan baby rites
Fire shootin' sparks to the stars above
Searing my soul with pagan baby love

I became a missionary on graduation
Saving pagan babies was my vocation
I boarded a boat for pagan baby land
And waded through the jungle to take my stand

But I wasn't there long before I realize
That pagan babies come in more than one size
Some grow up, the dancin' never stops
They don't wear much and they never wear tops

(refrain)

Lithe pagan baby with eyes so bright
Looked at me and said "you're mine tonight"
From the way I felt my poor heart's craving
I knew it was my soul needed saving

170

Moonlight sweatin' on pagan baby skin
Scents of the jungle floating in the wind
Mango juice on pagan baby lips
Grass skirts swaying from pagan baby hips

(refrain)

Sounds of the jungle ringin' in my ears
Been living here now for twenty-seven years
Seduced by a goddess and pagan baby charms
I found heaven in my pagan baby's arms

From our love came pagan babies three
Never baptized, living happy and free
They build their huts 'neath a baobab tree
Limbo's good enough for them and good enough for me

(refrain)

Acknowledgements

I would be remiss if I did not acknowledge my debt to four remarkable women without whose help, knowledge, and support this collection would not exist. I must thank, first of all, Donna Levin, a San Francisco based author and teacher. In the mid-1980s she allowed me to join her fiction writers' workshop in spite of the fact that I had never written a word of fiction. Several of the stories contained in this volume emerged from that delightful and illuminating experience and were no doubt much improved thanks to Donna's insightful comments and her love for the craft of writing. Now, some 30 years later, I am retired and living in a small town in Washington State. Though I had written nothing since those days in Donna's workshop, I was pleased to discover that two local women, NanLeah Mick and Annette Matrisciano, had organized a support group for aspiring writers in this area. I signed up. NanLeah and Annette, both very creative writers/poets/artists, rekindled the old desire to write. Many of these stories have benefited greatly from their kindness, critical comments, and encouragement. Finally I must thank Jo-Anne Rosen, friend, author, publisher and founder of Wordrunner Press in Petaluma, CA, who put this book together for me. Four beautiful, talented women. One grateful writer wannabe.

About the Author

Patrick Butler, a native of Washington State, moved to San Francisco after completing degrees in history and political science at Stanford University. He taught in the social sciences department of the City College of San Francisco for thirty years. Upon retirement in 1997 he returned to Washington where he lives with his wife Antoinette in a magical place on the shores of Puget Sound. He enjoys writing and performing songs in addition to writing fiction.

Made in the USA
San Bernardino, CA
20 May 2018

Praise for The Adventures of a Helicopter Pilot

"This is the journal of an honest, down-to-earth, self-deprecating, capable, and above all, courageous American in some of the most difficult circumstances in this nation's history. The pages fly by, and as they do, I see more clearly the superb character of a hero with a sense of humor. We need more like him and they are getting more and more rare."

–Ben Stein, Actor/Author

"Bill Collier knows what it means to go into harm's way, and he never hesitated when there was a hazardous mission to be accomplished. Just ask the guys he rescued and the Marines he served with."

–Major General Larry Taylor, USMCR

"Heroism, friendly fire, R&R, razor's edge flying, this book has it all. Bill Collier lets us accompany him on his trip to Vietnam as a young Marine Corps helicopter pilot. Nothing is sacred here, save perhaps Bill's love for his country and loyalty to his fellow Marines. He is frank about the merits and liabilities of his equipment, his leaders, and his own skills. If you want an unvarnished, understated, but nevertheless heroic tale of Marine Corps helicopter operations in Vietnam, this is a must read."

–John Phillips, NASA Astronaut and Naval Aviator

"These events are factual; some funny, some ironic, some tragic. There was no handbook to operate a helicopter in close combat. Lessons learned were, often as not, passed word-of-mouth from one pilot to another at the o'club bar. I served with Captain Collier for 10 months in both his squadrons."

–Lieutenant Colonel James B. Barr USMCR

"In *Adventures of a Helicopter Pilot*, Captain Collier provides a gripping account of his flying experiences in Vietnam. The reader has the opportunity to fly with Bill on harrowing missions that will leave his hands sweaty and senses on full alert! Collier provides a firsthand look at helicopter rescue missions that saved countless lives. So intense are Bill's accounts of his experiences and so keen his reminiscences, one gains an appreciation of the debilitation caused by Post Traumatic Stress Disorder. May God bless our U.S. Marines! Semper Fi!"

–Lieutenant Colonel Rich Faletto, USAFR,
Author **Four-Eleven: Planes, Pulaskis and Forest Fires**

"A realistic and down-to-earth personal view of our country's involvement in a none-too-popular war. My hat's off to Bill Collier for inviting us into a conflict with both humor and pathos. A must read for every student of history from a soldier's point of view."

–Ted Parvin, Retired Motion Picture Producer

"Thoughtful, funny, and full of death-defying escapades, *Adventures of a Helicopter Pilot* is a treasure trove of stories. Captain Bill's writing captures the feeling of sitting around a campfire with cold beer and old friends. The perspective and humility he brings to the narrative are those of a once-brazen young man who has lived to tell the tales. A great read."

–April Dávila, soon-to-be-world-famous novelist and mother of
two of the author's most adorable grandchildren

"Bill Collier gives a vivid and honest account of his time as a helicopter pilot in Vietnam and of a time and a war that many of us remember all too well."

–Erik Daarstad, Academy Award-winning Cinematographer
and Documentary Filmmaker

THE
ADVENTURES
OF A HELICOPTER PILOT

Flying the H-34 Helicopter
In Vietnam for the
UNITED STATES MARINE CORPS

Captain Bill
Captain Bill Collier, USMCR

Cover: An H-34 from HMM-161 lands atop the Rockpile, autumn of 1966, pilot unknown. Photo by the author.

Back cover: Sundown aboard ship. Somewhere in the South China Sea, early 1967, aboard the aircraft carrier USS *Princeton*, an H-34D from HMM-363 gets a rub-down after a hard day's work. Photo by the author.

Most of the more than 100 photographs and illustrations are from the author's personal archives. Those not from his personal archives are credited to their source.

Many of the photographs in this book can be viewed in full color at author's website: www.captainbillfliesagain.com

Captain Bill Collier
P.O. box 105
Port Hadlock
WA 98339

THE ADVENTURES OF A HELICOPTER PILOT:
Flying the H-34 Helicopter in Vietnam for the
United States Marine Corps

ISBN 978-1-500936-13-6

CONTENTS

About the Author

This is a spellbinding, firsthand account of what it was like to pilot a Marine Corps H-34 helicopter in combat during "The Helicopter War" in Vietnam.

As a brand-new, United States Naval Aviator with a mere 187.5 hours of helicopter flight experience, Second Lieutenant Bill Collier had many exciting adventures. Many were just a bit too exciting, some were horrific and a few were terrifying! Some were humorous.

Second Lieutenant Bill Collier after he completed U.S. Navy Flight School, mid-December 1965

This is the true story of his experiences during his 13 months in the war. Bill watched friends die violently and stood many times eye-to-eye, toe-to-toe, with Death himself.

Each time, Death flinched.

He was nearly killed six times during one 13-day period while on the ground with the infantry as a forward air controller.

Bill hauled about 375 wounded Marines out of the field.

He came home heavily decorated and with a serious case of post-traumatic stress disorder (PTSD).

He also had many fun and positive experiences as he bonded with his fellow Marine pilots to create lifelong friendships. He visited several countries in the Far East.

Acknowledgements

First and foremost I must thank my wife, Carla, for her continued love and support. She was most instrumental in my completing this book. She not only encouraged me to write this book, but without her help to get my life together, I am sure I would be living out in the woods in the Mendocino National forest in Northern California in a rusty old VW bus sitting up on blocks. Her unconditional love and compassion most likely saved my life. She still tolerates an occasional PTSD-fueled outburst.

In addition, I must thank I must thank my lovely and charming daughters, April and Summer, who continue to love their old father even though I was frequently absent from their lives both physically and emotionally. I must also acknowledge their mother, Michele, for her putting up with my PTSD-fired acting out for nearly two decades before finally setting me free. Over the years, she has become a good friend and a wonderful "YaYa" to our grandchildren.

I am grateful to my parents, Bill and Emma, and my step-mother, Betty. My brother Cal, who guided me into college-prep classes in high school, provided example and inspiration with his four years in the U.S. Air Force. Cal was the person who inspired me to become an officer. Dr. Albert Heppe taught me chemistry and physics at Sonoma Valley High School. Sophomore English teacher Beatrice Armstrong awakened my mind to the beauty and structure of the English language.

I am grateful to Captain Thatcher for recruiting me into the MARCAD program, and to my first two flight instructors, First Lieutenant Donny Evans and Captain Barry Schultz, for teaching me primary flying at Saufley Field near Pensacola, Florida. Also I appreciate the dozens of other instructors in Navy flight school who helped me complete flight training and to gain my Naval Aviator's Wings of Gold. Many thanks to the senior pilots at Marine Corps Air Station New River, North Carolina, who prepared me for flying in combat in Vietnam. Leon Elmore comes immediately to mind.

Many thanks to the Veterans Administration for providing free PTSD counselling for veterans. I specifically wish to mention S. Dudley, Randy Fowler and Stephanie Piekowski who were most instrumental in guiding me out of my clouds of confusion and self-destructive behaviors.

My love to all my fellow Marine Corps Aviators and crewmen who sacrificed much, sometimes all, to "accomplish the mission." Specifically, Gary James Connolly, Michael Hynes, James Stroupe, Jon D. Baker, Bill Ruth*, Bill Elmore, Timothy O'Toole, Michael Hynes, Daniel Smithson, Paul Sheehan, James Barr, Marin Baiz, James Depuy, Dennis Kawakek and many, many more.

Without our fantastic crew chiefs and ground support teams, none of this helicopter flying in Vietnam could ever have happened. Our crew chiefs flew all day with us, loading and unloading cargo and passengers, putting their lives in our pilots' hands hour after hour, day after day (some nights), landing after landing. Without them the machines would have deteriorated to un-flyable junk in less than a week. After working all day in the air, they many times worked all night to maintain the helicopters. Sometimes they had to wash blood off the cabin floor and sweep our maggots from dead Marines. They changed out engines overnight, replaced gear boxes, rotor blades and many other components – in the field at times. They filled about 100 zerk fittings with grease, most of them every night; there must be 50 zerk fittings on the H-34 rotor head alone. They did all the refueling whenever we stopped to refuel. These were the most dedicated crews that could possibly have existed, anywhere, anytime, any war. They never got enough thanks and credit for their sacrifices. Thank you crew chiefs, gunners mechanics, avionics and armory personnel.

Also, none of this could have happened without all the ground support Marines. The administration people kept the papers pushed and the money flowing. The intelligence guys kept us informed of the enemy locations and situations. The operations fellows scheduled

*Captain Bill Ruth died in the Pentagon on September 11, 2001. Semper Fidelis, Marine.

all the flights and coordinated the passengers to make everything move as efficiently as they did. The materials Marines kept the food, spare parts and other necessities flowing to us. And much, much, much, more to many, many, many more.

The Marines in the field gave us our reason for existing. We lived (and died) to bring them every support we possible could. God bless all the approximately 15,000 Marines who died in Vietnam.

Thanks to my daughter April Davila for her help with editing early on, and my daughter Summer for encouraging me to press on. Thanks to daughter Emily Aerni for helping with the early stages of formatting the manuscript. Thanks to Mary Sherer for her very professional final edit.

Thanks to the crew at Keokee for their work in formatting and finishing the final-final product. Chris Bessler and Billie Jean Gerke were invaluable with their skills and knowledge and Laura Wahl for her graphics work.

I wish to thank the following for reading rough copies of my book to give me feedback and/or a blurb for the front of the book: Lieutenant Colonel James Barr, USMC Ret; retired Santa Rosa, California, Firefighter Captain Ted Boothroyd; Academy Award-winning documentary cinematographer Erik Daarstad; soon-to-be-world-famous novelist April Dávila; Lieutenant Colonel Rich Faletto, USAF Ret; former grunt captain of Marines, Michael Kempf; cousin Leon Machell; retired motion picture producer Ted Parvin; former Naval aviator and retired NASA astronaut John Phillips; actor Ben Stein; and Major General Larry Taylor, USMCR Ret.

This Book is Dedicated to Leon Machell

My second birthday was V-J Day, so I grew up in the afterglow of World War II. To me, every World War II veteran who had been involved in the vanquishing of the evil countries of Germany, Japan and Italy was a hero. Growing up, I watched every episode of "Victory at Sea" many times. Only recently did I realize that I have my very own personal WW II hero-veteran in my family. Leon, the oldest of my 25 first cousins, graduated from Kings Point Maritime Academy, New York as a marine engineer in July 1943, the month before I was born. He travelled the high seas, both Atlantic and Pacific, not always in convoys, putting his life in the line of fire of enemy submarines and aircraft, just as much as any Allied soldier, sailor or Marine on the front lines.

Leon Machell, right, in his U.S. Navy lieutenant's uniform.

The warriors of the "Greatest Generation" truly saved the world. The Nazi Germans and the Imperial Japanese thought their races were superior to all other races and thought of them as sub-human. Had the Greatest Generation not vanquished the Nazis and the Japs, the whole rest of the world's population might have ended up in concentration camps, to be worked to death to benefit these "superior" races.

The citation below is from the World War II Registry of Remembrance, Part of the WWII memorial, which was dedicated in Washington, D.C. in 2004.

LEON FRANK MACHELL, U.S. MERCHANT MARINE, ACTIVITY DURING WWII, ENTERED KINGS POINT MERCHANT MARINE ACADEMY AT KINGS POINT, NEW YORK IN FEBRUARY 1942. GRADUATED FROM THE ACADEMY IN 1943 WITH A MARINE ENGINEER LICENSE. IN ADDITION TO AND SIMULTANEOUS WITH HIS MERCHANT MARINE SERVICE, HE WAS ENROLLED IN THE UNITED STATES NAVAL RESERVE, AND IN THE UNITED STATES COAST GUARD. HE SAILED ON LIBERTY SHIPS AND OTHER TRANSPORT SHIPS THROUGHOUT THE PACIFIC THEATER OF OPERATIONS DELIVERING AMMUNITION, FOOD, AVIATION GASOLINE IN DRUMS, AND OTHER SUPPLIES FROM SAN FRANCISCO TO MANY DIFFERENT LOCATIONS FOR THE ARMY, NAVY, AND MARINES. IN AUGUST 1945 HE WAS IN BUCKNER BAY, OKINAWA WHEN THE WAR ENDED. HE WAS DISCHARGED AS A LIEUTENANT IN THE UNITED STATES COAST GUARD IN 1946.

This citation is re-created from its original form, which was all in capitals.

Leon lives in Lodi, California, with his beautiful and charming wife of 72 years, Vivian. He celebrated his 93st birthday in 2014.

Happy Birthday, Cousin Leon – you are my hero!

In addition to Leon, shortly before publication, I remembered I had a second World War II war hero in my family. My Uncle Rudy Esposti, husband of my father's sister Opal, was a Marine in the South Pacific. He was with the Marines when they attacked the Japanese at Roi-Namur, the co-joined island at the north end of the Kwajalein Atoll. This was one of the major battles of the Pacific campaign. The Marines mopped up that Japanese stronghold in one day.

I remember that it was quite a family scandal when Aunt Opal decided to marry Rudy. Not only was he a Marine, he was Italian, too. The horror! Everybody quickly grew to love him for his charm, honesty and integrity.

In Memory Of:

Jon D. Baker
Richard Bassinger
Jeff Chestnutt
Phillip Ducat
Patrick Ott
Dean W. Reiter
Robert Schena
Gary Shields

And the 836 other United States Marines Corps
pilots and aircrew who lost their lives in Vietnam.

We have to ask ourselves the simple question:

WHY?

Prologue

Whenever two or more experienced combat helicopter pilots get together, they will inevitably start to swap flying stories. Every helicopter pilot has many. Somewhere, in the midst of these stories, one of the raconteurs invariably will say this phrase, "... and this is no shit!" The phrase will either be interjected into the middle of a story at an important point, or stated at the beginning of the story to validate the veracity of an otherwise implausible tale.

To many listeners it would seem to that the story being told is simply not possible, that the pilot is lying. It sometimes seems that what the pilot is relating could not possibly have happened.

To other helicopter pilots, it is verification that the speaking pilot speaks truth. The story will possibly have been modified and elaborated upon over the years, but the nut of the story itself is most likely very true.

This is a collection of stories of my experiences while flying for the Marine Corps in the Vietnam War from late July 1966, until mid-August 1967.

These are my stories ... and this is no shit!
(In chronological order, as best as I can remember.)

A fairy tale begins with, "Once upon a time ... "

An fighter pilot's war story begins with, "There I was at ten thousand feet when the shit hit the fan ... "

A combat helicopter pilot's war story begins with, "There I was, on short final, screaming into a hot landing zone, both machine guns blazing when ... and this is no shit ... "

Introduction

*April 27, 1964 Fetters Hot Springs, California, about 11:45 am.
(Sonoma Valley, 50 miles north of San Francisco)*

I worked as a carpenter apprentice, helping contractor Benedict Smigle build a small spec house on Buena Vista Avenue, just east of Highway 12. It was a balmy, beautiful spring day. My father's good friend, red-headed Louie Perryhouse, and I were preparing to raise a wall of studs that we had just assembled on the sub-floor.

My stepmother, Betty, came running across the street from her beat-up old green and tan 1949 Chevy station wagon. She waved a small piece of yellow paper in front of her, hollering excitedly, "It's here, it's here!" At first I had no idea what she was hollering about. Then she yelled, "It's here! Your orders are here!" The yellow piece of paper was a Western Union telegram, my official orders to U.S. Navy Flight School in Pensacola, Florida.

That telegram started my lifelong journey as a helicopter pilot. I had been selected for United States Navy Flight School on the Marine Corps Aviation Cadet (MARCAD) program.

I departed San Francisco International (SFO) on a National Airlines red-eye special late the evening of May 13, 1964. Early the next day, I reported to the U.S. Navy for duty, exactly three months before my 21st birthday. Nineteen months later, mid-December 1965, I became a Naval Aviator. (All Marine Corps pilots are Naval Aviators.) My girlfriend at the time, Marci Floyd, pinned my golden naval aviator's wings upon my chest.

Eight months after finishing flight school, I found myself flying the Sikorsky H-34D helicopter in combat for the United States Marine Corps in Vietnam.

I began helicopter combat flying with exactly 187.5 hours of helicopter experience.

Map of I Corps, Republic of Vietnam

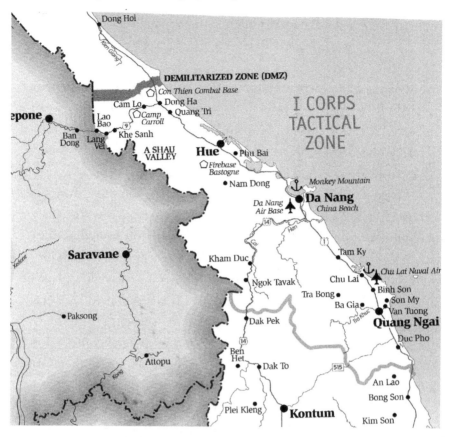

Map Excerpt from:
WARTIME VIETNAM
Courtesy of Vietnam Veterans of America, www.vva.org
Map design by Xande Anderer/Citizen X Design

1.
Dong Ha

"When a Marine in Vietnam is wounded, surrounded, hungry, low on ammunition or water, he looks to the sky. He knows the choppers are coming."

–Leonard F. Chapman, General, USMC
24th Commandant of the Marine Corps, from 1968 to 1972

My first night mission in Vietnam was so frightening that I suppressed it in my memory until mid-2007. This event came up after thirteen years of group and individual therapy sessions with a series of Veterans Administration (VA) psychological counselors. I started therapy in early 1994 for Post Traumatic Stress Disorder, for reasons best explained by these stories. I continue to go to group therapy monthly. A second hairy mission less than a month later compounded the problem.

A night medevac at Mutter Ridge
Hovering over a battle at night

29 August 1966, early evening.

*12 miles northwest of Dong Ha, Quang Tri Province,
in support of Operation Prairie*

Aviation has been defined as "Hours and hours of boredom interrupted on occasion by a few seconds of sheer terror!"

About 20:00[1] hours, well after dark in the tropics, we were called out on an emergency medical evacuation (medevac) at Mutter Ridge.

There had been a hell of a battle going on this hillside for weeks, as the 4th Marines were slogging their way up a hill, trying to dislodge the enemy from the high ground. In this ferocious battle there were many Marine casualties. Our squadron helicopters had been out there numerous times over the previous few days re-supplying the unit and rescuing dozens of wounded Marines. After going through the usual trio of telephone calls, my crew and another launched on a perilous mission.

A Rating System for Medevac Missions

We had a rating system for medevac missions. The three levels of medevac were routine, priority and emergency. Routine medevacs were for those Marines who had a minor wound or illness, but were in no immediate danger. Priority medevacs were for the fellows who were worse off, but were in no danger of dying right away; these could wait a few hours. Emergency medevacs were for wounded Marines who might die right away if not taken to a field hospital immediately. After full darkness it was too dangerous to go out into the hills and jungles to make a pick-up for any reason other than an emergency medevac.

The three-call scenario often happened like this. The field phone rang, and the duty officer would have a conversation with the unit in the field requesting a medevac. Usually his response was, "No. Sorry, we cannot launch out on a routine medevac at night; call us back at first light." Then he would hang up. About 20 minutes later, the shrill, irritating sound of the field phone would again awaken us from our uncomfortable sleep on the padded storage boxes that constituted crude ready-room seats. Again the duty officer would take the call, listen to the request from the field, and once again explain: "No, sorry we cannot fly a priority medevac until dawn. Call back at first light."

Not always, but frequently enough to make us nervous after the first call or two, the phone would ring for the third time. "Emergency medevac, pilots, man your aircraft!" While the command pilots gathered around the duty officer to get the briefing, the copilots

---

1 Military time starts at midnight and counts 24 hours. 20:00 is therefore 8 p.m.

rushed out to the rice paddy to start the helicopter engines, turn up
the rotors and begin the systems checks. We made every effort to be
off the ground in five minutes after an alert.

Many times, the sequence of calls was for the same trooper, but his
field sergeant kept upgrading the level of medevac until he got the
trooper a ride. Sometimes we went out to the field to see the "badly
wounded" trooper walk to the aircraft. Sometimes the trooper would
be carried to the helicopter on a stretcher, only to be miraculously
healed during the flight. Upon landing at Delta med, he would get
up off the stretcher and walk away. At times like this we learned that
the trooper had not gotten his orders until this day to go on R&R or
rotate home the next day and he did not want to miss his flight. We
always got a little perturbed when we put our lives on the line just to
see a healthy Marine the object of our emergency medevacs.

We copilots clambered up the sides of our Sikorsky H-34s, slid
into our copilot's seats and fired up the powerful Wright 1525 horse
power, nine-cylinder radial engines. The two pilots or helicopter aircraft
commanders (HACs) arrived from the detailed briefing climbed in and
took command. We blasted off into the black night sky. I was flying
copilot for a senior first lieutenant. He had flown out to Mutter Ridge
many times in the few days prior. He knew where we were going, he
knew what to do, and he knew well how to do it. I felt confident being
with him and that he would take care of me.

He did; much better than I could ever have imagined.

As we departed Dong Ha, we radioed "Landshark Charlie," the
disembodied voice in the ethers in charge of artillery in our area. At our
request Landshark took the precaution of shutting down the outgoing
artillery from near our base to the contested area. We would notify him
upon our return to base so that outgoing artillery could resume.

On the way out to the landing zone (LZ), there were no city
lights to brighten our way, no villages with fires burning to help us
discern terrain. No street or highway lights, no car lights. The moon
was just past full but had not yet risen. Once airborne, we navigated
our way by using our TACAN navigation radio. (This radio displayed

on instrument gauges our distance and compass radial relative to home base.)

We flew the 12 miles, west by northwest, out to the Mutter Ridge area and made radio contact with the grunts on the ground. Once we got near the LZ it was obvious where we were to try to make the pickup, as hundreds of tracers lighted up the area of the battle, and the occasional flash of a grenade or mortar explosion added to the fireworks. This LZ was hot, very hot.

I was a nugget, a brand new gold-bar second lieutenant. I was a newbie, a combat virgin, along for the ride. I had not yet been into a hot landing zone. I had not yet been out to Mutter Ridge. I had not yet done a high-hover hoist pick-up, and this was my very first night combat flight in Vietnam. My job was to watch the instruments when the lieutenant was busy hovering, to prevent his overboosting (too much power) or overspeeding (too many revs) the engine.

The pilot verified that they had a very seriously wounded Marine who needed to be rescued right away, or he might die. This was a genuine emergency medevac. At times, talking to the radio operator on the ground, gunfire in the background and his heavy, labored breathing told us things were less than cozy on the ground around him. This situation was most challenging. The problem presented to us was to fly down to the battle, establish a stable hover over ninety-foot tall trees, hold that hover for about five minutes while threading the rescue basket down through the trees to the Marines so they could load their wounded man. Then we had to retrieve the basket with the Marine in it. We must do all of this in near-total darkness.

It was going to be a very long five minutes. We spiraled carefully down to establish a hover above the Marines. While we descended, I extinguished all external lights to make us invisible to the enemy below. Once we were in a stable but precarious hover, the crew chief began operating the hydraulic hoist, unreeling the cable to lower the litter basket down to the Marines.

With our engine at nearly full power, I hoped the horrific roar of our engine was causing the enemy to hunker down in fear. I hoped they thought we would shoot back if they shot at us, as we could have. The crew chief and gunner each had an M-60 machine gun and were ready and able to return fire. Of course, should the crew return fire, our tracers would pinpoint us as a bright target for the enemy. Also, the crew chief was really too busy at the moment running the hoist to be shooting his M-60.

It was extremely difficult for the lieutenant to maintain a hover in the dark over these 90-foot tall trees. The only ground reference he had to relate to was the geometric plane created by sparkling tracers – red for the Marines and green for the enemy – whizzing across the battlefield, back and forth underneath us. But the terrain, our only plane of reference, was tilted at 30 to 45 degrees from level.

Normally, hovering a helicopter is a simple matter for any helicopter pilot with just a wee bit of experience. I remember well my first few attempts at hovering in the final stages of Navy flight school. I had recently finished the final portion of airplane training and had earned my Navy gold wings by landing my T-28C "Trojan" fighter-bomber on the aircraft carrier USS *Lexington*. Then I advanced to helicopter training at Ellyson Field, north of Pensacola.

My first few attempts at hovering were absolute frustration. I was all over the four sides of a mile-square field, bobbing up and down like a yo-yo. My instructor, Naval Lieutenant Bickum, let me go wild for a few moments until I was nearly out of control, then he calmly took over control of the machine, effortlessly put it back in the middle of the large field, and let me start over. After three or four attempts, I was able to keep the small Bell H-13 (Whirleybird) inside the limits of the mile-square field. By then, I was completely exhausted and drenched with sweat. I learned quickly after that with lots of practice.

BELL H-13 Helicopter   Source: Wikipedia

Hovering a helicopter requires something to hover in reference to; you cannot hold a steady hover unless you have something to use as a reference point. Think of looking up at the stars on a very clear night. A bright star looks so close it seems like you can reach out and pluck it from the sky. It is the same trying to hover a helicopter in the dark or over open water, there are no real reference points. Distance and height are difficult to assess.

The lieutenant was having great difficulty holding a stable hover. Trying to hover over the sloping ground caused him to repeatedly tilt the helicopter away from the vertical, causing us to drift away from the Marines. If we drifted too far in a northerly direction, we might drift into trees on the upslope, infested with the enemy. We also might drag the basket through the trees, endangering the wounded Marine now in it, and even perhaps entangling our cable in the tree tops. The mission was in jeopardy, as were we. To make things even more interesting, occasionally an errant burst of tracers would rise vertically, some of them passing uncomfortably close to us. We knew each visible tracer bullet represented four or five bullets.

There was only one solution. The lieutenant asked me, "Bill, do you know where the hover/flood light switch is?" My first thought was that there was no way he was going to ask me to turn on those lights. To do so meant certain, instant death for the whole crew! So I answered him with a simple: "Yes, sir." A millisecond later I realized, *Ohmygod! He is going to have me flip that switch! When those lights come on, we will be the biggest and brightest target in all of Vietnam. We are hovering over who-knows-how-many hundreds or thousands of NVA [North Vietnamese Army troops]. We are going to be so shot full of holes that we will explode into a ball of fire!*

Then the lieutenant said to me ... and this is no shit! ... "When I tell you, turn on those lights."

I placed my fingers on the toggle switch on the overhead panel. I knew I was done for, but what could I do? Refuse an order? I was a Marine; "Death before dishonor" was our creed. I was duty bound to do what my pilot in command told me to do, even if it meant my immediate, fiery death. *This is it! I am going to die in this war, right here, right now!* I only hoped that I would get shot and die quickly and not bounce down through the tall trees in the thrashing and crashing, flopping and chopping, slicing and dicing, whirling ball of exploding, flame-spewing helicopter as it tumbled down through the trees, to be burned to death, most painfully and slowly!

He told me to turn on the lights. Without argument or discussion, I dutifully toggled that switch.

Now I die!

The results were amazing. Absolute silence! Every single man on the ground, Marine and enemy combatant alike, must have thought he was the most exposed fellow on the planet. Each one, feeling that he was going to be the next soldier to be shot, threw himself into the nearest foxhole or behind the nearest tree. The battle completely ceased for at least 90 seconds while we hovered there, fully lighted up like a light standard at a Friday night high school football game. It seemed like forever.

Nothing happened. Nothing! We never once got shot at! Why the enemy soldiers on the ground did not roll over on their backs and give us full salvos of hundreds of 7.62 mm. AK-47 bullets, I will never know. I would not have been surprised to have a Marine shoot at us, to protect himself and his fellow Marines from our floodlights. (But then, the Marines knew one of their own was being rescued.)

How a Helicopter Flies

So just how does a helicopter fly, you ask? Have you ever driven along in a car with the window down, your hand playing in the air? Who hasn't? Remember what it was like? Just try it next time you drive somewhere on a nice day. Put your hand out the window into the air. The faster you go, the stronger the "wind" on your hand. This is called "relative" wind because if the car is not moving, there is no wind. The wind is relative to the speed of the car. Remember moving your hand around to make your hand go up, then down? Well, in that little bit of playing around, you are learning about the basics of aerodynamics.

If you hold your hand flat, fingers and palm parallel to the ground, your hand will slice rather nicely through the air. If you hold your hand perpendicular, your hand will catch a lot more air, and it will require much more effort to keep it in place.

Now put your hand out parallel to the ground again, and curve your palm and fingers so that your hand is slightly cupped. You have now created a simple airfoil (wing), and you will find that your hand will want to rise up, because of the lift created by your airfoil/hand. Lift is created because the impact of air on the bottom of your hand is greater than the pressure on the top; the hand tends to move in the direction of less pressure.

Aerodynamic engineers will tell you that the lift is caused because the pressure on the top of the hand is less; therefore, the hand moves in the direction of less pressure. I have always thought it was easier to visualize that the pressure on the bottom of the hand is greater, pushing the hand up. Six of one and half a dozen of the other, I say. So that is how a wing works.

Now delete the word "helicopter" from this discussion. Replace it with "rotary wing." A helicopter is simply an airplane whose wings go around the rotor mast faster and faster until the wings create lift and the aircraft rises. The rest is simply adding various controls to harness the thrust so you can go where you want to go.

Hovering is a delicate balance between several forces. The primary balance is lift versus gravity. The engine powering the rotors must generate enough lift to keep the helicopter at the same altitude, balanced between climbing and descending. At the same time, the thrust must be evenly balanced so that there is no component of it tilted from the vertical, or the helicopter will follow that tilt vector and drift left, right, forward or aft.

The crew chief finished hoisting up the wounded Marine and pulled him into the helicopter. When the lieutenant could see that the victim was clear of the trees, he told me to switch off the lights. With great relief I did so, amazed to be still alive and not a crispy critter in a heap of steaming, smoking rubble on the hillside.

We delivered the wounded Marine to Delta Med, the field hospital. We never got any feedback on these missions. We never knew if the Marines we rescued lived or died, unless one died on board. This did happen on board my aircraft at least once.

I, the new guy on the block, a brand new gold bar "nugget" second lieutenant, combat virgin, had no idea what a courageous and heroic thing the lieutenant had just accomplished. I thought that this was an every day routine kind of thing, something that these more experienced guys did all the time. I knew I soon would be expected to do similar work. I wondered if I was up to it.

In my own time, in my own way, I was.

It was only decades later that I realized what a tremendously brave and wondrous thing the lieutenant did that night over Mutter Ridge, how courageous he had been. He put his life (and mine, and the crew's) on the line to rescue a fellow Marine. If I'd had any idea at the time, I would have written him up for a medal. This mission was worthy of at least a Silver Star, if not the big one, the Congressional Medal of Honor.

I feel his heroism was equal to that of Admiral Spruance in turning on the lights of his aircraft carrier to recover his planes at the end of the Battle of Midway in World War II. He risked torpedo attack by Japanese submarines, but in doing so Spruance recovered his experienced pilots and their aircraft. Those pilots were vital to our victory in World War II.

This rescue was such a traumatic event for me that I blanked it out of my memory until recently. The lieutenant's name isn't listed in my aviator's logbook. I must access some unit records somewhere, to find out who he was. If I learn who he was, I may yet write him up for that medal. But at the same time, our attitude was: "We are not here to get medals; we're here to rescue wounded Marines." As Gunnery Sergeant Massey (one of my drill sergeants in the earliest stage of flight school) would have growled, "Don't thank me. I'm just doing my job."

Here is the Command Chronology entry for this exciting event:

"29 August, 1966. ... One medevac was particularly noteworthy, as it necessitated a 90 foot hover at 1,000 feet of altitude and a basket pick up of a U.S. wounded. This was completed without incident."[2]

This is somewhat of an understatement!
(This event occurred two weeks after my 23rd birthday. I had been in Vietnam about four weeks.)

8 August. Corporal R. L. Belnap was killed when the aircraft in which he was flying in as aerial gunner was riddled by enemy fire while on an emergency resupply mission approximately 50 miles NW of Phu Bai."[3]

During August of 1966, squadron HMM-161 flew 1,264.3 hours, carried 5,011 passengers, hauled 221 tons of cargo, and hauled 227 medevacs out of the field. We changed 14 engines this month. I personally flew 51.2 hours.

"Friendly Fire!"

Dong Ha, South Vietnam 25 Sept. 1966, about 1915 hours – almost a full month after the previous frightening night medevac rescue.

The shrill, irritating ring of the field phone jarred us out of whatever had us occupied, calling us out on another perilous night medevac. Much like the frightening mission of 29 August, the location was about 265 degrees, 11 miles from Dong-Ha; Mutter Ridge again. More seriously wounded Marines with Second Battalion, Seventh

---

2 Texas Tech, "HMM-161 Command Chronology, 29 August, 1966." Document No. 1201079199
3 Texas Tech archives, Command Chronology HMM-161, 8 August, 1966

Marines (2/7) desperately needed a ride to Delta Med. We manned our two H-34s, called Landshark Charlie to quell the outgoing artillery, and flew out toward the hot landing zone.

In this case, I was riding copilot for senior Captain Peter Janss. As flight leader, he commanded the flight of four helicopters, two H-34s and our armed escort, two Huey gunships. Their call sign, "Klondike." They trailed behind our two H-34s in loose formation in case we needed to have them suppress enemy fire while we descended into the hot landing zone.

The second H-34, carrying a Corpsman, would fly into the hot LZ. Again, I was along for the ride and felt very safe. We, in the lead helicopter, would not be required to go down into the hot LZ unless No. 2 crashed or was shot down. I felt there was slim chance of that happening, as it was being flown by a very aggressive, very experienced junior captain, Phil Ducat. I was pretty comfortable with the whole mission. Flying on our wing in No. 2 position, in YR-3, were pilot-in-command Ducat and copilot First Lieutenant Dean W. Reiter. Crewmen were the crew chief Arthur W. Green, gunner Vernon H. Parker, and Navy Corpsman Robert P. Bossman. I had known Dean through most of flight school, knew his wife, and had partied at their house in Marine Corps Air Station New River, North Carolina, prior to Vietnam.

As we neared the LZ, we switched radio frequencies to communicate with the ground troops. The grunt radio operator confirmed that this was indeed a true emergency medevac. We heard the sounds of gunfire in the background. The radio operator grunted and breathed heavily over the radio as he exerted himself to avoid getting shot.

He instructed us to orbit for a while, as they were not ready for us yet. This was another huge understatement. They were being overrun by the North Vietnamese Army troops.

We were relieved to not have to go into the hot LZ right away. Captain Janss put us into a race-track pattern at a nice cozy, safe 4,000 feet, well above small-arms fire range. We orbited about five to six miles from the raging battle, roughly halfway between the battle and our home base. Here we waited, monitoring the radio, waiting for the call that would reactivate the mission. It seemed things could not be safer. We were over an area of high brush, the valley of the Cam Lo River. If we had an engine failure, we would have probably been able to land in the river bed, where our wingman would swoop down to rescue us. As engine failure was always a possibility, we always kept the location of any nearby emergency landing site in the backs of our minds. We were there for him as well, should his engine fail.

I was enjoying the night scenery, what little there was of it. Mostly, it was dark and gray outside. I was lulled into complacency by the continuous loud drone of the huge 1,525-horsepower, nine-cylinder radial engine. The unmuffled exhaust exited the engine about six feet from my left ear. The constant roar was mildly numbing.

As we orbited in our "fat, dumb and happy" complacency, we suddenly flew into violent turbulence. I was nearly shaken out of my seat. It was like riding a bicycle off smooth pavement and riding between the rails onto the cross-ties of a railroad trestle. A split second after the turbulence began, there was a mighty whooshing, roaring sound, like the sound you would hear if you were standing right below that railroad trestle with your head between the tracks as a high-speed freight train rushed by overhead. A speeding locomotive passed right through my helmet! I was scared and wanted to react, but I didn't know what to do or how to do it. Captain Janss was flying the helicopter, and he was the mission commander. Nothing was under my direct control. There was not a thing I could do but stay put, strapped tightly down by my seat belt and shoulder harness.

Before either of us could click the mike and say the usual "What the fuck, over?" The noise and turbulence ceased as abruptly as they had begun. They were replaced by an intense, bright glow flooding the cockpit coming from my left. I turned my head to see its source. What I saw was burned into my memory forever, and will never leave me. YR-3 had exploded and was burning up in an intense sun-bright fireball right there off my wing, not 200 feet away.

As the aircraft burned, it began to lag behind us, plunging from the sky, dripping molten bits as it disintegrated. At about 1000 feet below us, I watched the entire rotor system depart the helicopter and spin off into the darkness. The still-spinning rotor blades, illuminated by the diminishing flames of the burning hulk, flickered a farewell. Plunging further down into the black abyss, the fireball grew smaller and smaller and became less white hot until it cooled down to yellow, then to a glowing red ember, then winked out, perhaps as it hit the ground.

This whole incident took less than 15 seconds. The two pilots, the two crewmen and the Navy corpsman never had a chance. They were incinerated alive.

I triggered the mike and said to Captain Janss, "They shot down our wingman, sir!" Then I had an instant of sheer panic as I realized that if they could shoot down our wingman, they could shoot us down in the same manner, as well! I did not want to die horribly, right here in the sky of South Vietnam, as my five squadron mates had just done. Had I not been tightly strapped in, I might have tried to jump out. I assumed that the enemy had somehow shot down YR-3 even though we had been flying at 4,000 feet above the ground, an altitude we usually felt was safe from small-arms fire. Did the enemy have some new weapon capable of shooting higher, a missile perhaps? We scrubbed the rest of the mission and returned to base.

The cause of this mishap was miscommunication. While we were orbiting, the Marines on Mutter Ridge were being overrun by the enemy. The battle had devolved to hand-to-hand combat. In this case, the grunts called for emergency artillery, calling artillery right into their own position. This was an act of absolute desperation on their part. The grunts knew that some of their own would die from the self-inflicted artillery, but if they did not call it in, they would all die at the hands of the enemy. The emergency artillery request overrode our previous request to Landshark to hold fire. Because we were off frequency, or perhaps because Landshark forgot to broadcast the emergency mission, we were not aware of it. The safe place Captain

Janss chose to orbit was right in the path of the huge 155mm artillery shells. We in the lead ship had flown right between two salvos of the huge howitzer rounds. Our wingman was not so lucky. This catastrophe was not due to direct enemy action.

An incident like this is called, "Friendly fire."

To make them light in weight, the H-34 helicopters were constructed of magnesium-aluminum alloy. This alloy is very difficult to ignite, but once ignited, the whole helicopter will burn to ash in 15 seconds on the ground. Here in the night sky, with the fire fanned by the 100 knot forward speed of the helicopter and fed by 100 gallons of high octane 115/145 (purple) aviation fuel, I don't think the fireball lasted more than ten seconds before the entire machine and crew were totally consumed

I have since read the account[4] of the Klondike gunship escort helicopter pilots. They were closely following YR-3 and had a front row seat to this incident. They report that the artillery shell passed right through the cockpit of YR-3. I do not believe the shell exploded; it simply passed through the helicopter, ripping electrical lines and rupturing fuel cells. I was very wrong about the enemy being responsible for this, but "they" had almost got us, too. I also read in archives recently that the bodies of the two crewmen were found on the ground. They must have been blown clear, or jumped to their deaths to avoid incineration in the violent fire. (I have read that in World War I, air crews would often choose between "wet" or "dry" death as their flaming aircraft plunged from the sky. Perhaps these two chose to die "dry.")

We returned to Dong Ha. I have no idea if another set of crews went out to help the wounded Marines on Mutter Ridge. After landing, I went to the tent, but I felt a need to be alone. I slunk out back by the bunker, wanting not to talk to anyone about this terrible thing I had witnessed. I looked west, up into the dark night sky that had just consumed my five buddies. I tried to make sense of all that

---

4 www.popasmoke.org. Reference, Texas Tech, "Command Chronology of HMM-161, September 25, 1966." Page 6. Item No.1201079200

A Burnt Up H-34

All that is left are the remains of the tips of the rotor blades, the tail section which fell away, and the big black lump of ash containing the engine and transmission. These two parts were made of steel. There were many such piles of ash scattered about South Vietnam. (I flew this same aircraft not long before it was destroyed.)

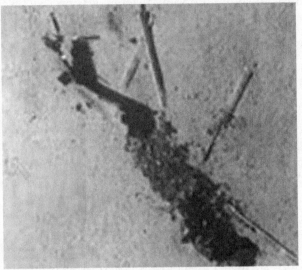

Picture of an H-34 that burned up on a beach.

"This photo was taken the day after our helicopter, YZ-62 (148058), was shot down by a 12.7MM on 21 Dec 67. The crew was Lt Col Sam Beal the MAG-16 XO, Major Gene Salter Jr., Cpl William D. Carpenter, L/Cpl George T. Curtis (MGySgt USMC Retired & POPASMOKE member) and HM2 Albert Villanavua (corpsman). The aircraft was on an Emergency Medevac mission for Mike 3/7 'BEACHNUT Team Mike' in the Arizona Territory. The crew and 5 Emergency Medevacs were rescued off a Sand Bar under intense heavy enemy fire by Lt. Col William " Bill" Beeler in a CH-46. DFCs, Silver Stars and Purple Hearts were awarded. The 4 page story with combat illustrations by (POPASMOKE'S) Major A. Mike Leahy appears in the April 69 Leatherneck Magazine."

had happened. Why? Why them, not me? How did this happen? It was the beginning pangs of survivor guilt.

This was my second hairy mission in just a few weeks. It was another huge shock to my psyche. I sunk into a state of emotional numbness. I immediately assumed that there was no way I was going to survive this war. I had been in Vietnam only about eight weeks and had come very close to a fiery death twice in this short time. I still had 11 months to go. I felt doomed. There was no way I would ever survive.

It was the beginning of PTSD.

After pondering on it for a few days, I decided that I could not give up. I would do my job as best I could. I would be vigilant and careful. Maybe, just maybe, somehow, I might survive this war.

Somehow I did, but not without several more hairy events.

During September of 1966, pilots of HMM-161 flew 1,460.9 hours, carried 3,284 passengers, 320.2 tons of cargo and 782 medevacs. We changed six engines. I personally flew 64 hours.

The day after YR-3 and crew were incinerated, I got a much needed day off. Because I'd slept in, I got to the showers late, after they had already been taken over by the Vietnamese maids who used the showers to do our laundry. I had two choices; I could skip a much desired and much needed shower, or I could shower in front of a bunch of, what seemed to me, old hags. These older Vietnamese women had the habit of chewing betel nut, which stained their teeth black; this made them very unattractive to us, probably by design.

I decided I had to have a shower, even if I had to get naked in front of this group of black-toothed old hags. I took my clothes off and had a long, luxurious cold shower. As I soaked, I reflected on the fact that I was able to feel the cold water splashing on my skin, and that I had something to be a bit embarrassed about, while my friends who had been incinerated the night before would never, ever again feel anything, either physically or emotionally. I would complain little about anything after that.

The night after YR-3 burned up, Chaplain Fullilove (yes, that was really his name) held a memorial service for the dead crew members. It was short and to the point. When one of the fellows died, (two usually, as helicopter pilots tend to die in pairs), we would have a few soothing words from the chaplain and then we'd hold a wake and get very drunk. Every time the wake degenerated into a wild, raucous, drunken, singing, happy party. It was the only way we could deal with the tragedy and "continue the march." The mentality of a Marine in combat is one of "Let's live for today, for the now," and the rest will happen if it is meant to be. It's really difficult to think about tomorrow when your attitude is that tomorrow may never come.

We all knew it could be us next time, but each of us individually knew secretly that we were invincible. Of course, we also knew that those other guys, the guys who just died, had each thought himself invincible, too. We tried not to think about that too much.

In combat, you know that every day could be your last. There are days when it is the last for some of your buddies, and you drink at their wake, toast them into the next adventure, and get on with the program. Combat doesn't stop just because some of the players are killed. We had a mission to accomplish. We had to press on. We had Marines in the field to support. We were Marines; we could not cry or seem weak or emotional in front of our comrades.

We were never afraid. Not fearless, just never afraid. We could not allow ourselves the luxury of feeling fear. To feel fear was to have a distracting thought. We could not afford to be distracted while flying these perilous missions. A lot of emotion got stuffed over the months. Fear we locked up in the far recesses of our mind, in a tiny strong box encased in solid heavy mental steel, wrapped in a heavy chain with a stainless lock that had no key hole nor key.

Anger was our way of dealing with fear. We got angry when one of our fellows died. We wanted to take it out on the enemy, even if the cause of the friend's death was (more often than not) an accident or a mechanical failure. "Goddamn gooks!" we would say. If it weren't for them, we wouldn't be here, and our friends would still be alive.

Besides anger, we allowed ourselves to lust a bit occasionally. We had little use of lust as we rarely saw any woman worthy of that emotion. All we ever saw were the hootch maids who washed our clothes and swept our hootches for a few pennies each week. Older, with their ugly black teeth from chewing betel nut, they were very unattractive to us. Only the chaplain's assistant, a beautiful young woman in her red *aou dai* outfit, got our full attention. She was an exotic knock-out. Of course, as the chaplain's assistant, she was unapproachable. Surely it must be some sort of serious sin to lust after the chaplain's assistant. There was no chance to have any privacy either. *She is probably a Viet Cong spy anyway*, I rationalized.

My experience with women at this point in my life was nearly nil.

About startle reflex

Most people have heard stories of veterans who, at the sound of a car backfiring or some other loud noise, throw themselves down for protection. This is called startle reflex. It is a major symptom of PTSD. I had to stifle my startle reflex because I was sitting in my helicopter, strapped in. There was no way I would throw myself to the ground or into the nearest foxhole. That stifled reflex has stayed with me forever. I still never react quickly to anything.

2.
Phu Bai

The previous two horrific incidents took place near Dong Ha. I was actually based at Phu Bai at the time. Dong Ha was an out-station about 50 miles north, where we deployed for a few days at a time.

Phu Bai hootch living

Top: Our hootch and our maid. Officer's club, right, background.
Bottom: Officer's country. Right: my corner living "suite."

We lived in structures we called "hootches." They were plain plywood floors, with corrugated metal walls up to four feet, then screen up another four feet. Metal shutters could be propped up or left down, depending on the desires of the occupants. We usually kept the sides down to keep the noise, dust, and light out. Many times if we had had night medevac duty the night before, we slept during the day. It was rare to have an actual day off, so we were almost never home during daylight hours.

Eight Marine Corps officers lived inside each of these shacks, which were 16 feet by 32 feet. Basically we had two sheets of plywood, or 64 square feet to each officer. We each had a standard army cot, with a pillow, a blanket and sheets. We had an upright locker beside the cot. A few empty ammunition crates were nailed to the uprights as shelves to keep shaving gear, letter writing materials and a few personal items. I was lucky in most cases because I managed to get a corner "suite" and I was able to build a semblance of a desk against the end wall.

I kept my harmonica on the shelf, but lost interest in learning it when one of my hootch mates told me he saw our black-toothed maid putting it to her mouth. I had learned rudimentary versions of "Happy Birthday" and "The Marines' Hymn," but I could never put that harmonica to my lips ever again.

In the lockers we hung such things as our rarely-used khaki uniforms. The weather in Phu Bai and all our bases in Vietnam was almost always so very hot and humid that anything left out would turn green with mold in just a few days. To prevent mold, we kept a small light bulb burning in the bottom of each locker. The constant slight warmth of the bulb kept things inside dry and mold-free.

Outside the door was a small table with a can of water, and maybe a mirror and a light for shaving in the pre-dawn. I traveled light. I carried a toothbrush in the pencil pocket of my flight suit, because I never knew when I might be spending the night somewhere else. While flying, my flight gear, consisting of flight helmet, flight gloves, map case, .38 caliber revolver and flak jacket was my total baggage.

The hootches were in neat rows around the ubiquitous central parade ground with flagpole. The area was all sand; in one corner of the parade ground was a movie screen where we had a movie almost every night.

For the privilege of living in these tents, we officers relinquished our basic housing allowance, about $85 per month. Across a field, about 200 yards away, was some kind of Army base called the 8th R.R.U. (Radio Relay Unit?). The enlisted kids working at this unit lived in air-conditioned trailers, two guys to each small trailer, with private bedrooms. For this they got sub-standard housing pay. Go figure.

We had maid service, for which we paid a minimal amount extra. The mama-san made our cots, and did our laundry for us. The maids would always gather in the showering facility to do laundry together. As mentioned above, if one slept in and then wanted to have a shower, he had to shower in front of six to eight Vietnamese women. It was difficult to do the first few times; one had to gently push a maid out of the way to get a shower. After awhile this became routine.

We had a bit of a rat problem in the hootches. One friend actually had a rat fall out of the rafters and fall onto his stomach and bite him as it fled. This pilot had to go through the precautionary series of rabies shots. We put out traps and tried to kill them, but we weren't very successful. Whenever we heard the loud "SNAP" of a rat dying in one of our traps, we quickly took it out side, doused it with gasoline, and set it on fire. We knew the rats could carry the fleas responsible for bubonic plague. We danced around the burning rat in our underwear like a bunch of drunken hellions. We *were* a bunch of drunken hellions.

Medicinal Brandy

6 August, 1966

"At approximately 1740, 4 aircraft were involved in a recon insertion for Operation Prairie. After landing, the fourth aircraft, YR-9, experienced problems and subsequently crashed into trees. The aircraft burned, but the crew escaped. The pilot received moderate injuries, the crew chief minor injuries, and the other crew members were unhurt."[5]

My hootch-mate Hugh Smith had a bad day flying copilot for Stan Pechalonis in the above crash. From his account, they landed heavy, long and hot in a hilltop landing zone. They did not have enough reserve power to go around. Going too fast to stop, they rolled off the knoll and plowed right into the trees in front of them. Hugh's foot was trapped in the helicopter as the structure of the instrument panel crumpled around him. He showed me the tip of his steel-toed boots. The leather was gone, the steel toe insert was gone, and the sock was missing from the top of his toes, but he was unscratched. He had no memory of the exact cause of this, but we surmised that the instrument panel smashing into the cockpit must have trapped his foot. In a panic, in his haste to escape the possibility of the crashed helicopter igniting into an inferno, he must have jerked his foot out of the entrapment, ripping his boot and sock open, but leaving his foot unscathed.

Our flight surgeon, Doc Hassletine, prescribed a drink of medicinal brandy for Hugh's nerves. Several of us retired to the doc's medical hootch to have a drink with Hugh. But of course once we broke open a container of that medicinal alcohol, we had to drink it all, else it might spoil. There was absolutely no sense in letting it go to waste.

We were about three-quarters blasted when a flustered young trooper came rushing into the tent and asked for the doctor. "What's the problem?" asked someone before the real doctor could speak up.

---

5 Texas Tech. University, Command Chronology for HMM-161, 6 August, 1966

"I'm going on R&R tomorrow," said the young trooper, "and I must have my shot card up to date or the gunny [sergeant] says I can't go." This was serious. Everybody needed R&R, and it was within the doc's power to help this young man with his urgent need. But instead, Doc Hassletine just nodded toward Smith and said, "Well, doc, why don't you take care of the boy?"

Smitty picked up on the doc's meaning right away and went along with the game. The real doctor talked him through the procedure. He told Smitty where he could find the needed serum in the refrigerator, talked him through the filling of the hypodermic and instructed him on just how to stick the needle into the trooper's arm, and then how to slowly push the drug into the man's tissue. The trooper must have thought that Smitty was a medic under training. He wasn't going to do anything to endanger his R&R, so he never questioned or whimpered about "Doc" Smith giving him his shot.

One of our scarier missions

Recon insertions and extractions were always our more exciting missions. Recon Marines sneaked around in the jungle and hills, shadowing the enemy, reporting his positions and activities. Their mission was to not engage the enemy, but to observe and report. We always tried to insert them a few miles from where we thought the enemy was so they could sneak up to and observe enemy strongholds.

Sometimes that did not work out well. Once in a while the recon Marines would be discovered by the enemy. Then the chase was on. They had to try to escape from the enemy, and they called us for help. It was always scary when we went out in the jungle-covered mountains to pick up one if these teams and the radio operator was whispering, or, worse yet, there was gunfire in the background. Anything could happen. Fortunately for me, I never got involved in an insertion or extraction that was the culmination of a running gun battle.

Booze and Music

When I arrived in Vietnam, I was not much of a contemporary music fan. I had grown up on the music of the Beach Boys, the Kingston Trio, New Christy Minstrels, Joan Baez, and Peter Paul and Mary. The strains of those folk songs and ballads still touch my heart. I was not a great fan of the then-emerging music geniuses, the Beatles. I had never been a fan of country and western music. All of this was about to change.

Our main form of recreation was drinking alcohol. We simply got drunk almost every night. Most evenings, wherever I was, I went to the officers club as soon as I finished flying. On a rare day off I would go to the bar as soon as the club opened. Drinking was encouraged by 25-cent beers and 35-cent cocktails. Usually we drank in moderation, but occasionally someone would get ripped. One night a friend found me passed out in the sand next to my hootch. It was the hootch nearest the club, but somehow I had not made it to my cot. He helped me off the ground to my bed.

The officers club was very much like our living tents, with screen walls and a tin roof. To one side sat an L-shaped bar and a few tables and chairs scattered around on the cement floor of the open area. It was nothing fancy, but a place to gather and drink and swap stories. I learned a lot of good flying techniques in those drinking sessions.

The only entertainment of any sorts at Phu Bai was a reel-to-reel tape recorder with three (count-em: three) tapes. One tape was an early Beatles collection, the second was Johnny Cash, and the third was Christmas carols. Evenings always started out with one or the other of the first two tapes, playing it again and again. When we were thoroughly saturated with that first one, we switched off to the second. Sometimes we alternated between the two tapes, but no matter how we arranged them, we still had just those two tapes. Between Johnny Cash's "I see that train a-comin' " and The Beatles "I wanna hold your hand," I became thoroughly brainwashed to love both Johnny Cash and the Beatles.

Later at night, whenever a serious "alcohol front" had moved in, and we had all we could stand of the first two tapes, some fool would put on the Christmas tape. Usually by then it was late, we were all somewhat drunk and melancholy, and we would sit around the bar and sing along mournfully with the Christmas songs that reminded us of home, family, love, and all the good things we had left behind. No one seemed to care that it was August and the weather outside was closer to that of the Sahara Desert than it was to "White Christmas."

Pilot Jim Hatch played a mean guitar. He frequently broke it out to entertain us. This was great for morale. He wrote and sang a take-off of the song "The Green Beret" by Barry Sadler.

A CD including this song and several more of Jim Hatch's great morale-boosting music may be available at: http://www.popasmoke.com/px-music.

With permission from Jim Hatch:

"WE ARE THE MEN OF MAG 16"
(Sung to the tune of "Green Beret" by Barry Sadler)

We are the men of MAG 16, Pretty rough and fighting mean,

From way down south we came this way, Don't give a shit about the green beret.

We fly in choppers, are real meanies, Don't need no chute or green beanies.

And while you jump, we fly through hell, of course we know, the Marines are swell.

With these hard hats upon our heads, we'd rather fly than end up dead.

So take your caps and silver wings, Hang'em in your ass, with all your things.

We fly on missions and fly away, on medevacs both night and day.

One hundred men were hauled today, not a goddamn one had a green beret.

We too have wings upon our chest, and can compete for America's best.

Our wings are gold we have caps of green, Rather than a beret, I'll be a Marine.

Back on Okinawa, a neisan waits, lifts up her skirts, jacks up her rates.

She's counted out eight months flight pay, and won't put out for the Green Beret.

I know this song won't be no hit, But a good Marine don't give a shit

But when it comes to glory and fame, we'll kick your ass and take your name.

Landing on the Rockpile

When I first arrived in I Corps, during our trips to Dong Ha, we occasionally had to resupply and support the Marines at the observation post (OP) atop the Rockpile. Initially no platform existed on top of this tall limestone karst. The available flat space was only about 5 feet by 20 feet. To correct for this, we landed crossways to the tiny strip, placing our wheels (with our brakes locked) on the small pathway, letting our tail float out over the abyss. It took a bit of finesse to keep the helicopter steady. As Marines got off the machine, we had to delicately lower power a bit to keep from lifting off. On the flip side, we had to carefully add a bit of power each time a Marine got on board to keep us from falling over backwards down the hill.

Later, someone carried up the lumber seen in the pictures. The wooden platform was slightly larger than the helicopter's wheel stance, so we could sit solidly down. It was always a bit scary flying close to the limestone karst, because we knew it was a honeycomb of holes and tunnels. This was a great opportunity for an enemy soldier, hiding in one of the holes, to pop out and stitch us full of bullets on final approach to the platform.

That would have been a disaster.

An H-34 from HMM-161 lands atop the Rockpile, autumn of 1966, pilot unknown.
Photo by the author also appears on the cover.

Phu Bai Fragments

At each base we had a crude pilots' ready room, similar to our living hootches. Inside were several rows of plywood benches, covered with red Naugahyde cushions. In the corner by the door was a plain linoleum-topped gray military desk with a field phone on it. An operations duty officer sat at the desk. While we waited, we wrote letters home, read books, ate our meals brought from the mess hall, talked among ourselves, played cards or napped as best we could on the hard benches. Here we waited for the phone to ring to call us out on a mission of mercy.

A snake in the cockpit!

There was a small green snake in Vietnam called the "bamboo krait." Its nickname was the "two-step snake." Rumors had it that if this snake bit you, you would survive for only your next two steps. One day, shortly after take-off from Phu Bai, a small green snake appeared out of our radio control panel between the pilots and crawled around the radio console. It then slithered up the instrument panel to disappear through a crack in it, never to be seen again. What a surprise. Was that one a bamboo krait?

A scary thought

Flying around I Corps, during the fall of 1966, I had a very prophetic thought. I was quite aware that the jet fighter pilots had an air-to-air missile called the Sidewinder for shooting down enemy fighter aircraft. Much like the rattlesnake after which it was named, this missile could home in on the infrared heat signature of its prey. My thought was, *If the enemy comes up with a hand-held, heat-seeking missile, this war will be over. They will blow our helicopters out of the sky in droves!*

This idea was so frightening to me that I never shared this thought with anyone for fear it might come true. A few years later, well after I departed Vietnam, while I was flying for Air America in Laos, my premonition did come true. The Pathet Lao soldiers began using the small, hand-held heat-seeking "Strella" missile.

Another story for a later time.

I am a Boy Colonel

One morning right after I arrived in Phu Bai, I was in the ready room waiting to depart on a flight. Because it was one of the rare cool mornings in Vietnam, I was wearing my Navy leather flying jacket. A young sergeant came into the ready room on business. He took one look at me, physically flinched and his face blanched as he backed out of the room and disappeared. For a while I could not figure out what it was about me that caused such a visceral reaction from this trooper. Later I realized that my leather jacket was covering up the last half of my name tag. What the trooper saw was the first half of my name, "Lt. Col..." The rest of my name tag was hidden by the overlapping jacket. He must have thought I was the youngest lieutenant colonel in the entire Marine Corps. If so, I must be a real hard-ass; therefore, he did not want anything to do with me.

A Skyraider crashes

Another day, shortly after my arrival at Hue Phu Bai, I was walking the flight line, near the parked helicopters, when an H-34 hurriedly taxied up next to me. The pilot, "Furgie" Furgesen, was yelling at me and banging on the side of the helicopter to get my attention. Over the noise of the rotors and engine, I could not tell what he was saying, so I climbed up the side to better hear him. "Get in!" He ordered me into the copilot seat. I motioned that I had no flight gear and no helmet. "Never mind," he said, "just get in, NOW!" As I climbed into the copilot seat, before I was even strapped in, he leapt us off the ground and flashed us across the runway and headed south. This was highly unusual. As I hastened to strap in, I saw what all the excitement was about.

A Vietnamese Air Force A-1 Skyraider was on short final for landing at the Phu Bai airport. His engine shot out, his propeller still, his landing gear not down, this pilot was coming down for a dead-stick belly landing. Fortunately, the Vietnamese pilot skillfully slid the big fighter-bomber in on its bottom without mishap. Furgesen had been out on a solo post-maintenance check flight, heard about the evolving incident from the control tower, and wanted me along so I could hop out and assist the Vietnamese pilot, if need be.

The excitement over, Furgie returned me to my place on the flight line, to whatever I had been doing before this interesting distraction.

Another time at Phu Bai I watched as an H-46 brought in a stripped-down H-34 from somewhere out in the field where it had been abandoned by its crew. The H-46 pilot somehow managed to drop the H-34 from about 30 feet in height. It crushed as it smashed onto the runway. Write that one off.

One night I flew copilot for Peter Lepo on a medevac for a Vietnamese civilian who had been badly injured. While we were sitting in the LZ, Peter instructed me to draw and cock my .38 pistol, just in case a sapper might decide to run up and throw an explosive charge at the helicopter. Fortunately, nothing happened.

I found it amusing that I had to qualify with a .45 automatic pistol before leaving for the war, but once I arrived I was issued a .38 revolver that I had never practiced with.

Other than these minor incidents, things were quiet around Phu Bai. We did admin runs to Da Nang for mail, parts and supplies. We flew routine medevacs, both for our military and for Vietnamese civilians nearby. We moved some Vietnamese army units around. We rarely got shot at. All the real action was further north near Dong Ha in support of Operations Prairie, Hastings and Pawnee.

While at Phu Bai, I tried to read Bernard B. Fall's *Street Without Joy* about the experience of the French army in Vietnam. I had to put it down while wondering if any of our leaders had ever read it. They might have learned something. I couldn't finish it; I never have.

I also read Joseph Heller's *Catch 22*. I felt I could read a chapter and then put the book down and watch a chapter. Except for the absolute absurdities depicted in *Catch 22*, I felt the same insanity was happening right there, all around me.

3.
How I Arrived in Vietnam

After a very long flight on a Northwest Orient Airlines charter flight from Travis Air Force Base in northern California, I landed in the Republic of Vietnam at Da Nang airport. I was taken in a large truck called a six-by, to the First Marine Air Group (MAG) Headquarters. On that truck ride I observed a truism I had heard about World War II: "War is choking on dust while being knee deep in mud."

I reported to the group operations (S-3) officer, a major. He asked me where I wanted to go, which squadron I wanted to be in. I had no clue what I was getting into, what I might want to do, or where I might want to go. I knew nothing about what was happening in the war. I was flabbergasted by the fact that he gave me choices. Lately I compared my feeling to what it might be like if you took a fifth-grader, plunked him down in the middle of a big high school and began to ask him what classes he wanted to take.

When I looked up at the major's Plexiglas status board, I noticed that every squadron under his control was listed, with the names of the pilots assigned to each squadron beneath each one. I saw a name I knew – the only name I knew – Tom Knowles. Tom and I went through flight school together as fellow cadets, albeit not in the same class. "Oh, I'd like to go to HMM-161," I told the major, feeling I wanted to go somewhere where I knew at least one pilot. That is how I chose HMM-161 (Helicopter Marine Medium Squadron 161) at Hue Phu Bai.

Just a few short weeks later, Tom changed squadrons. He volunteered to retrain to fly Huey gunships and was gone from my life for a while, but by then I had made many friends in HMM-161. Our paths would cross again.

For the first three weeks or so, there were no available accommodations in the regular tents for new guys, so I spent this time living in the transient officer quarters near the ready room. I roomed with Hugh "Crash" Smith, and Neil "Hoss" Snider. Both became very good friends.

4.
An H-46 Helicopter Disappears

6 October 1966, after dark

Usually after two days of hard flying at Dong Ha, our aircraft were tired and used up. Replacement crews relieved us to allow us return to Phu Bai for much needed repairs. Often, as we left Dong Ha, the mechanics cannibalized our aircraft to steal whatever bits and pieces they might use for the relieving aircraft. The crews removed non-vital parts like batteries, inverters, generators, and starters. Once started, these departing machines would function well for the short trip home without those parts.

After a normal two-day tour at Dong Ha, it was my time to rotate back to Phu Bai. I was to be a passenger, as my helicopter was being left behind. It was either a replacement or it was hard down, not flyable. I was ready for some rest and was anticipating the possibility of a rare, but much-needed, day off. I gathered my gear and wandered out to the rice paddy where our helicopters prepared to depart. Drat! My ride home was not ready to leave yet. The mechanics waited to relieve it of its starter; but, ironically, the machine would not start. The mechanics dinked around with it for about 15 minutes, with no success. It was getting late; I was tired.

A hundred yards across the rice paddy, a Boeing Vertol CH-46A Sea Knight "Phrog" (squadron number EP-154) cranked up for the short flight south to Da Nang, with an intermediate stop at Phu Bai, my home base. It was a simple matter for me to pick up my gear and walk a hundred yards to board the now-turning H-46. I actually picked up my gear and took a few steps toward the other machine.

Then, for some reason, I decided against taking that hop. I sat back down in the rice paddy, passing up a chance to get home faster and in more comfort than with my squadron mates. As the H-46 took off, I lamented, *Drat, if I had gone with them, I would be home before we even get this damn H-34 started.*

H-46 "Sea Knight" ("Phrog")

How wrong I was. That H-46 departed east toward the South China Sea ... never to be seen again! Somehow it simply disappeared. Search parties scoured the area for the next few days but never found a trace of this missing machine. The H-46, a crew of four and perhaps some passengers, were gone. No search aircraft ever found so much as an oil slick or any debris.

Whenever we flew up or down the coast, we often flew out over the water to be out of range of any "One-shot Charley" who might pop off a quick round in our direction given the opportunity. We surmised that the H-46 pilots must have accidentally flown into the sea, leaving no trace. Whatever happened to that H-46 is still a mystery.

I missed a ride to oblivion.

During October of 1966, the H-34s of HMM-161 flew 1,081 hours, carried 3,264 passengers and hauled 205 tons of cargo. We carried 740 medevacs. We changed four engines. I personally flew 69 hours.

5.
Background of a Small Town Kid

"Whether we call it sacrifice, or poetry, or adventure, it is always the same voice that calls."

–Antoine de Saint-Exupéry

So how the heck did I find myself in these situations? I certainly did not set out in life with a goal to be hovering precariously over a raging battle at night, nor to watch comrades die by incineration in an exploding helicopter, nor to risk severe liver damage by getting drunk every night.

I was just a small-town kid growing up in the small, quiet, agricultural town of Sonoma, 50 miles north of San Francisco. Sonoma was a little bit of a touristy town then, but mostly it was the center of the budding California wine industry and a prune, pear, hop and apple growing area. I attended several primary schools in the valley and graduated from Sonoma Valley Union High School with the class of 1961. As anchorman for the top quarter of my class, I did not really excel in anything and was too small and uncoordinated to be active in sports. I ran, poorly, for the cross-country team in my senior year. I was a flop in that because, as I later realized, my legs are way too short for my long torso and I just did not have the stamina to compete with the other boys who could get much more distance out of each stride.

In my senior year, despite getting cut from the team, I earned my letter in football by being the team manager. I earned my big green 'S' letter as much as the other member of the team. I sacrificed many a lunch with my buddies to stay in the equipment room to repair broken equipment, sew torn jerseys, or run errands for the two coaches, Edsell and Koache. (Yes, one of our coaches really was named Koache.) At games I was the water boy.

I grew up in the afterglow of World War II. VJ day was my second birthday. What a party! Too bad I don't remember it. I was enamored of anybody who had been in the war. Some of my best childhood memories were of marching bands strutting down Sonoma's Broadway, bass drums booming, on Flag Day or the Fourth of July, or Veterans Day in honor of veterans. One of my uncles, Vern Campbell, was a war veteran and a member of the American Legion. My cousins, Ron and Larry Collier, lived next door and often invited me over to their house on Saturday mornings. Between cartoons and "Ramar of the Jungle," we watched many times over every episode of the "Victory at Sea" documentaries about World War II naval action.

Many times when we played outside we played "guns." All the neighborhood kids would break into two teams, separate, and then "go on patrol" looking for each other. I think the only rule we had was that the bad guys, the Krauts or Japs, had to die every time. We used sticks for guns, and improvised the sounds of a "burp gun" or a "Tommy gun" with our voices. Sounds of BRRRAAAPPP!! BRRRAAAPPP, you're dead!" "NO! I'm not, you missed!" echoed around our neighborhood many times as we played war. I thought just maybe I would like to be a war hero too, someday when I grew up. These influences created within me a desire for a military life.

It was a rare day when my father was able to slip me a fiver that wasn't needed for food or household bills. If I wanted or needed anything, I pretty much had to earn the money myself. I generally worked some job or other after school. I started making all my own money for school clothes and pocket money by the time I was in third grade. I was one hell of a good prune picker. A few times I picked up 30 large lugs in a single day. At 30 cents a box, I was making big bucks for a 12-year-old in 1955. My weekly allowance was only one dollar, but for that I could have two candies and a soda at our local theater in Boyes Hot Springs, while watching a movie and an installment of the newest serial thriller. I would have enough left over to buy a couple of candy bars during the week. Candy bars and Cokes were five cents each from vending machines away from the theater. I worked doing yard work for neighbors and from there, by referral, for people around town.

At one point my father bought me a big power lawn mower to mow our huge country lot, one of my many chores. This led me to start hiring myself out to neighbors to mow their properties. This became a prosperous little business for me. In 1960, after I got my first car, a 1952 blue two-door Chevy coupe, I could throw my mower in the trunk, and mow a couple of hours after school. At one time I put an ad in the local paper, "Have Mower Will Travel," after one of the popular westerns on TV at that time, "Paladin, Have Gun Will Travel." I charged $3 per hour for me and my mower, fuel included. I got a lot of calls, stayed busy and kept my pockets full of spending loot. All this hard work never hurt me a bit.

I really wanted to go to college, but my family was not well-to-do. In a way, I got tricked into preparing myself for college. One day near the end of eighth grade at El Verano Grammar School, our teacher, Mr. James Healy, told us that high school counselors were coming the next day, and we should be prepared to talk to them. I had no idea what I wanted to take in high school; I didn't even know that in high school you had choices. That night I asked my big brother, Calvin, what I should do. Because I had great grades in grammar school, even being the top of the honor roll one quarter in the seventh grade, Cal told me I should take college prep classes. He said that they were the same as what the other kids took, but more in depth. He said I would find it more interesting. I signed up for college prep classes. I took only the required minimum of shop classes, and no auto repair classes or agriculture classes, subjects that the non-college prep kids were taking. It was only about halfway through second semester senior year that I realized the only thing I had prepared myself for was to go to college. Crap! I had not really planned on going to college because I thought I couldn't afford to go.

I decided to try to attend a military academy, where I could get a free college education and prepare for a military career. I sat for the exams for West Point (Army), Annapolis (Navy), the US Air Force Academy, and for the Kings Point Maritime Academy in New York. I even took the exam for the California Maritime Academy in Vallejo, California. The only exam on which I did well was the California Maritime Academy. Here, I actually was accepted, but this was the single academy of the lot to charge tuition. I came from a poor family, and there was no way I was going be able to pay $1,400 a semester to go to college. It just did not fit into my mentality to be able to pay that kind of huge money. I did not know about student loans, so I never even bothered to go to the acceptance interview. My family had no political contacts or clout whatsoever to use to gain a political appointment to any of the other academies. (I still have on file a franked letter of rejection from then Vice President Richard Nixon.)

The main reason I didn't do well in the exams was that my math scores were poor. Someone suggested that I go to the local junior college and take some advanced math classes, improve my math skills and take the academy exams again at a later date. It sounded like a good idea. I realized that I could afford to attend a local junior college by working part time.

After graduating from high school in June of 1961, I worked the summer in construction with my father, Bill, in Shingle Springs, near Lake Tahoe. That fall, I quit the construction job and enrolled in Napa Junior College for the coming semester. I got a job driving school buses for the local school system. It paid fairly well, so well that at the age of 18, I was able to support myself, and the job worked well around my class schedules.

After attending Napa Junior College for five semesters, I found myself floundering, not really sure what I wanted to do with myself. I knew I wanted to be an officer in the military, and I knew that required a four-year degree. I could not seem to focus on a major. Initially I wanted to be an engineer but found out right away that calculus, college physics and advanced chemistry were not my forté. I changed majors a few times, finally settling on "undecided, liberal arts, teaching maybe." About the end of my second year there was a Marine Corps recruiter on the Quad trying to sell students on a career in the Marine Corps. He was all dressed up in his Marine Corps greens, all spit, polish and shiny brass and short hair. He had some kind of large, fold-out display he was showing to some kids. I was not at all interested in enlisting. I gave him a wide berth.

A semester later, looking at a sixth semester at a two-year college and still undecided about where I was going in my life, I stopped to talk to that same Marine Corps recruiter, Captain Thatcher. Captain Thatcher was recruiting for the Marine Aviation Cadet (MARCAD) program through which a young man could go to Navy flight school for 18 months and receive both his Navy wings of gold and his commission in the Marine Corps. What got my attention was not the fact that he was selling Navy Flight School in Pensacola, where I could attend for only 18 months and come out as a pilot, a naval aviator, no less. No, what got my attention was what he said about being commissioned as a a second lieutenant in the United States Marine Corps when I completed flight school.

Here was a quick and easy way to become an officer without having to complete four years of college. I became quite interested and began the process of joining up. I was one and half units short of the required 60 units, but Captain Thatcher thought he could get me a waiver for that slight deficiency, if I kept my current grades (B's) up to the end of the semester. I did; he did.

I drove my 1955 white-and-maroon, four-door Mercury down to the Naval Air Station Alameda one Saturday in early 1964. There I took a battery of aptitude, ability and intelligence tests. I took a physical exam. Captain Thatcher had promised me an orientation ride in a T-34B Mentor airplane, but that day it was down for repairs. (I found out later that it was *always* down for repairs.)

My final decision whether to join or not was made when a former Napa J.C. student, Mike Shrimp, who had preceded me into the MARCAD program, came home on leave during a break from flight school. I saw him around the campus in his leather Navy flying jacket, with his pretty blonde girlfriend, Suzy Berger, on his arm. When I asked him about the MARCAD, program, he gave it a big "thumbs up." I was convinced that this is what I wanted to do. I signed up. (I think Suzy and Mike later married and cooked up a couple of Shrimp-Bergers.)

During my five semesters at NJC, I had been the president of my fraternity, Chi Lamda Rho, for two semesters. I also drove school buses for the local school system as a part-time job. I think these two activities were very much in my favor to get me accepted into the MARCAD program. I was a bit of a leader; I could operate heavy machinery responsibly.

Once I had signed up, I expected to get orders any day. Since I already had the required number of college credits and was bored with school, I dropped out. As soon as the school bus manager found out I was no longer enrolled in school, he fired me. The bus driving jobs were for enrolled students only. I took a full-time job with Ben Smigle, a local contractor, working as a carpenter apprentice with my father's good friend, Louie Perryhouse.

It was late April 1964, while I was working construction in Fetters Hot Springs on one of Ben Smigle's spec homes, that my stepmother, Betty, came running across the road where I was working, framing a small house. Waving a yellow piece of paper in the air, she was very excited and yelling: "It's here, it's here!" At first I had no idea what she was yelling about. Then she said "It's here, your orders are here!" The yellow piece of paper was a Western Union telegram – my orders to report to U.S. Naval Air Basic Training Command, Pensacola, Florida. I was to report there in mid-May.

> "You are never given a wish without also being given
> the power to make it come true."
>
> –Richard Bach

The next thing I knew I was driving to San Francisco to pick up my ticket to Pensacola for flight training, to join "the cream of the crop," in flight school. It wasn't until months later that one of the guys finally figured out what crop we were the cream of, and then it seemed very appropriate. We were the cream of the crop of America's college drop-outs. This attitude of being the best of the least or the least of the best was one that would follow us MARCADs the rest of our Marine Corps aviation days.

I was very impressed that the government would spend $165.78 to buy me an airline ticket to Pensacola. Early on the evening of May 13, 1964, I boarded National Airlines' red-eye special flight from San Francisco to Atlanta, then on to Pensacola. It was a Boeing 707 with only two other passengers on the whole airplane. One of them was Stephen Corrie, also a recruit of Captain Thatcher's. From the East Bay, Steve was to be a classmate of mine in class 20-64.

The Captain had put us in touch with each other a few days earlier, and we had a rendezvous at SFO. Those were the good old pre-hijacking days when the pilots left the cockpit door open. Steve and I were able to visit the cockpit and talk to the pilots.

I embarked on this adventure, and the Marine Corps hired me for it, strictly on the strength of my physical health and scores on the various mental and physical aptitude tests.

I had never before seen the inside of an airplane.

"Whatever you can do, or dream you can do, begin it.
Boldness has magic, power, and genius in it."

–Goethe

First Air Medal

After I had been "in country" for a few weeks, the squadron had an award ceremony. I was awarded my first air medal. I was to earn 22 more.

Phu Bai, September 1966. 2nd Lt Hugh Smith, 1st Lt Neil Snider, 2nd Lt Dan Smithson, Major Samaras, 2nd Lt Eddie Allen, and 1st Lt Paul Havens also received their first air medals.

6.
On the Move

After the first two frightening events flying out of Dong Ha, the rest of my time while based in Phu Bai was pretty quiet. I have no recollections of any more interesting events. On the last day of October 1966, we uploaded our entire squadron onto the small aircraft carrier USS *Valley Forge* for what was supposed to be a short cruise to the island of Okinawa. At this time, this was a normal three-month rotation to Marine Corps Air Station Futenma. An amusing series of events is summed up nicely in the combat chronology[6] for the next two days:

1 November 1966

The squadron was taken off the USS *Valley Forge* after only one day on board and from want of a place to go, unloaded to the Da Nang Air Base taxiway, where the squadron gear was left overnight. Sixteen aircraft carried 65,000 pounds of cargo and 75 passengers.

2 November 1966

Today the squadron moved from the Da Nang AB taxiway to the USS *Iwo Jima*. Sixteen aircraft moved 65,000 pounds of cargo and 75 passengers.

[The combat chronology terminates at this time, as we were no longer in combat.]

We sailed for Okinawa. I learned in 2014 in a personal e-mail from Lieutenant Colonel James Barr, Ret., the round-bottomed ship rolled to its maximum in the tropical storm we encountered. Had *Iwo Jima* rolled any further, we could have rolled over and sunk.

In Okinawa we engaged in another sort of combat. This

---

6 Texas Tech, Command Chronology HMM-161 October 1966

entailed lots of beer, whiskey, dancing at the officer's club with hordes of beautiful young American school teachers employed by the Department of Defense to teach the children of military personnel. Also, we had to attend to a large number of charming airline stewardesses who routinely passed through on Military Assistance Command (MAC) flights, carrying troops to and from Vietnam. Okinawa was heaven compared to the war.

During November of 1966, HMM-161 helicopters flew 125.7 hours, carried 925 passengers, and hauled 75.0 tons of cargo. None of this was combat flying. I flew only 18.0 hours this month, none of it combat.

Okinawa, Futenma Marine Corps Air Station:

A Covert Mission

I was involved in an interesting covert mission while we were in Okinawa. Since our squadron was scheduled to be in Okinawa for two or three months, several of the young married fellows flew their wives over to join them. Somebody came up with the idea of giving the wives a helicopter ride. It was strictly forbidden for us to carry civilians, but our colonel obviously was in on this nefarious plot for he was the pilot for this escapade. I was the copilot.

The colonel had a special H-34 towed into our hangar. This particular older H-34 had until recently been the presidential helicopter in Washington, D.C. It was fitted out with extra soundproofing, airline type windows, and airline seats. Once the aircraft was inside the hangar we loaded about eight wives, and then the tow vehicle pulled us out to the aircraft parking ramp.

We started up the helicopter, called the tower and made a normal departure. The colonel and I gave these beautiful young women a grand tour of Okinawa Island for more than an hour. When we returned to the base, we taxied back to our hangar and shut down. The tug towed the helo back into the hangar out of sight of prying eyes. The young women deplaned, and no one was the wiser. I am sure all the wives had a memorable ride and loved their tour of the island, and got a small insight into what their husbands did for a living. So far as I know, we got away with this trick. If we hadn't, I am sure the colonel would have been relieved of duty.

Our main recreation during this slow time was going to the officer's club and ... what else? ... drinking. One night a cute little redhead walked up to me and asked, "Are you Bill Collier, former student at Napa J.C.?" That I was. Here I reconnected with a beautiful young red-head Carla L, who used to ride the school bus with me from Sonoma Valley to Napa Junior College. She was now a stewardess with Continental Airlines. We had a few drinks and danced the night away. We exchanged addresses. I called her after I returned to the U.S., but we did not get together.

Another night in the club, I encountered a young teacher whom I recognized from North Carolina. Just before going to Vietnam, I spent six months in North Carolina at the Marine Corps Air Station New River, adjacent to Camp Lejeune. Here I learned the basics of practical combat flying from pilots who had already spent time in Vietnam.

Her name was Faye. She was curly-blonde, blue-eyed, big-busted, attractive, if a little on the plump side. She had dated my friend David Golding while we were based at New River. From Dave, I had a little inside information about her. I knew she liked to drink gin and tonic and that she was friendly. I bought her a couple of drinks. We talked for a while. I got her address in the single teacher's housing. After she left the club, I bought two gins and tonic, and put them into the side pocket of my sports jacket. I went to her dorm, knocked on her door. When she answered, I asked her if she would like to have another drink with me. She hemmed and hawed about it getting late and not wanting to return to the club. I said, "No problem," and produced the two drinks from my pocket. I didn't leave until early the next day.

I also met and dated a beautiful dark-haired school teacher from Dubois, Pennsylvania, named Jean. I remember fondly the times we spent dining out and dancing at various officer clubs at different bases.

Hotsi Bath

Many times after a hard night's drinking and partying, I went across the road from the main gate and enjoyed a hotsi bath. This usually required a wait of at least 30 minutes, but I easily passed that time by having another 22-ounce Japanese Kirin beer. When called for my bath, I entered to a small bath room that contained only a tiled bath tub, a steam cabinet and a small stool. The female attendant had me disrobe and get into a steam cabinet, with only my head out. I sweltered in this box until I thought I was going to have to scream for help. It was almost hotter than I could stand. About the time that I thought I was going to have to break my macho reserve and scream for release from the cabinet, the attendant appeared magically through the door and pulled me out. Then she placed me into the tub of very hot water, and repeated the torture. She let me soak in this tub until I once again was seriously thinking of screaming for relief. Again the woman magically appeared and saved me. I think she must have been watching through a peephole in the wall to know exactly when to reappear. After dragging me out of the tub, she sat me on the stool. Dipping hot water out of the bathtub, gave me a complete scrubbing down.

By now I was melting, but she was not done with me yet. She dried me off, had me crawl onto a massage table and gave me a wonderful massage.

After one of these hotsi baths, I was so relaxed that it seemed that I floated back across the road, through the gate and back up the hill to my quarters. Each time, I think I was asleep before my head hit the pillow.

The cost for this hotsi bath was $2, not counting the beer, which also cost $2.

Habu Pack

While on Oki, a group of us bought small motorcycles from Slim's motorcycle shop just outside the gate. We thought we needed transportation to get around the island. I bought a little Honda 90 trail bike.

We had a lot of fun rat-packing around and exploring various corners of Okinawa. We visited Shuri Castle and the caves on the south end of the island where the Japanese troops made their last stand during World War II. Thanksgiving of 1966 found about five of us at the extreme north end of the road on the west side of the island. We realized that we were too far out to return to base for Thanksgiving dinner, so we ate at a local Okinawan pub. Our meal consisted of the small, delicate but very tasty native bananas and Kirin beer.

We called ourselves the Habu Pack because Habu is the Okinawan word for snake. We even found a local pub called the Habu Bar, so we frequented it at times. Perhaps a better word might be "terrorized."

The motorcycle made it easier for me to socialize with Jean and other American school teachers.

Back to Vietnam

"When starting an aviation career it is not unusual to be overwhelmed, terrified, suffer from lack of confidence and be just plain scared. As experience grows, self-confidence replaces fear ... but after a time, when you think you have seen it all, you realize your initial reactions to flying were correct."

–Author unknown

After only about five weeks our situation changed; our stay in Okinawa was cut short. Higher powers decided that our squadron should be inactivated, that our squadron flag would return to the States. In the United States, a new squadron was to be formed around our flag, utilizing the Boeing H-46 Sea Knight, the new tandem-rotor helicopter which was gradually replacing our venerable H-34s.

The old machine we had grown to love so much was being phased out.

Instead of going back to the war as an intact squadron, we returned to Vietnam on individual orders, our members to be scattered amongst several other squadrons. After a long C-130 ride from Okinawa, we reached Da Nang once again. There were so many of us there that it took a while for all the orders to be cut and for transport to be arranged for all of us to go to our various new duty stations. We were stuck once again on the tarmac at Da Nang airport. This time we were assigned to an empty hangar, so at least we did not have to sleep out in the open. There for three days with little else to do, we drank a lot of alcohol.

One of our fellows awoke the last morning at Da Nang with a terrible hangover. While he was off to the head, someone played a prank on him by rolling a 60-pound sand bag into his military suitcase (B-4 bag). He was not pleased upon unpacking at his destination three days later to find that he had been carrying around an extra sixty pounds. He simply thought the bag seemed heavier to him because he was extra tired from being very hung over. Also, he told me recently (May 2011, at a reunion) that when he arrived at his new squadron it was raining and the pierced steel planking (PSP) was slick. When he slung his heavy bag off the helicopter, the extra, unexpected weight caused him to slip and fall down – right in front of his new commanding officer.

What a way to make an impression on a new CO.

7.
Ky Ha

I arrived at my new assignment about 15 December, 1966. I was assigned to HMM-363. This squadron was situated on a peninsula jutting into the South China Sea called Ky Ha, adjacent to Marine Corps Air Station Chu Lai. This was in Quang Ngai province, about 50 miles south of Da Nang. We flew in support of Operation Sierra and the ROK (Republic of Korea) Marines and the Marines of 2/7.

Several of my friends from HMM-161 were also transferred to HMM-363 with me, and I knew several of the officer-pilots in the new squadron from flight school and North Carolina prior to Vietnam.

One serious implication of all this moving around and changing squadrons was that I lost a lot of seniority toward becoming an aircraft commander. Just before we left Phu Bai, I was nearly due for my helicopter aircraft commander (HAC) check ride. All the time in Okinawa I did little flying. As a new member of HMM-363, I dropped down the seniority list. All this delayed my check ride for weeks after it should have occurred. This explains why many of my experiences were as copilot rather than pilot in command.

One of the normal rotations of duties at Ky Ha was flying over to Marine Corps Air Base Chu Lai, to standby as the search and rescue (SAR) helicopter. It was only a two-minute flight from our peninsula at Ky Ha, but the base commander always wanted two helicopters right there on the airport, right next to the runway, available for immediate dispatch should there be a need for us. For 24 hours we lived in a hootch beside the runway. For those 24 hours we were intermittently serenaded by the take-off and landing noises of F-4 Phantoms, F-8 Crusaders, A-4 Skyhawks and C-130 transports. By now, used to various loud noises, we could sleep almost anywhere.

I found no flight-hour statistics for HMM-363 for December, 1966 in the archives. I did not start flying with my new squadron until 19 December, but I flew 45.3 hours in the next 12 days. Several times I flew with Tim O'Toole, a former flight school classmate.

We Lose a Full Crew, Plus Six Marines

11 January 1967

Only a few days after my arrival at Ky Ha, First Lieutenants Mike Schena and Gary Shields were orbiting just offshore from Chu Lai when their engine failed. They dumped into the stormy water near the beach with a load of six troops. Not one of the 10 Marines on board survived. For several days afterwards, whenever our missions took us near the beach, we would fly low and slow along the beach and look for bodies. One day I spotted one, so we stopped and pulled it into our helicopter. The smell of his rotting body was enough to gag a maggot. All the bodies of those who drowned were recovered.

Command Chronology for that event:

("Millpoint" was the radio call sign for HMM-363 aircraft.)

Two Millpoint aircraft launched from Ky Ha and were proceeding to the Quang Ngai airfield to stand night medevac. YZ-74 had to make a passenger pickup at the admin pad before continuing on to Quang Ngai. The section leader radioed his wing man in YZ-76 to orbit over the beach at Chu Lai to wait for YZ-74. While the lead aircraft was on the Admin Pad a radio transmission was received from YZ-76 stating that the aircraft was down and that the pilot was returning to Ky Ha to get another aircraft. The section leader rogered this transmission. A period of 30 seconds elapsed when the pilot of YZ-76 radioed that he had lost his engine and was ditching in the water off Chu Lai. The pilot of YZ-74 lifted out of the admin pad and arrived over the downed aircraft. YZ-76 hit the water at the surf line and due to heavy seas and surf, the aircraft was breaking up very fast. There were no survivors to be found on the surface. Millpoint SAR aircraft arrived over the scene minutes later and assumed command of the rescue operations. YZ-76 went down with a crew of four and six Marine troops aboard.

I had gone all through flight school with Gary Shields, and got to know Bob Schena during the last stage of flight school (helicopters) at NAS Ellyson Field, just north of Pensacola. Gary's nickname was "Squak" because he had a very loud, piercing, booming voice. Someone said of him, "He could be heard through a stone wall a quarter of mile away." He was one of the few MARCADs who was married while going through flight school. (The contract we agreed to when we joined said that we were not allowed to be married until we finished flight school.) Somehow Gary was able to conceal his wife (and two kids by the time he finished!) from the officials until such time as it was no longer a factor to wash him out.

A Tragic Medevac

On 12 January 1967, while based at Ky Ha, I flew on a night medevac mission with Steve Howell. Everything went routinely. We flew out to an LZ somewhere to the west, picked up a wounded Marine or two and returned to Ky Ha. So far as we knew, we were not shot at during this flight. Crewmen were always under strict orders to not fire their M-60 machine guns unless they had explicit permission from the aircraft commander.

Our young machine gunner, probably an admin clerk flying a few missions to earn himself an air medal, got trigger happy. On short final approach, right over the village just outside the base, he saw lights flashing. The flashing was simply lights blinking as we flew past tree branches, wires and posts between us and village lights. He thought the flashes were enemy fire. Without warning, he suddenly opened up with his M-60 machine gun and returned that imagined fire. Unfortunately, before Steve could holler over the intercom to order him to cease firing, his burst of machine gun fire killed a little Vietnamese girl asleep in her bed.

Steve, as aircraft commander, was in serious trouble for the gunner's actions. An immediate investigation revealed that Steve had followed proper procedure by briefing the gunner that he was not to fire until given permission. I believe the gunner was into some serious trouble, but I never heard any follow up. I am sure that somehow the Marine Corps paid some compensation to the family of the little girl, and this incident was soon forgotten.

Steve became very distraught over this incident, and there is no telling whatever else he had experienced prior. He took the responsibility to heart. He began drinking more than usual, got sullen and morose. I now know he, too, suffered from PTSD.

Rescue of A-4 pilot off Chu Lai

15 January, 1966

It seemed as if it was going to be just another routine night of SAR boredom. It would be a good time to catch up on our sleeping, our letter writing and just generally sitting around and talking with our buddies. This was much safer than night medevac duty. SAR was rarely called out to perform, and this night we were in the midst of a tropical storm. Forty knots of east wind blew off the South China Sea, boiling the sea, driving 20 foot swells onto the beach. There was a low ceiling, a solid overcast of clouds just a few hundred feet above the sea. How many bombing missions could there be on this stormy night, anyway? Don't bombers have to see the ground in order to drop their bombs? We anticipated a quiet night.

Our previous uneventful SAR standby had been on Christmas Eve, 1966. To improve morale, Tim O'Toole, the flight leader, slipped over to the officers club and brought back a bottle of Champagne. We decided to toast home, families and Christmas. We had no glasses to drink our bubbly. Being Marines, we quickly came up with a good field expedient. We rapidly opened cans of C rations, dumping out servings of crackers with cheese or pound cake until we came up a small can for each crew member. We poured each man an ounce or two of the bubbly. There were nine of us (two crews of four plus a Navy corpsman) so no one was worried about getting too much to drink. No chance of our abilities getting impaired. This little drink was a huge morale builder.

Just prior to midnight on the 15th, the control tower called us, ordering us to man our aircraft and stand by. An A-4 Skyhawk fighter-bomber pilot was in trouble and might need our help. We immediately ran out to our two H-34 helicopters and cranked up the powerful engines. We checked out our systems and warmed up our radios. We dialed up the Chu Lai control tower frequency for further instructions.

As we listened to the conversation between the tower and the A-4 pilot, we began to get the whole picture. The A-4 had just taken off with a full load of bombs on a radar-controlled bombing mission. [That's how they did it.] Upon trying to retract his landing gear, the pilot got an unsafe gear indication - the gear would not retract. This meant he could not proceed on his mission because his aircraft would not accelerate to normal flying speed. This also meant he might not be able to land, depending on what the problem was.

The pilot tried the basic emergency procedures that he knew and had no luck. Fortunately he had full fuel so he had plenty of time to work on the problem. We sat on the ground with our engines idling and listened to the situation unfold.

The tower called the executive officer of the A-4 squadron up to talk to the A-4 pilot. Then the commanding officer of the squadron came up to try to help. Those two were puzzled by the problem, so they then called the squadron maintenance officer, who also could not help. Those three called in the technical representative from the Douglas Aircraft Corp. The four of them put their heads together to try to figure out how to solve the dilemma. Trying to recycle the landing gear lever did no good. Trying alternative hydraulic systems did no good. Pulling up abruptly on the stick did not dislodge the stuck gear.

One thing that really impressed Tim and me and the other helicopter pilots was that most of the suggestions brought up by the would-be helpers on the ground had not yet been tried by the pilot. We were negatively impressed that this A-4 pilot really knew almost nothing about his aircraft's emergency procedures and back-up systems.

For about an hour nothing changed; we sat, idling. The aircraft stranded in the air was flying perfectly and still had at least another hour's worth of fuel on board. There was no need for anyone to panic. All the while the pilot repeatedly kept saying, "I really don't want to have to jump out of this thing!" (Eject.) Finally, the pilot flew a low pass by the tower and those in the tower observed that the main landing struts were badly bent. There nothing that anybody on the ground could do or suggest that would alter that fact. The lame gear would neither retract nor extend.

The pilot had hit some object on the runway as he took off. Later investigation revealed that a bomber taking off prior to this A-4 had accidentally released his bomb racks full of bombs onto the runway. These racks full of bombs are what damaged this pilot's landing gear on take-off.

After much discussion and debate, the consensus was that the pilot would never be able to land the A-4. It was too risky for him to try to belly land it in the strong cross winds with the landing gear partly down. Despite his misgivings, he would have to eject. In preparation, he flew several miles out to sea, and dropped his racks of 250 pound bombs into the South China Sea through the overcast. Now at least he didn't have racks full of high-explosive bombs to worry about.

The pilot, flying in circles above the clouds, knew where he was by using his TACAN navigation radio. His A-4 flew at a speed well in excess of 100 knots. It would be difficult for him to eject with any certainty that he would come down onto the base. If he drifted beyond the base perimeter to the west, he would come down into what we called "Indian Country." No one wanted to be outside the friendly lines at night. In addition, there was a minefield surrounding the base. He certainly did not want to float down into the minefield. We all considered either option to be certain death.

He homed back in on the TACAN signal, made a U-turn, headed out to sea once again. When the instruments told him he had passed over the radio beacon, he then timed about one minute. This should put him a couple of miles to the east over the ocean and we all hoped that the strong winds would carry him back onto the base.

Before ejecting, he put the aircraft on autopilot, so it would continue to fly straight and level to the east after he ejected. (So far as we know, that aircraft is still out there, flying east on autopilot.)

We coordinated a rescue plan with the A-4 pilot by radio. Then we waited and watched. We spotted the flash of his ejection seat through the overcast as he departed the doomed jet. We then positioned ourselves where we knew we could be of immediate assistance and so that our rotors could not be a threat to his parachute as he floated down through the dark clouds and splashed into the churning waters beneath. This was going to be a difficult pickup. A hovering pick up is a challenging maneuver at any time, but to do it over a boiling sea at night is near impossible.

He landed in the water probably a mile from the beach. Another sign of his unpreparedness: he carried no emergency flares with him. At least he had one of those very small one-cell flashlights clipped to his survival vest. Only this small single-cell, white light made it possible for us to find him after he splashed down.

Tim flew confidently to the pilot and hovered right over him with all of our hover and flood lights turned on. There was never any doubt in either of our minds that we would rescue this pilot. In preparation, the crew chief in the belly of the helicopter had rolled out 100 feet of cable from the hoist and attached the horse collar to the end. All we had to do lower this horse collar down to the pilot wait for him to slide into it and reel him up like a big fish. Piece o' cake. During the day, with calm seas and good visibility, it would have been a cinch. This was not daytime, this was not good visibility, and we had the turbulence of gusty winds of the tropical storm to deal with. Our potential passenger was bobbing around like a beach ball in a fan factory.

Tim made several tries to get the horse collar to the reluctant ejectee. Every time he failed. Each time that Tim placed the collar almost within the pilot's, reach the wind whipped it away. Sometimes wave tops collapsed under the pilot, and he slid down a wave, away from the collar. This was very exasperating for Tim and the now soaked and rapidly tiring pilot. We had to be successful soon, or the pilot would drown.

My job was to monitor the instruments and make sure that all the machine's limitations were respected. Tim was pushing those limits. The operating manual for our helicopter said the limit on the nine-cylinder Wright Cyclone engine was five minutes at full power. We were fairly heavy as we had a crew of five and nearly full fuel. It took nearly full power just for us to hover in that situation. After more than 10 minutes at this high power, Tim pulled back from the hover and flew a quick circle around the pilot and then went back down for another hover at full power. "The book says full power for only five minutes, it does not say you cannot go right back to full power after rolling back to cruise power for a little while," Tim said, once again establishing a hover. Several more tries of getting the horse collar to the drenched pilot ended in failure.

At one point while we hovered over the sea, a bit of motion caught my eye to my left. I looked up in time to see a huge roller coming right at us at eye level. In his focused attention to rescue the A-4 pilot, Tim had inadvertently followed the slope down the face of a big wave into a deep trough between huge waves. I reacted quickly and lifted up the collective lever to raise us above that wave. The wave kissed the bottoms of our tires as it passed beneath us. It would have slapped us out of the sky like a gnat hit by a fly swatter. Fully dressed in flight gear and boots, we would not have survived a violent crash into the turbulent sea.

We hovered back over to the bobbing, bouncing pilot. After several more attempts, Tim was finally able to get the horse collar to him. Nearly exhausted, he was able to grab it and slide into it. The crew chief hoisted him up to the chopper and pulled him in to safety. We returned the exhausted and soaked but unharmed pilot to his unit at Chu Lai. I give credit to Tim O'Toole's extraordinary piloting skills that we completed this mission.

We did not receive any medals for this rescue as it was all in a day's work. Sikorsky Aircraft Company awarded Tim and me each a Sikorsky "Winged S" for using one of their aircraft to save a life on this hoist rescue mission. One of the best sayings that evolved from our time in Vietnam was, "The best medal is a live man's smile."

Picture of Sikorsky Winged S courtesy of George McKee.

Another time, I was scud-running (flying along the bottom of the clouds) southbound along the coast at night, returning to Ky Ha from Da Nang. We were flying wing on our leader but lost him in the fog. We followed proper procedure in this case, slowing slightly and making a slight turn to the right, to keep us from running over our leader should we overtake him. After a brief time who should appear out of the fog but our leader, who swooshed right past our left wing headed in the opposite direction less than 100 feet from us. Our leader had decided that the weather was too bad to proceed down the coast. He had made a 180-degree turn without bothering to tell us, and nearly ran head on into us with a closing speed of about 200+ knots! He assumed we were still with him. This near mid-air collision was also partly our fault for not communicating to him that we had lost him in the fog and that we were no longer following along tightly on his wing. It has been well established that a mid-air collision will ruin your whole day.

While based at Ky Ha, we occasionally flew to Tam Ky for overnight medevac standby for the Marines in that area. As I recall, I never launched out at night from this place.

At Tam Ky, a 155mm howitzer battery was located right next to our tent. Intermittently it fired directly over our tent without warning. When it did, the sound was deafening, and the entire tent shook with the concussion from the big rounds leaving the tube just a few feet over our heads. The first few times were frightening, but we got used to it, and soon we could sleep through the explosions. We learned what "outgoing" sounded like. This information would come in handy in just a few weeks.

A 155mm howitzer at Khe Sanh with a flat tire.

We also worked with the ROK (Republic of Korea) Marines in this area. They were very tough fighters and hated Communism. It was rumored that if they took fire from a village, they attacked and did not return without an enemy body.

One day I flew a mission where we hauled 18 dead Marines from a small dirt airstrip back to Chu Lai. The dead were not in body bags, but exposed. They had been killed the day before in a skirmish with the V.C. It seemed to me that each of the dead Marines was younger than I. It was a sobering day.

Just before departing Ky Ha, I was informed that I was promoted to captain along with dozens of my contemporaries. What a difference from a few months before when I was based in North Carolina. There we were told that if we put in our first tour without any problems, if we did a good job as first lieutenants, (and maybe did a little brown-nosing) then we might, just might, maybe, be offered captain if we shipped over (re-enlisted) for another tour. Now we were being promoted to captain with minimum time in grade. I really did not yet have a clue what a second lieutenant should be doing, and here I was about to become a captain. War does that to the military machine.

During January of 1967, the pilots of HMM-363 flew 799.2 hours, carried 192.5 tons of cargo, 2514 troops, and 311 medevacs. I personally flew 36 hours.

About the food

For the most part our food was adequate and plentiful. At Ky Ha especially the food was always terrible. Many times we would get feedback from the first few guys who went to the mess hall. If the breakfast report was bad – more often than not powdered eggs and powdered milk – we broke out the C-rations from our personal stash under out cots. These were usually preferable to the food at the mess hall. The REMFs[7] got all the good food at the larger bases in the rear.

My favorite C-ration was spaghetti and meat balls. The least favorite to most guys was the "Bean, lima with ham." The prize meals in each case of 12 were the ones that had the canned peaches or canned pound cake in them for dessert. We often would save up those two desserts until we could eat them together. The phrase "peaches and pound cake" became our euphemism for good times. When things were going well we said, "Everything is peaches and pound cake."

A case of C-rations. Source: wikipedia

Ubiquitous at every meal was "bug juice." This was a fruit-flavored, highly sugared version of Kool Aid in bright red and green colors.

---

7 REMFs: Rear Echelon Mother Fuckers.

8.
On the Move Again

After my short stay at Ky Ha my new squadron was sent aboard the USS *Iwo Jima* (LPH-2) on 19 January 1967. We sailed first to Keelung Harbor in northern Taiwan. En route we had a training session of night carrier landing practice. I was not on the flight schedule for this night practice flying, which did not disappoint me a bit. Flying around in a very dark, moonless night over the South China Sea did not appeal to me at all. During this night flying practice I sneaked up to the catwalk at the edge of the flight deck, and I took several pictures of helicopters landing on the deck at night. Using the "B" (open) stop setting on my camera, I captured some unique time-lapse exposures of action on the flight deck. I captured the landing signals officer (LSO) dancing around in his electrically lighted suit, and pictures of helicopters in motion over a few seconds of time.

I did not really know that being up on the edge of the flight deck during flight operations was quite illegal, although it did make a lot of common sense that I should not have been out there. Had a helicopter crashed, flying debris and bits of helicopters would have acted just like shrapnel from an artillery shell, and could have chopped me to bits or knocked me into the sea.

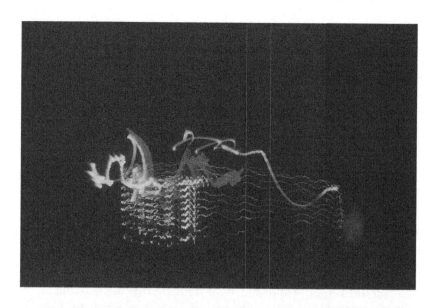

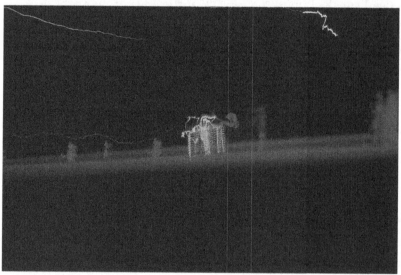

Elapsed-time photos of the Landing Signals Officer (LSO) in his suit of lights with wands, giving directions to a helicopter landing at night on the carrier. These photos may be viewed in full color at the author's website: www.captainbillfliesagain.com

Taiwan

Our ship docked in Keelung Harbor near the delightful hot springs resort town of Peitou. We rented the entire floor of a small hotel and had a raucous squadron party. I have incriminating pictures of several squadron mates that I could use for blackmail, but of course, I would never. After a couple of delightful days there, on January 31, 1967, we sailed for the Island of Okinawa.

Before leaving Taiwan, several of my friends and I took the opportunity to visit the Chinese National Museum, which contains much of the national treasure of China, taken to Taiwan by the Nationalists when they fled the mainland. On display were a small fraction of the thousands of antiques and artifacts from eons of Chinese history. Some of the things I saw there really do fall into the category of "...and this is no shit!" I specifically recall seeing a glass display case that held something under a large magnifying glass. Viewing through the glass I saw a carving of a large horse fly, made of jade, about the size of a real-life horse fly, carved in extreme detail. The magnifying glass was so that museum visitors could see the details of the tiniest parasite of some kind that inhabited the fly's body. These little mites were also carved out of jade, also in exquisite detail, almost invisible to the naked eye.

I also saw what seemed to be, at first glance, a birdcage. It was actually a picnic basket made for the emperor of another past Chinese dynasty. It was made entirely of ivory, with intricate details carved all over it. The placard on this piece said that a Chinese artist worked his entire lifetime to create this basket for the emperor; however, he died before he could complete it. The artist's son then took over the project and spent most of his lifetime finishing the project.

From Taiwan the ship sailed to Okinawa, where I was able to again hook up with one of my favorite school teachers, Jean C. from Dubois, Pennsylvania. My first night back, we were enjoying a nice meal at the officer's club, when one of my friends informed me that I was officer of the day. That was a surprise to me. As OD, I should not have a date and be drinking wine with my meal.

We hurriedly finished our dinner and slipped over to my room, hoping for some privacy. It was not to be. As the officer of the day, I had the squadron mail. All the men kept coming to my room to ask for their mail. There was no way Jean and I could have a quiet time together. I gave her taxi fare and sent her home.

After just a few days back in Okinawa, we again took off, sailing toward the Philippine Islands. At sea we once again had day and night ship landing practice. I again missed out on night flying, this time because I contracted conjunctivitis, "pink eye," in my right eye. I did not like the flesh colored patch Doc Houts gave me to protect my eye, so I used a black marking pencil to color it black. From this I got the nickname "Black Patch." For a while, my other eye started to bother me. I feared I was going to have to wear patches over both eyes and have to be led around the ship by one of my fellow pilots. Fortunately, that did not happen.

Olongapo City, Philippine Islands

There was a problem with the aircraft fuel storage tanks being contaminated, so we cruised to the huge U.S. Naval base at Subic Bay, to get our fuel tanks cleaned and refilled. We had time on our hands here, so we continued to party and drink to excess on the base and in Olongapo City (the "Po"), the city just outside the gate of the base. This place had a reputation rivaling that of Tijuana, Mexico. You could get anything you wanted there. And maybe some things you didn't want.

We started each day at the Bachelor Officer's Quarters (BOQ) swimming pool with Bloody Marys and eggs, then hung around the pool, where we drank San Miguel beer to excess, and got to know some of the American school teachers working military contracts in that area. At night we went out to the village and partied. I was still wearing the patch over my eye. Dancing with the girls, I told them the VC had shot out my eye. I got lots of sympathy.

We usually frequented a bar called the "Blue Willow." It was just another beer bar where the beer and the girls were cheap and good.

The rules of the Subic Bay naval base were that no one could be out in the village after midnight. That did not mean we could not stay out overnight; it just meant that we had to lay low if we stayed out past midnight. So we each simply paired off with a working girl and went to her "crib" to spend the night with her. We could legally be back on the streets at 0600, so we could easily make morning muster aboard our ship before beginning another day of the same debauchery.

One night several of us got caught out after curfew by the Shore Patrol (Navy military police), in the Blue Willow Bar. I lied and told them I was attached to a different ship that I knew was out in the harbor. I knew we were to leave in a couple of days and that we would be gone before anything could come of my giving them the wrong info. Chances are the commanding officer of that ship gave my name to the CO of the Marines on board his ship, that officer checked his roster, did not find my name, and threw the report away. It was war time; they could not be bothered with such trivia. At least that was my hope. Judging by results, I was correct. No repercussions.

We drank a lot of beer, danced with many lovely young ladies, and otherwise enjoyed ourselves. A significant song at the time by "The Animals" goes:

We gotta get out of this place, If it's the last thing we ever do
We gotta get out of this place. Girl, there's a better life for me and you.

When we sang along with that song our hearts, minds and spirits were in tune.

A Not-So-Secret Mission

"The only fair way to judge anything is by results."

–Thomas Willhite

Unlikely as it may seem, it was on a street corner of Olongapo that my next great aviation-related adventure began. Bill Ruth and I were standing on a street corner waiting for a taxi when two friends drove by in a Jeepney taxi and offered us a ride. We didn't really care where they were going. We were out for a good time, so we hopped in. As soon as we boarded the taxi, one of my friends introduced us to the two beautiful young Filipina women accompanying them. They both spoke English fluently, were articulate and well educated, which was very common for the working girls in Olongapo. It was more fun and a lot more profitable for them to come to Olongapo and be bar girls for the GIs than it was to be teachers or nurses in their home villages. As we taxied to our destination, one of the young ladies said something to the effect "I understand that when you return to Vietnam you're going on an operation in Quang Ngai province." That was a surprise to us because we had no idea what was next in store for us. Even our commanding officer, Lieutenant Colonel Keith Huntington, had no idea what or where our next operation might be.

After about three weeks of the ongoing debauchery in the Po, we sailed once again for Vietnam on the USS *Iwo Jima*. Once we were safely out to sea, where everything was very secure on the aircraft carrier, our colonel gave us a secret briefing about our next assignment. We were quite amazed to learn that the "Po" bar girls were right; we were indeed scheduled for an operation in Quang Ngai Province. I am sure we told our CO of our information and he passed the information up the chain of command, but nothing changed. We sailed on toward our destiny.

I was concerned, because I thought that if the bar girls in the Philippines knew our destination, then, sure enough the enemy had to know we were coming. They would be waiting for us. I foresaw a huge ambush ahead of us. Again, I worried that my life was in serious jeopardy. I felt compelled to find some way to avoid flying in this upcoming operation, but I could not simply be a coward and ask not to fly. I did not want to surrender my coveted, hard-earned golden wings and quit flying permanently. After all, our creed was "Death before Dishonor."

On Quitting

All military pilots are volunteers. No pilot is required to fly aircraft against his will. We could turn in our wings at any time with no repercussions. Can you imagine the carnage if non-willing fellows were required to fly those (then) high-tech machines? But the flying, and its resulting adrenaline rush, got into our blood, and we were driven to be there for our Marines out in the field. Marine Corps helicopter pilots are like that. Marines are like that.

The one pilot I knew who quit flying in Vietnam did not quit out of fear. Captain Dick Black, a fellow former MARCAD, was a special case. Before joining the service, he had worked his way through college in Florida by going into the Everglades swamps to capture poisonous snakes to sell to serpentariums. These entities bought the snakes so they could milk them for their venom, which is used to create anti-venom. He said this was written in his medical record: "Bitten by poisonous snakes six times; twice accidentally." He had allowed himself to be bitten under controlled circumstances so that he could build up immunity in case he should be bitten while out in the swamps alone.

He volunteered to become a full time FAC because he loved snakes, and he wanted to be out in the field to get close to the local snakes. While in the field, he was wounded by a land mine, but his injuries were minimal compared to his nearby radio operator who died from the same blast.

Dick Black on deck of Subic Bay O'Club, Philippine Islands.

THIS PAGE INTENTIONALLY LEFT BLANK
(Only prior military people will appreciate this bit of humor.)

9.
Quang Ngai Province

I Become a Forward Air Controller

As chance would have it, while we were in the Philippines the battalion landing team (BLT 1/4) that we were scheduled to support on the upcoming operation came up short two forward air controllers (FACs). One of them had become ill, and the second FAC had disappeared somewhere into the village of Olongapo. Our skipper, Lieutenant Colonel Keith Huntington, asked for volunteers to take their places. He promised us that if we went out as FACs we would only be out there for this operation and no longer. He promised we would not be kept out in the field for the rest of our tour in Vietnam, which was our biggest worry. Colonel Huntington was older, very much a father figure in his gray crew cut and calm demeanor. We trusted his word. So Jerry Norton and I jumped at the chance to become FACs to avoid flying in the upcoming fiasco known as Operation Deckhouse VI.

The job of an FAC is to be the liaison between the grunts and the airdales, to facilitate communications between two very different military cultures. Normally the job of Forward Air Controller is one that nobody wants. It's a non-flying job, out in the field with the grunts, dirty, full of bugs, malaria-carrying mosquitoes, snakes, punji pits and other hazards to one's health, not to mention the biggest threat of all ... the enemy. It was rumored that the normal life expectancy of an FAC out in the field with the grunts was measured in single digits of weeks. But I had the premonition that if I went flying in this operation, I was doomed. My apprehension overpowered another of our credos, "never volunteer."

It turned out that this period of 15 days in the field, from 16 February to 3 March 1967 was the most harrowing and dangerous of my time in Vietnam. That I am aware of I was nearly killed six times in those 15 days. How many other close calls I had that I was never aware of, only God knows.

I was assigned to Battalion Landing Team of the First Battalion, Fourth Marines, (BLT 1/4), a grunt company aboard the USS *Cleveland*. I flew across to the ship as a passenger in one of our own helicopters. Here I met Captain R.D. Kelly, the company "C" commander, who showed me down several decks into the bowels of the ship. In the junior officers bunk room, I met all five of the other young lieutenants of this company I was going to support. They were friendly and made me feel welcomed and at ease. I began to prepare myself for the next day when we would assault the beach with landing craft.

Helicopters of HMM-363 land aboard the USS *Cleveland*
while landing craft circle beside the ship.

After supper, the other lieutenants elected to go to a movie and invited me to join them. I declined with some lame excuse that I wanted to be alone. I let them assume whatever they wanted.

Embarrassingly, in all my Marine Corps flight school training, I'd never packed a combat pack. I was a "college" MARCAD, I had no grunt training, and I had never been to boot camp or to OCS. I had no idea how to arrange my pack to make it look like and, more importantly, function like a grunt's pack. I waited until the other young officers departed to the movie, then I took one officer's pack apart, observed how it was put together, and then rebuilt my pack to match his. Now I was ready for action.

For this mission, I had my choice of US-made weapons. I absolutely did not want an M-16. I had seen and heard that this rifle was a piece of junk and was susceptible to frequent jamming in the field. What I really wanted was the enemy's weapon, the AK-47, but there were none in our armory. I chose instead a .45-caliber "Grease Gun." This was very much like the Israeli Uzi, which put out a lot of stopping power without much chance of it seizing up in a battle, should I encounter an urgent need to fire it. It also had the advantage that it used the same ammunition as the 1911 .45-caliber handgun strapped to my side. I was well armed.

Hitting the beach!

The plan was that the battalion would hit the beach the next morning at first light. I slept fitfully and awoke at zero-dark thirty. After breakfast about 0430, I descended deeper into the bowels of the ship, where I found my unit, a squad of Marines that I was to accompany to the beach.

The landing craft was a sizeable rectangular motorized metal box on tracks, much like a floating tank. Each motorized box would take a squad of combat-ready troops from the ship to the beach, where the front ramp would then rattle down, and we would storm out and overwhelm the enemy. He would be ours! This was to be reminiscent of all the World War II Pacific beach landings where all my childhood heroes dwelled. This was my chance to experience the glories of Tarawa, Tinian, Saipan, Okinawa and Iwo Jima! Now I was beginning to feel like a real Marine, just like in the movie *Away All Boats*. I had to contain my excitement and maintain my cool, as if I did this sort of thing every day.

The amphibious landing craft lived underneath the helicopter flight deck of the ship in a huge cavern, much like an aircraft hangar. Except in this case, the deck was steel and there were no windows. There was a steep decline to the huge swinging "barn" doors at the stern of the ship, where water sloshed at the foot of the decline. After we loaded up, the giant gates in the back of the ship swung open. One by one, the lumbering steel boxes clanked on their tracks down the steep ramp, then floated out into the South China Sea, like awkward ducklings eperiencing water for the first time.

Once in the water, we circled beside the mother ship with the other landing craft, eagerly waiting for our attack on the beach to commence. With all the delays in getting everybody ready and getting off the ship, it was well after first light before we finally even clanked our way down the ramp. We began to circle beside the ship. Then we circled some more. Then we circled more yet. It seems that we circled for hours. And then we circled some more. This was supposed to be a surprise attack at first light. How in the hell can we surprise anybody with all these big ships offshore, all the circling about, and all this noise? We did not hit the beach until almost 0900.

The landing craft were small inside, and we had more Marines than seats. Since I was an officer, it was a courtesy to let me board last. Consequently, I did not get a seat. I had to stand in the corner, right under the hatch where the driver sat, topside. The trouble was the damn thing was only about five feet in height on the inside. Being over six feet tall, I couldn't stand up straight. I wedged myself into the corner, semi-standing with my neck tilted down and my knees slightly bent. This was most uncomfortable; but I hadn't seen anything yet.

As we circled and circled and circled some more, the sea state was probably three to four foot swells, close together and choppy. The little craft rocked and rolled. Guess what happens when you get a bunch of men in a small space crammed together, with no windows, very little fresh air, and then start getting bounced around in a choppy sea? In the Marine Corps it is considered uncouth to throw up on your buddy (unless of course you have been out drinking until all hours – then it is somehow okay). The Marines began vomiting into their helmets. I heard retching, saw helmets full of vomit. The acrid smell assaulted my nostrils. No one could possibly have avoided losing his breakfast under such conditions. I did so only because each time, just as I was going to upchuck my breakfast, the landing craft rolled under a huge wave and about 10 gallons of cold sea water came crashing through the hatch and poured right down my neck and spine. The shock from the cold water took my mind off being sick for a while. That scenario repeated itself several times over about 90 minutes, until I was thoroughly soaked, cold, miserable, and ready to shout, "Drive this s.o.b. onto the beach, drop the door, and let me get the hell out of here!"

That seemed like a good idea until we finally stopped circling and headed for the beach. A few hundred yards out from the beach, the Marine beside the driver, manning the .50-caliber machine gun on top of the vehicle, began to fire. Ka-chunk! Ka-chunk! Ka-chunk! The .50-caliber machine gun has a very distinct sound to it, unlike an M-16 or any other small arm.

OHMYGOD, *they're shooting at us!* screamed the silent voice in the back of my brain. I knew that if the Marine topside was shooting his .50-caliber at the beach, that meant the enemy was there and they were shooting back. If we had a .50-caliber machine gun, then they must have .50-caliber machine guns. A .50-caliber bullet is as large as a man's thumb and can blow someone apart. Sometimes these projectiles are filled with explosives and are small bombs that explode on impact. At this point I knew for certain that once the door lowered down onto the beach I was going to die. We would all be mowed down by huge, explosive .50-caliber bullets, like clay rabbits at a carnival.

Afraid, I said a little prayer: "Dear God, please don't let the door come down. Please make the door stick in the closed position, and keep that barrier of steel between us and the enemy. Please,

please, make it so that we have to go back to the ship for repairs!" No such luck. My prayer went unanswered. The landing vehicle rolled up onto the beach, the door clanked down and all the Marines in front of me ran out.

I was doomed.

I ran out of the vehicle, prepared to do battle. I was surprised to not hear shooting; nobody was running or taking cover.

The landing craft on the beach.

Against all combat instructions, all the Marine officers were standing around in a group, consulting a map. This was contrary to everything I had ever read or seen in the movies about the dangers of grouping together during combat. "One grenade will get you all!" They were trying to figure whether we had been dropped on the correct beach. We were safe, no enemy in sight. All the machine gun firing had been just in case, for practice, for fun.

But of course there were no enemy troops.

They knew we were coming.

At the Officer's Club of Subic Bay.

FAC "Black Patch 1-4 Actual" in the field.

Flying the H-34 Helicopter in Vietnam

After we organized on the beach, we moved inland a bit and established a battalion headquarters. At this time I was feeling pretty secure because I was with Captain Kelly and the other officers, surrounded by a battalion of U.S. Marines. What more safe and secure place could there be in the whole world than surrounded by a battalion of U.S. Marines? This seemed much better than being in the air in a helicopter, an easy target. Especially since the enemy knew we were coming.

My two radio operators, Hughes and Higgins, were enlisted men who had both been in the field for about six months. Each man carried a radio of a different tactical network. Each knew his job better than I ever would and could call in an air strike or a helicopter flight better than I could. They had been doing it for months. But they could not do this without an officer there to give the Okay. That was my job. I was just an official presence. I got the needs for air support from the grunts, told Hughes and Higgins what the needs were, and they did the radio calling. I was simply a communications middle man.

Corporals Higgins and Hughes, my radio operators.

As it turned out, it might have been a lot better for me if I had been through official FAC school. In fact, it would have been beneficial for me if I had been through basic infantry training and officer training at Quantico, too, but I had not. As a "college" MARCAD, I had gone directly to flight school. (To this day, my military friends are both amazed and appalled when I tell them, "I got out of the Marine Corps as a captain, but I never went to boot camp or OCS.")

After flight school, while posted at New River Air Facility adjacent to Camp Lejeune, I signed up for correspondence courses to learn what I needed to become a real officer. I studied them for a while but I was going off to war. I knew I might not survive. My attitude became, "Hell, why bother?" If I survived the war, then I would apply myself to the learning of how to be a real Marine Corps officer. Rather than study, I found I preferred walking over to the o'club to drink beer with my friends and watch Batman or Barbara Streisand performing one of her specials on TV. I did apply myself heartily to learning all I could about flying the H-34.

A mysterious visitor

At one point, shortly after the landing, I was walking inland through a scrub pine forest, along a sandy path. There was no underbrush for the enemy to hide in. The trees were too skinny to hide behind. The soil was sandy and seemed too soft and crumbly for the enemy to build one of his insidious trapdoor spider holes. I felt safe because on all sides of me, as I walked toward the company headquarters, I was surrounded by experienced combat Marines. About a half mile away I could hear and see huge black clouds as the jet bombers worked over the landing zone where the helicopters from my squadron were scheduled to soon land to discharge their troops, the helicopter-borne assault landing I had finagled to avoid.

As I walked along, I heard a strange noise. It was not unlike the whirring of helicopter blades, but much softer and quieter, almost a whispering. It sounded very near and was approaching quickly. It was difficult to tell from which direction. I puzzled over it for a few milliseconds and reasoned that whatever it was, it was coming down from the sky, directly toward me. I had to decide which way to jump, run or fall. I did not want to throw myself off the trail into the woods because there might be mines there. I wanted to stay on the trail where many Marines had just recently trod. I did not want to run back from the noise and appear fearful. I should have thrown myself down forward on my belly in the trail, but I stood there, indecisive.

Shortly, my decision was made for me. Ka-thump! Something landed right in front of me about eight to 10 feet away, exactly where I would be, had I thrown myself forward into the prone position on the trail. The heavy visitor hit hard. I approached to look at it, being very cautious to make sure it was not explosive. It *sizzled*! I was both amazed and puzzled. After it cooled enough to touch, we inspected it and found it to be a piece of cast iron about 2.5" x 4" and about 3/4 of an inch thick, weighing about two pounds.

That mystery piece of metal had very sharp and uneven serrated edges, much like irregular saw teeth, some almost an inch long. I realized this piece of metal had most recently been semi-molten and while spinning itself to this place, it had actually formed these teeth as molten metal tried to fling itself away from the central mass. It had English writing on it. Soon a couple of Marines were there, trying to help me figure this thing out. Our first thought was that this was perhaps from a mortar that the enemy had shot at us, using stolen U.S. ammunition. (The enemy never captured ammo, they stole it. We, on the other hand, never stole anything, but captured it or liberated it.) Finally we realized its origin. It was a piece of one of the 250-pound bombs that our bombers were dropping a half mile away. It had simply blown over to us for a visit.

I decided to keep it for a souvenir, but, after a few days out on patrol carrying my 25-pound pack in the oppressive heat and humidity, my Grease Gun, and lot of ammunition, I decided it weighed too much. To lighten my pack I dumped it. It would have made a great paperweight and a wonderful conversation piece on some future desk. It would have been a simple matter for me to label it and send it to myself in care of my squadron.

At the same time, my squadron mates were involved in the helicopter portion of the vertical envelopment. Vertical envelopment was the theory that we would catch the enemy between those of us landing on the beach and the airborne troops landed behind the enemy by helicopters. We would catch the enemy in a pincer movement and squeeze them into a confrontation or force them to surrender. The situation at the landing zone was nearly the exact situation that I had visualized in my fearful premonition.

Planning one of these operations must have taken weeks and weeks. The landing zone had been picked out well in advance, probably months before. Overflights had been made, aerial photographs taken, poured over and marked with strategic plans. That much planning time gave lots of opportunity for information to be talked about with friends. These friends would then talk to others, then to others, until the strategic importance of the planning and the need for secrecy was forgotten. This is probably how secrets get blown. The World War II admonition, "Loose lips sink ships!" comes to mind. This is how the bar girls in the Philippines came to know of our operation well before we ever did.

Prior to our landing, bombers had dropped tons of bombs on the LZ to prepare it for the helicopters. Naval artillery had zeroed in on the place and shredded it to bits with tons of high explosives. Rocket-firing barges offshore had fired additional untold thousands of pounds of high explosives into the landing zone. Before our helicopters approached to bring in the airborne troops, the Huey gunships sprayed the area with machine-gun fire and rockets to kill the last living thing down there. How could anything survive all that?

This procedure is something that the Marines learned the hard way in Tarawa in the beginning of the island hopping campaign in the South Pacific during World War II. In their first landing on a beach against the Japanese, the Marines had not used enough artillery or naval gunfire preparations before the Marines landed. Consequently the Marines got slaughtered on the beach and in the surf. The next time the military wanted to take an island, they bombarded the island heavily and experienced dramatically fewer casualties.

After all this bombardment, my entire squadron of H-34s came swooping in to land in the LZ without me. The helicopters were full of combat-ready troops, geared up to go into action against the theoretically dead or shell-shocked Viet Cong. Lieutenant Colonel Huntington, leading the way, lined up on final approach, coming in with precision to the landing site, landing well forward in the zone as to leave lots of room for the other helicopters behind him. They were committed to a landing as they were too heavy to easily fly away ... full of troops and fuel.

There was only one small problem. Lieutenant Colonel Huntington made a slight mistake. He landed in the wrong landing zone, about a half mile short of the designated, well-prepared zone. The zone he landed in was not the place that had been worked over so well by all the tons of wonderful high explosives. At this landing zone there was a welcoming party. The enemy opened up with a multitude of AK-47 rifles and machine guns. Bullets flew everywhere. They knew we were coming.

I heard later that every single one of our helicopters was shot full of holes. Several choppers in the flight went back to the ship, pilots screaming "MAYDAY! MAYDAY!" over their radios. Eight of the thirteen sustained enough damage that they had to shut down for repairs. Every helicopter in the flight was streaming some kind of fluid, be it hydraulic, fuel, oil or blood. Fortunately, every helicopter made it back to the ship. Not one had to ditch into the sea.

As fate would have it and with perhaps some kind of karmic justice because he was the one who led the helicopters into the ambush, the only man wounded of all the crewmen involved was Lieutenant Colonel Huntington. His left Achilles tendon was blown apart by a bullet. He walked with a limp forever after. Overall, the initial landing of this operation was not the disaster I had seen in my premonitions. Contrary to my premonitions, no one was killed. However, this was only the beginning of a two-week operation and it was off to a poor start.

Short Round!

Meanwhile, back at battalion headquarters somewhere in the scrub pine forest not far from the beach, I was standing around talking to a bunch of Marines. The mortar crew behind us had been repeatedly firing 60mm mortars over our heads in support of the Marines out on point, advancing toward the landing zone. It was only a few minutes after the scary incident with the bit of molten bomb shrapnel when someone shouted the words, "Short round!" Not having been to boot camp or officer's training at Quantico, it took a few milliseconds for the full meaning of this phrase to penetrate my consciousness. During that brief time, everyone who had been standing around me simply disappeared. This is strange, I thought before I realized what was happening.

The short mortar round impacted about 20 feet from me in the sandy soil. Just before it hit, I threw myself down onto the ground, but the flat ground was poor defense against a mortar so very close. Fortunately, the mortar had not been in the air long enough to arm itself and it fell harmlessly, a dud. Had it armed itself and detonated, I would have had some minor, perhaps major, wounds. I might have been killed. This was my second close call in less than half an hour.

I began to question whether being on the ground surrounded by a battalion of Marines was really so much safer than flying after all.

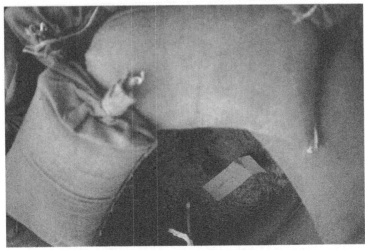

The short round surrounded by sandbags awaiting disposal by EOD.

My home for my first night in the field. Note the foxhole in foreground.

I spent the night near a foxhole, under my shelter half.

We spent the night without event. No infiltrators, no sappers, no human waves of Viet Cong charged through our perimeter defenses.

The next day we captured a potentially vicious Viet Cong attack dog and held him prisoner. Unfortunately, even when bribed with our best "C-Rations," he refused to bark us any information about the local cadre of Viet Cong. As we moved on, we released him back to his own, unharmed and uneaten.

Lieutenant Smith with captured enemy dog, "Sniper."

THE ADVENTURES OF A HELICOPTER PILOT

On Patrol

The next day, we went out on patrol, to find and engage the enemy, to find him and kill him. We were going hunting for the hardest game of all, our fellow man. Our game was also armed with automatic rifles, mortars, and perhaps more, just like us. The enemy was not sitting around, passively waiting to be killed. He had the advantage: he knew we were coming. He waited in ambush for us.

We were also the hunted.

The main advantage we had was a weird track-driven, tank-like machine called the "Ontos." Mounted on top of it were six 106mm recoilless rifles. These were huge cannons, but instead of firing like artillery or bullets from a gun, the rounds in these rifles were rocket powered. This meant no recoil, which theoretically made them more accurate. This provided an enormous amount of firing power for a company to have in the field. It was very dangerous to be behind this machine whenever it fired rounds because the back-blast from the rockets could be fatal. (Perhaps that is why this machine was phased out soon thereafter.)

The formidable, six-tube Ontos Source: Wikipedia

We had naval gunfire and rockets at our disposal. We had Marine Corps and Navy bombers on call, orbiting overhead to be called down immediately for whatever our needs might be. We had Huey gunships on call. We had the helicopters of my squadron on call. My job was to coordinate the airplanes and helicopters.

Patrolling to the west, we emerged from the pine forest. We passed through a small village. I was impressed with the small, perfectly round boats the villagers made out of woven palm leaves. They were nothing more than large baskets about four feet in diameter and about 18 inches deep. These people used the baskets for their subsistence fishing.

We swept west until we came upon Highway 1, the major (and only) north-south highway in the country. It was a thin two-lane ribbon of asphalt, hardly a country road by U.S. standards. Two large vehicles meeting on this road would have to pass very slowly and carefully. Because of the war, the road had no traffic at all. The peasants were using it as a space to dry their sliced cassava root, a main staple. The South China Sea lay to the east, and the Annamite Mountains to the west. There were large ditches on either side three to flour feet deep, with water in the bottoms. There was nothing much but rice paddies on either side of the highway. We turned north, following the highway, looking for trouble.

We found it.

We came to a place in the road where it passed between small hills on either side. It looked like a perfect place for an ambush. Things were too quiet. There were no people visible. These were not good signs. Sure enough, we began to take sporadic sniper fire from the narrow pass. For all we knew, the sniper was a simple rice farmer up there with a single-shot blunderbuss. But it could have been a battalion of Viet Cong.

It was hard for us to pinpoint the exact source of the sniper fire. The Marines immediately returned fire by shooting hundreds of rounds randomly into the hills on either side of the pass. If nothing else, it was a good release of tension for the troops to be able to shoot at something. When we tried to advance again, we received more sniper fire. This time it was more than single shots and more than one rifle firing. We knew two things. First, there was more than one Viet Cong up there, and second, all of our shooting had been for naught.

The officer in charge of the patrol decided that the way to handle this tactical situation was bigger firepower. We needed artillery. The artillery forward observer (FO) called back to the battalion headquarters. By now, the 105mm howitzers had been brought ashore and set up on the beach, awaiting our call. The FO gave our coordinates to the big guns. The arty officers calculated their trajectories, loaded their weapons, and fired a single round into our neighborhood. This one round was to determine if their calculations had been made correctly and what adjustments might be needed. The first round was about a hundred meters short, falling very close to our guys.

I have read old veterans' descriptions of artillery rounds "tearing apart the sky," but now I understood what those stories were trying to tell. Imagine that you rip a strong piece of cloth, quickly and violently. Then magnify that noise by about a thousand times. This is what artillery sounds like when it passes close overhead. The big shells actually do tear the sky apart. It was frightening, and it was not even coming very close to us. Yet.

That is when thing got really complicated and busy all at once, as they are wont to do in battle. "Add 100, and fire for effect," the FO radioed to the arty-firing Marines on the beach. That meant they should add one hundred meters to the range and let go with a full salvo of rounds. That should have put the huge 105mm howitzer shells right on top of the enemy snipers in the pass. That should blow those particular bad guys to bits, and the pass would be ours. It all sounded good on paper.

Between the poor radios, and perhaps some other

miscommunication, the arty shooters *deducted* a hundred meters off their initial calculation, and proceeded to fire a whole salvo. They dropped six rounds right smack down onto our front line troops before the arty observer could shout, "CEASE FIRE!" No one was killed, but we now had three seriously wounded Marines on our hands and it was time for me to do my FAC thing, to call in the medevac helicopters. I instructed Hughes and Higgins to do that, and they acted superbly. It seemed only a few seconds before the H-34s from my squadron were on their way.

My official call sign for this operation was "Gold Lemon 1-4." But I had created my own personal call sign so that my squadron mates in the air would know that they were working with me. During the cruise from Okinawa to Subic Bay I had had a case of conjunctivitis and had to wear a black patch over my right eye for about a week. So I picked up a nickname of "Black Patch." After I volunteered for this FAC mission, one of my friends suggested that in the field I use the call sign "Black Patch 1-4 Actual." I liked the idea, so I used it.

A week later, here I am in a very real combat situation, standing in the middle of Highway 1, guiding in my squadron mates on an actual combat medevac. I grab the radio, and I'm talking directly to Major Owlette, the flight leader of the four helicopters. "Barrelhouse medevac, this is Black Patch 1-4 Actual, I have you in sight. Continue straight ahead, and come in on my smoke." What a glorious, hot-dog position to be in. I am loving this. This was a role to be played, and I was playing it to the limit, showing off in front of my squadron mates.

"Roger that, smoke in sight," said the major. I used standard hand signals to guide the helicopters down the final approach to the highway.

A smoke grenade guides in the flight of four H-34s.

The major brought the helicopters beautifully down, landing right in front of me. Three other helicopters settled down on the road behind him. A fleeting thought quickly flashed across my mind to wonder why there were so many helicopters since we had only three wounded. Two helicopters would have been sufficient, but I was too busy to think through that question right then.

As the major decreased his power and brought the helicopter to idle, his crew prepared to take on the wounded Marines. I thought this would be a good time to continue playing the John Wayne role to the hilt, so I leapt into the ditch beside the highway. Just as I hit the dirt, a burst of AK-47 bullets passed through the space where I had been standing not two seconds before. Those same bullets passed about 18 inches over my head and splattered into mud on the bank on the other side of the ditch, not five feet from me. Had I not decided to play John Wayne, I would have been the recipient of one or more of those bullets. Several of the bullets hit the nose of Major Owlette's aircraft, fortunately not doing any great damage. Once again, I came very close to being a medevac in one of my own squadron's helicopters.

I learned later that Major Owlette was extremely angry at me. He thought that I knew that there was great danger of him taking the hits, and that is why I jumped out of the way. No, I was just playing the role of combat Marine as I had seen it in the movies.

Soon, the reason for the two extra helicopters became evident. Once again radio messages had gotten garbled. The battalion officers still aboard ship thought that because we had taken some battle casualties, we were heavily engaged with the enemy. We therefore must be in need of reinforcements. The extra helos brought us a dozen fresh troops. But our casualties had been self-inflicted. This was another "friendly fire" incident.

Shortly after the helicopters departed, we returned to the task at hand. The snipers in the pass persisted, pinning us down, and we needed to neutralize them. As we refocused, a group of peasants from the village came hustling down the road toward us. They were making sad, wailing noises that sounded like a wake. They were carrying something big. As they passed me, I saw what it was. An older peasant woman, caught near where the artillery impacted, had been hit in the chest by a piece of arty shrapnel. It looked like she had been shot with the bone from a T-bone steak. She had a deep "T" shaped hole in her chest, right into her heart. She was very dead. There was very little blood as her heart had experienced "sudden stoppage." This we called "collateral damage."

In the next permutation of trying to rid ourselves of the snipers, the officers leading the patrol decided to bring in the A-4 bombers. These aircraft carried Snake Eye bombs which are really just regular 250-pound bombs, with a spring-loaded retarder attached. When the bombs are released, these spring-loaded arms extend, making an X-shaped tail on the bomb. These arms slow the bombs down enough to ensure the pilot time to get away and not blow himself out of the sky. The need for these had been learned the hard way in World War II and Korea, where pilots had actually blown themselves out of the sky with their own bombs.

A few years later, while flying for Air America in Laos, I had a long conversation with Captain Al Swartz of Continental Air Services. He told me that while flying F-4U Corsairs in support of Marines in Korea, he actually blew himself out of the sky this way. He said after he dropped his bombs there was a loud BOOM! and his engine stopped. Looking down between his feet he could see the ground! He belly landed in the rice paddies behind enemy lines and just barely managed to avoid capture by the Red Chinese before being rescued by the grunts.

The bombers made several passes, dropping Snake Eyes into the hills. The enemy knew he was doomed, so he began to shoot at the bombers. What the hell, he knew he was going to be blown to bits anyway, he might as well try and shoot down the bomber. The Marines then began to shoot at the enemy shooting at the aircraft. Then the young officer in charge of the Ontos began to fire 106mm recoilless rounds. It was pure pandemonium for a while.

Another A-4 zoomed overhead to drop another rack of bombs. This pilot made a slight miscalculation and dropped his bombs a few yards short of the pass. Once again several of our Marines received wounds. I called in yet another medevac. More "friendly fire casualties." This time the snipers held their fire. More likely they were dead.

Finally, someone realized it was getting late in the day, and we should think about getting back to the safety of our battalion command post a few miles to the south. The young officer in charge of the patrol radioed back to Captain Kelly to ask for instructions. We hoped our orders would be to return to the command post in the pine forest, which seemed, by now, a much safer place to spend the night. It was not good to be out in an exposed position late in the day, for the enemy knew that he could attack with impunity in the approaching darkness and be much less susceptible to arty and bombers. We had not come prepared to spend the night away in the field.

The young officer in charge of the patrol got orders from Captain Kelly. We were to stay put for the night. It was too dangerous for us to hike back to the CP as dusk approached. We might get caught out in the open on Highway 1. Getting off the radio, the officer, who thus far had been in charge of the patrol, asked me, "Bill, what is your date of rank?" After I answered him, his next statement caused a ball of fiery horror to well up inside me. It started at my anus and speared up my insides like a hot flame and then exploded under the bottom of my heart and spread sideways into my stomach! I could hardly breathe. "You're a few days senior to me. You are the senior officer out here," he said. "You are in command, skipper!"

"Oh, shit!"

I had never been to boot camp. I never attended officer training school at Quantico. Suddenly I am in charge of this patrol in a combat situation with minimal knowledge about grunt things, responsible for the lives of about 25 Marines. I knew nothing about strategy, tactics, etc. My entire field experience was the previous 30 hours I'd spent walking around following these guys and being their FAC. I had no confidence that I should be in command. After a few milliseconds of near panic, I said to the young officer, "Well, Bob, you are next in seniority. That makes you my XO. What do you think we should do?"

"We should hunker down right here for the night and make do the best we can," he said. "Good, let's do that," I replied. He seemed relieved to take charge, and I was relieved to let him. We pulled back a few hundred yards from the pass to settle in for what promised to be a very long and interesting night.

Our situation was weak, but not dismal. We had not anticipated being out all night, so we had very little equipment or food. Not one of us had even a single entrenching tool to dig in with. We moved to the west side of the highway onto a small peninsula that jutted out into the water-filled rice paddies. We thought this gave us a bit of security because we had water on three sides of us and the openness of Highway 1. Here we found the remnants of a concrete foundation of a large house, probably the remnants of a chateau left over from the French colonial days. The six-inch high, stubby, concrete foundation walls gave us a bit of protection from the attack we fully expected. We had our formidable Ontos.

Charlie was famous for his night attacks, sneaking past or stealthily killing sentries, then getting in close enough to throw hand grenades into the sleeping troops. Thoughts of such things were in our minds as we did our best to set up a perimeter guard for the long night ahead.

Some Marines who had brought along a few cans of C-rations shared them, so no one went hungry. After supper, we settled in for what was to be one of the longest nights of my life. We had no sleeping bags or blankets, not even shelter halves to keep us dry should it rain. We had left all those creature comforts back at the CP, expecting to return. We did not need those things. We were young and healthy. We slept on the bare ground with our boots on. I think some of the fellows even hoped for us to be attacked during the night. We were Marines.

Sometime in the wee hours I was awakened by my XO as he said to me in a loud whisper, "Skipper, come listen to this." I bolted up quickly from my attempt to sleep on the hard ground, instantly on alert. I expected to hear the sounds of hundreds of Viet Cong charging up the hill. Except there was no hill, and there was no enemy charge. We crept out to a sentry post at our perimeter. "There, hear that?" Bob said. I listened, still expecting the worse.

Yes, I could clearly hear what sounded like 60mm mortars launching. They were very close, and we expected them to impact in our area within a few seconds. Except there never was the follow-up sound of mortars impacting or exploding anywhere. We heard it again: 60mm mortars being launched within easy range of us. But again, no impacts, no fiery explosions in our small camp. This was very spooky. Even if the rounds were duds, we should be hearing the quiet thumps of the dead rounds hitting the ground around us. Even if the rounds were being shot directly away from us, we still should have heard them exploding in the distance. Nothing. We heard nothing. We racked our brains trying to figure why we did not hear the impacts. This mystery was never solved for us. We slept little for the rest of the night.

The next morning we returned to the battalion command post. Somehow taking the pass from the enemy was no longer important. As we walked south on Highway 1, we came upon a funeral procession. Contrary to my limited experience with the few funerals I had attended, all the Vietnamese mourners were dressed in white. The ceremony was for the woman who had been killed the previous day by our arty. I was amazed that there seemed to be no animosity toward us from the villagers for her death. It was as if to them we did not exist. To us they were unreal. We all just seemed to inhabit the same space, but there was no communication between us and them at all. My guess is that they were very afraid of us, that we might on a whim decide to kill the rest of them too.

On patrol we made it a point to follow in the tracks of the Ontos. We hoped the weight of the Ontos would destroy any mines, booby traps or punji pits in our way.

One of those days in the field, while on patrol with the battalion, I realized I had lost my operational map of our area. It had probably been blown away by a resupply helicopter or simply slid out of my pack as I walked. The map had secret tactical markings on it that would be valuable to the enemy. I feared that it must be in the hands of some shadowing enemy trooper. I thought I was in big trouble. I had inadvertently aided the enemy.

I knew I must correct this problem to protect our Marines. I must tell Captain Kelly, so he could inform battalion headquarters that some of our top secret operations information had been compromised. I had no idea what plans might have to be changed, what tactics reorganized, or how many other complications I might have created with my carelessness. But I had to tell on myself because the lives of the Marines were in jeopardy if I did not. Even though I thought I was in big trouble, I could not keep this secret to myself Just as I was about to approach Captain Kelly to tell him what a dunderhead I was, one of the grunts walked up to me and said: "Sir, I believe you dropped this a ways back." He handed me my map.

At one point we patrolled close to the ocean and climbed to the top of a small hill overlooking our part of the province. There was an expansive view of the countryside from here, and it was a great place for the arty observer and me to do our business.

Just for practice, the FO allowed his assistant to call in artillery on a small village about a mile away. We had not been to that area, we had no information of any enemy activity in the village, and there was absolutely no reason to call arty onto that village that I knew of, except it was in an area known as a "free fire zone." This meant the whole area was assumed to be controlled by the Viet Cong and it was open to bombing, no exceptions, no questions asked.

I knew it was wrong, but I did not know what to do or how to say the words to stop him. I have always been sorry that I didn't speak out. The FO assistant dropped several rounds of high explosives in on a peaceful, quiet village for no obvious reason except for the assistant to have the experience of seeing his own handiwork. I was saddened by that experience. I have no idea if anybody died or was injured in that event.

On our map the village was named "Phouc Me." We did.

From atop the hill, looking south into an area being patrolled by another company, another FAC was doing his job. Could it be my friend Norton? We watched bombers circling and dropping their bombs and could see the resultant mushroom cloud of smoke.

An A-4 Skyhawk is barely visible in the top, left tip of the mushroom cloud as it bombs the enemy in Quang Ngai Province.

As my unit patrolled the countryside, we tried to again engage the enemy with little result. We burned a few hootches and found some enemy food stashes and ruined the food. I wondered how the Marines could tell enemy hootches and enemy food from friendly hootches and friendly food. Again, our assumption was that anything and everything in the area was enemy.

One day we had a short firefight at the base of the hill. The enemy fired a few dozen rounds into our midst, hitting no one. We returned fire with hundreds of rounds of M-16 bullets. During this fire fight, a young sergeant about 20 feet from me, experienced a very close call when his watch got blown to bits. Rather than wear his watch on his wrist, he wore it on the dog tag chain around his neck. An enemy bullet passed between his flak vest and his chest, from his shoulder to his sternum, then out the open zipper, missing his body entirely. The bullet hit the watch on the dog tag chain hanging off his chest, exploding it into bits of shrapnel. Bits of the watch wounded the Marine beside the sergeant slightly.

My radio operator Hughes took a bullet right in the middle of his back, on his radio. The impact pushed him over onto the ground, unhurt. We had to order a new radio to be delivered by the next helicopter. Better to need a replacement radio than a replacement Hughes.

Upon arising on my last morning in the field, after sleeping for the very last time ever in a foxhole, I discovered a large scorpion hiding in the webbing of my helmet. Had I put my helmet on without seeing the evil insect, I would have had a very painful, perhaps fatal, scorpion bite on my head. Once again I avoided being a medevac in my own squadron's helicopters.

Both Lieutenant Norton and I survived the FAC gig and returned to the ship. I fulfilled my goal of self-preservation by honorably avoiding flying for the operation. We were each awarded the Navy Commendation Medal with combat "V" for valor to reward us for volunteering to take the risky missions as FAC. Because of his wounds, Lieutenant Colonel Huntington had been replaced by Major Day. Major Day honored Lieutenant Colonel Huntington's promise to make sure we did not return to the field. I was glad. I did not like being out there in the field. I now knew for sure that my place was in the air. I would face any future risks from a cockpit at the controls of a helicopter.

Upon returning to the ship, I decided to reward myself with a long, hot shower. All water aboard ship has to be distilled from sea water, and it is always in short supply. While aboard ship we were normally required to take very short "Navy" showers. A Navy shower is when you wet yourself down, then turn off the water while you scrub down with soap, and then you turn on the water once more to quickly rinse away the soap. I rationalized that since I had been without a shower for two weeks, I could now take one longer shower, which I did. One of the majors caught me wasting all this water and chewed my ass. "Yessir!" I said, as he told me to secure the water.

My mental way of being subservient and at the same time rebellious was to say silently to myself, "Yessir, yessir, three bags full."

Full of what ... you can guess.

Navy Commendation Medal
Source: Wikipedia

For operation Deckhouse VI, which ended 3 March, the helicopters of HMM-363 flew 1,124.7 hours. They hauled 5,426 passengers, carried 418.1 tons of cargo and carried 267 medevacs.

For the entire month of February 1967, I did no flying at all.

Return to flying status

After the FAC experience, I returned to flying status. On 30 March 1967, I finally was able to get my aircraft commander (HAC) check ride out of the way and become an aircraft commander. I had been in country for eight months, but the check ride had been delayed by changing squadrons and all the shuffling around between Phu Bai, Okinawa, the P.I. and the FAC tour. Now I would not have to be copilot all the time and be at the mercy of some other pilot's bad decisions.

I could now live or die by my own bad decisions.

After my HAC check I still occasionally flew copilot. I had an exciting ride with Mike Hynes. After Deckhouse VI we were supporting the Marines in Operation Beacon Hill I, somewhere south of Da Nang. Mike and I flew out to an LZ and picked up a load of wounded troops. Returning to the ship, we found that the ship was smothered by a blanket of heavy fog. All we could see was the top-most mast of the ship sticking up out of the fog layer, slicing a groove in the fog as the ship sailed forward. The ship was not at flight operations. Mike was not to be deterred; we had wounded Marines on board who needed to get to the ship's hospital, RIGHT NOW!

Mike came up with a clever solution to this problem, the Navy and all its anal flight operations rules be damned. He flew out about a mile behind the ship, descended slowly down through the fog flying toward the ship. We watched our radio altimeter until we got low enough to see the foamy wake of the ship, then leveled off about 50 feet above the water. Then Mike slowly followed her bubbly trail until we could see the huge hulk of the ship as it appeared out of the fog above us. From well below the level of the flight deck, Mike added power and climbed up and planted the helicopter on the flight deck near the superstructure, beside the hatch leading to the on-board hospital below decks. The captain of the ship was not pleased, as the ship was not at flight quarters, but Mike justified an unauthorized landing because we had seriously wounded Marines on board. So far as I know, Mike did not get into any trouble for his daring approach and life-saving landing.

The USS *Iwo Jima* from overhead during good weather.
Two H-34s sit on the deck, far left. Hueys on the right.

During this phase of our carried-based flying, we encountered a curious Navy custom. The Navy officers on board the ship had two sittings for evening mess. Uniform standards were strictly enforced, and dinner started exactly at 1700 hours (5 p.m.) for junior officers, which all of us junior helicopter pilots were. If we were not at the table on time in the proper uniform, we could not join the Navy officers for supper, even though we had to pay for it.

Most days we flew as long there was daylight, supporting the Marines as needed until darkness precluded any more flying. Many times, we returned to the ship just at or shortly before 1700. Sweaty from flying in the tropical heat all day, we did not wish to rush to our rooms and put on our better uniforms just to go to supper. Sometimes there was not time to do even that. The captain of the ship was adamant about sticking to Navy protocol and would not allow us junior Marine Corps aviators to attend evening mess in our flight suits. Our commanding officer, now Major Day, tried to reason with the captain of the ship, to no avail. The few times we missed the formal dinner, we went down into the bowels of the ship and bought greasy cheeseburgers from the small snack shop. It irked us to have to pay for two meals, and then to eat food inferior to that served at the officer's mess.

The entire ship existed for one reason: to support our helicopter squadron. We, the pilots of those helicopters of that squadron, were not allowed into the officer's mess for supper.

Approaching and landing sequence to the USS *Iwo Jima*

Four helicopters from HMM-363 approach the USS *Iwo Jima*; the first one is already firmly down on the deck.

Getting closer

Closer still.

About to touchdown ...

... touchdown.

Marine Corps H-34s from HMM-363 wait for the haze to clear a bit before lifting off the USS *Princeton* on a strike mission.
Springtime 1967.

Once I flew over to this U.S. Navy destroyer and landed on its after end.

This was my view from the helipad. Navy gunners, please hold your fire!

Two pictures from the only USO show I saw while in Vietnam.

THE ADVENTURES OF A HELICOPTER PILOT

Two Helicopters Down

22 March 1967

We were still operating off the USS *Princeton*, but working out of Dong Ha. It was the monsoon season, with strong winds and rain falling in torrential sheets. Ceiling (height of clouds above ground) was about 150 feet. You wouldn't send your worst enemy out flying in weather like this.

The Marines of 2nd Battalion, 7th Marines (2/7) were heavily engaged with the enemy. They were in dire need of an ammunition re-supply and they had wounded to come out. They called for help; the medevac helicopters launched into the black night sky.

First Lieutenant Mike Hynes was the leader of the two-plane medevac section that took off from the Dong Ha airport. He used his TACAN to get his aircraft into the general vicinity of the imperiled grunts. He circled around trying to establish visual contact with them, while dodging the bottoms of the clouds and the uneven terrain below.

These Marines were located very near the DMZ. A slight navigation error could end up with the helicopters going into North Vietnam, and it made us nervous to fly so close to that border. Even though the enemy had no known helicopters, interceptors, or even any appreciable anti-aircraft capabilities in the area just across the border, it made us feel uneasy that we might inadvertently wander over the border. Should we crash or should the engine fail, we would surely be captured by the North Vietnamese Army – at best. At worse, we might find ourselves guests of the Viet Cong. With the NVA we might find ourselves in a terrible POW camp. With the Viet Cong, we felt torture was certain.

Flying around in the torrential rain in helicopter YZ-78, Lieutenant Mike Hynes, with copilot Dick Ericson, noted that he had drifted dangerously close to the border. He thought it best that he turn around. Lieutenant Jim Stroupe with copilot Paul Sheehan followed closely behind in tight formation.

Hynes pushed the stick gently and began a very slow, very shallow turn to the left, toward the south all the while trying to stay below the low cloud ceiling and above the helicopter-crunching ground. Just as he started his turn, he hit a radio tower. Suddenly there was a lot of terrific loud crashing noises, a great rending of aluminum-magnesium alloy as the helicopter began to disintegrate around them. Mike did not know what exactly was happening, but he knew he had sustained major damage, they were going down, and he had almost no control of the machine.

When the first of the four rotor blades hit the tower, the impact curled that blade up over the rotor mast, like the arm of a pirouetting ballet dancer. In this position, the blade was no longer a factor in the lift vs. weight component of the aerodynamic formula, being completely neutralized by its position out of the rotor disk. This terrific imbalance, caused by the loss of one blade in four, should have been disastrous for the helicopter. It should have instantaneously thrashed itself to pieces.

Somehow as the helicopter continued through the radio tower, the second blade of the four missed the tower entirely. The third blade hit the metal tower with full force. Its damage from the collision was completely different than the first blade. It must have slid along the structure for the length of the blade. All of the lift-producing portions of the blade were stripped neatly from the blade, leaving only a naked, non-lift-producing spar in the stead of the previously perfect rotor blade. The fourth rotor blade missed the tower, too. Something, probably the now-falling radio tower, perhaps one of the rotor blades or a guy wire, sliced off the tail of the helicopter, leaving it dangling and swinging by the rudder control cables. Lieutenant Hynes was now attempting to fly with only two rotor blades, the tail nearly severed, disabling any semblance of directional control, and falling into enemy territory!

Hynes rolled on full throttle and pulled the guts out of the engine. He hauled up on the collective with all his strength, and pulled full back stick to counter the upset center of gravity of the machine, to try to cushion the crash that he knew was inevitable. Miraculously, due to Mike's quick reactions – and a lot of luck – the aircraft alighted almost delicately on its tires. The remnants of its mangled tail flopped forward onto the ground beside it, still attached only by the rudder control cables.

The copter splashed into a rice paddy in about 18 inches of water. It really was a miracle that it got down to the ground at all without exploding, without one of the damaged rotor blades cutting through the cockpit or the cabin, and without spinning out of control for lack of a tail rotor. Hyne's instinctive reactions made the difference between a crash that the crew all walked away from, and one that should have gone "splat, splash, crash, burn, die" on impact.

Miraculously, no one was seriously hurt. The crew had to dig the Navy corpsman out from under the boxes of resupply ammunition that had fallen all over him, but he, too, was unhurt, discounting minor cuts and bruises.

Hynes' H-34 after hitting radio tower.
Tail of helicopter is on the ground in front of the H-34.

All they had to do was get on the emergency radio and call in Lieutenant Jim Stroupe in the second aircraft to come down and rescue them. That is why two helicopters were always sent out together; in case one went down. Simple as calling mum; it says so, right here in the helicopter handbook.

Lieutenant Stroupe was one of the best. He had a good sense of balance between caution and aggression, great headwork and superb eyesight. He was aware that his leader had gone down, and he was quick to come to the rescue. Stroupe took the time to get out a radio call that his leader was down and he was going in to retrieve the crew. Word immediately spread throughout our camp, and the whole squadron went on full alert, ready to launch in a flash to assist in any way we could.

I had flown all day with Tim O'Toole. Tim was one of the best helicopter pilots ever, bar none, a natural. He was eager to get into the air and go out to see if he could help Mike. I was reluctant to be too over-eager. We already had two helicopters down in the area, for unknown reasons. The weather was as abysmal, and I just did not see any odds in adding to the carnage that I could imagine lying out there in the field. Tim was Mike's brother-in-law, which explains why Tim was so eager to go to Mike's assistance. I just knew I was going to be right out in the middle of this fiasco very soon. We had a term for this kind of situation; we called it a "shit sandwich."

Lining up into the wind and making a beautiful textbook approach to the crash site, Lieutenant Stroupe could see that the area in which Mike had crashed was all open rice paddies. No trees, no hootches to hide enemy troops, no visible hazards. Stroupe could land right on the highway and not even get his tires into the knee deep water. Then they could all go home for a cool one.

As he went in for a nice smooth landing, Stroupe and Sheehan both failed to see telephone wires stretched between poles. As his rotor blades engaged the wires, the resultant torque rolled his helicopter over on its side, and it skidded close to Mike's wreck. Once again Lady Luck rode as a crew member in the final seconds for this second aircraft also did not burn or explode. The four Marines from the second crashed helicopter scrambled out of it and gathered with the crew of the first.

Lieutenant Stroupe's aircraft after hitting telephone wires.

Now we had two crashed helicopters and nine men on the ground, (four pilots, four crewmen and one Navy corpsman), possibly in North Vietnam. Three of the four M-60 machine guns carried by the two ships were lost in the dark, and the fourth one was unusable because no one recovered any ammunition for it. The entire armory available for their defense now consisted of the four .38 caliber handguns carried by the pilots, with six rounds each – 24 bullets total!

As they gathered together to assess their situation, Lieutenant Hynes was obviously the leader. Not just because of his having the senior date of rank of the four officers present and being the flight leader, but also by the fact of his natural leadership abilities. Men in any situation would gravitate to Mike to get them through a scrape, anytime, anywhere. He was that kind of natural born leader. Hynes took control. Hynes said: "We are down in North Vietnam. We surely attracted the enemy's attention with our air show, and we can expect visitors. We'd best do whatever we can to create whatever we can in the way of a defensive perimeter."

Beside the highway they found a burial mound a few yards in diameter. It was only a circular heap of dirt a few inches higher than the surrounding rice paddies, but even this little elevation was better than hunkering down in water. It offered a minimum of protection from bullets should enemy soldiers come visiting.

The airmen didn't have to wait long before they heard troops moving north along the highway toward them. The troops advanced closer. Were these Viet Cong or North Vietnamese Army regulars? The airmen soon could make out distinct shapes moving toward them in the dark. They held their fire. If they were going to die here, they were going to take as many of the enemy with them as they could. Hynes, from Boston, gave what he fully expected to be the last order of his life, "Don't shoot until you see the whites of their eyes!"

What a shame it was going to be to live through that spectacular dual helicopter crash just to be shot down like dogs in the middle of a cold, dark wet rice paddy in an unpopular war, in a dingy little country a long way from home, hearth and family.

Just as things were looking most bleak, Mike heard the sound of a vehicle engine. It sounded to him like the engine of a Jeep. "Hold your fire!" Hynes ordered. Lieutenant Stroupe took the precaution of moving a few yards from the others in case he should draw fire, and yelled, "Does anybody speak English?" Someone answered in English. It was the friendly troops from the small Vietnamese Popular Forces (local militia) base nearby. It was their antenna that Mike's rotor blades had struck.

They were saved.

The Popular Force soldiers took the nine crewmen back to the safety of their small base where they all then endured an intermittent barrage of mortars. The men were able to radio out to our base and report they were in safe hands. I expressed a huge sigh of relief as I learned I did not have to go flying out in such awful monsoon weather with Tim to try to rescue his brother-in-law. As it turned out, not one of the nine men had anything more serious than a scratch or a bruise from this entire incident. They returned to our base at Dong Ha the next day.

Looking south over the dual crash toward friendly P.F. outpost. Dual crash photos provided courtesy of Lieutenant Paul Sheehan, who was copilot in the second H-34 to crash.

Recovery crews came out to the crash site and prepared the helicopters for removal. With the rotor blades taken off, the engines out, and the tails removed, the helicopters became light enough to be lifted out by an H-46. These two crashed helicopters were later rebuilt and returned to service.

After the war, both Lieutenant Hynes and Lieutenant Stroupe stayed in the Marine Corps. Both re-trained in jets and each planned a career in Marine Corps aviation. Captain Mike Hynes was killed in a mid-air collision while flying an A-6 Intruder somewhere in the Southern United States. Lieutenant Stroupe, also promoted to captain, was killed one night when the engine in his A-4 Skyhawk exploded over the desert somewhere near Yuma, Arizona. They both left young widows.

In May of 2004 dual crash survivor, Paul Sheehan communicated with former Sergeant Mike Hoskins, who had been attached to a Marine Corps artillery unit at Gia Linh at the time of the dual crash. Hoskins was writing about his unit's artillery duel with the NVA across the DMZ when he ran across Paul's account of the dual crash. Here is what Hoskins had to say about that night:

There were also 6,000 NVA soldiers within 1.5 miles of Gia Linh, mostly concentrated west/northwest of the firebase. They were staging for an eventual ground attack on the firebase that came in a half-hearted attempt the early morning hours of 28 April after they attacked a second time with artillery. We did not fare as well that night due to a change in battlefield tactics by the NVA.

Your part in this? You crashed in the "middle of" those 6,000 NVA regulars. The DMZ was also crawling with NVA artillery personnel, pulling their weapons back out and remember, we were probed almost every night by gook ground forces, who would have had to pass by you coming and going to Gia Linh the night of the 22nd.

Also, after being hit so hard on the 20th and 21st, we were not hit the night of the 22nd. The four mortars you received was (sic) probably a message telling you they knew you were there. I also believe from my research, the probable reason they did not come after you and your crews was they were still trying to move their artillery under the cover of darkness.

Most of it was towed by animals and would require a great effort on their part to relocate it. We had caught them towing the 105s with elephants north of the Ben Hai in two northeast quadrants on the 21st, we took out the 'Dumbos' [elephants] and their artillery. They had no choice at that time because we had found them the night before but they were still trying to save their 100s from us and night was the only time they could somewhat safely move. I think that is what saved you from death or imprisonment; fate is a funny thing, literally, the odds were 6,000 to 6-8? All were reported to be within walking distance to the PF hamlet you were in.

Another crash

26 March, 1967

In ongoing support of Operation Beacon Hill I, while attempting to take off from a hot LZ after an emergency medevac, one of our helicopters, YZ-69, crashed into the trees. Because of the high trees around the zone the enemy situation, the crew and medevacs were not picked up until the next morning. Although the machine received "strike damage" (was destroyed) no injuries were reported in the crash. The machine was blown up by demolition experts.

10.
Back to Dong Ha

15 April, 1967 we debarked from the USS *Princeton* and installed our squadron at Dong Ha, the place where I had seen so much action the previous fall and the dual crash in March. This remote, dusty, humid place had grown up to be a substantial base in our absence. It now had about 40 hootches, a mess hall, a water treatment plant, an operations tent, helicopter maintenance and parts storage tents, and an admin office tent. It was like any small Marine Corps air base anywhere in Vietnam. We had a small base exchange where we could buy cigarettes, candy and such. There was even a barber shop. That was a huge improvement from when I had been commuting there while based at Phu Bai.

The hootches were the same kind as those we had at Phu Bai and Ky Ha. I staked out a corner and built myself a small desk and bookshelves from discarded ammunition crates. I bought an oscillating fan and placed it right above my cot. Some hot nights I left it running on the high setting all night long, blowing directly down onto me just so I could sleep in the oppressive heat and humidity.

My corner palace at Dong Ha. Note the oscillating fan above my cot.

Myself and hootch mates George Hadzewycz, Eddie Allen, and James Barr.
Missing: Gary Connolly, Mike Hynes, Tim O'Toole, Dan Smithson.
We usually wore only boxers and tee shirts (or not) in the hootch to beat the heat.
Look how skinny we were!

Dong Ha now even had an officer's club in the making. There was a plywood platform for a floor, but the walls were not yet up. Most of us had by now acquired some sort of folding lawn chair, so every evening we gathered on this deck. We sat out in the open and enjoyed the balmy evenings while drinking copious amounts of cold beer and rehashing the events of the day.

SAMs

One of those warm, humid, tropical nights with clear skies, sitting on that deck drinking beer, we watched as a pair of A-4 Skyhawk jets streaked overhead toward the DMZ. We knew they were A-4s by the distinctive whine of their engines. We were only eight miles south of the DMZ, so we knew that those two jets should have to turn around soon. These aircraft were not allowed to cross the border into North Vietnam.

Sure enough, still in our sight, to avoid crossing into North Vietnam, the jets peeled away from each other, scribing a huge horizontal scrotum high in the sky with their contrails. The two pilots intended to re-join formation and fly south. Just as they exposed their tails to the north, two trails of light streamed up from the ground and streaked toward the airplanes. At first we thought they must be nearby parachute flares, but instead of falling earthward as flares do after igniting, these lights kept rising up faster and faster. Soon the streaks were moving much faster than the jets, which we knew were traveling in excess of 250 knots. These had to be surface to air missiles launched from North Vietnam - SAMS!

Like watching a movie, we could see the missiles closing in on the airplanes. It immediately became obvious to us that the two pilots were also aware of the now supersonic high-explosive death headed their way, because the jet pilots once again peeled off in different directions and began evasive maneuvers to escape the jet-hungry missiles. One jet jinked west, the other, east. Only one escaped. We sat and watched the missile close in on the second one. We cheered for the unfortunate pilot, trying to save him with our yells and grunts, but the missile found him and exploded violently as it found its prey, blowing the jet out of the sky. A few seconds later there was another great explosion, which we assumed to be the fuel tanks of the doomed jet blowing up. There's nothing like having a front-row seat to watch one of your compadres blown to bits.

The whole incident took maybe 15 seconds, from initial tallyho of the northbound jets to the second explosion. We were rather demoralized by the incident, but there surely was not a whole lot we could do about it, so we ordered another round of drinks. "A toast to the pilot," said Tim O'Toole, as he raised his beer. "A toast to the toasted pilot!" Dick Basinger quickly added.

For a few seconds we drank in silence and contemplated fate. There was a good chance that the downed A-4 pilot was someone we knew from flight school in Pensacola, and that we would later learn who he was. Or ... more precisely ... who he had been. With just a slight twist of personal history, that could have been any one of us up there that night.

Douglas A-4 Skyhawk From Wikipedia. This is the same type aircraft that the pilot ejected from at Chu Lai.

The next day one of our helicopter crews, flying support missions out in the area just south of the DMZ, picked up a call on the emergency radio frequency. It was the pilot of the A-4 that had been blown out of the sky the previous night. He survived the double explosion. The second explosion had in fact been his ejection seat jettisoning him away from the disabled airplane to safety, not his fuel tanks exploding as we had assumed. He had ridden his parachute to the ground and hid in some bushes all night, waiting for one of our choppers to wander nearby. The rescue crew brought the rattled pilot back to our base, and he eventually returned to his unit, unharmed, with a hell of a story to tell his grandkids.

The next day my mission was to go out to recover the remnants of the SAM missile so that the intelligence people could have a look at it. A good portion of it was still intact.

My blurry picture of remnants of the SAM missile.

During April 1966 the helicopters of HMM-363 flew 1,224.5 hours, carried 4,489 passengers, hauled 194.6 tons of cargo and rescued 662 wounded Marines from the field. I flew 77.5 hours.

External Loads

One reason we were able to carry a lot of cargo in a short time was the capability of the helicopter to carry external loads, also known as "sling loads." On the bottom of most helicopters is a cargo hook.

Loadmasters bundled cargo into manageable loads and wrapped it up in cargo nets. Each cargo net could then be hooked to the cargo hook on any helicopter and snatched off the ground easily and quickly. This made delivery very easy as we did not have to load and unload cargo. All we had to do was punch a button on the cyclic control stick to release the load.

In case that system failed, we had a manual release to drop the load. The mechanical release was triggered by the pilot stomping down on a spring-loaded pedal beside his right foot. Somehow a release activated by foot was called a manual release. (It seems to me that perhaps this should have been called a "footual" release.)

An Army H-34 carries an external. From the Army -10 manual.

Of course, there was always the danger of something falling out of the net, and sometimes the entire load fell from the helicopter without us knowing why. We blamed it on static electricity or hook malfunction.

One incident was quite amusing. My friends Mike Hynes and his copilot Paul Murray were carrying a small all-terrain vehicle to the Marines out in the field in the hills above Khe Sanh. Flying out to the delivery point, Mike briefed Paul on the delivery. "Do not release the load until I say 'Pickle.'" ("Pickle" was our word for pressing the button to release the load). Paul must have been sleepy or tired. All he heard was "pickle," so he pressed that button. The ATV dropped from about 800 feet. Tires bounced high in the air as the ATV impacted the ground and smashed to smithereens. "Oh, well. Let's go get another one."

Paul died in Alaska while flying a Bell Jet Ranger helicopter on the North Slope of Alaska in 1969. On take-off, his skid slid under a root of a bush on the tundra. As he lifted up, the helicopter rolled over, killing him. It was his first civilian job.

Enemy Helicopters!

Occasionally we were sent from Dong Ha to Khe Sanh to support the Marines who held positions atop the hills surrounding Khe Sanh airport, just as we had once been sent to Dong Ha from Phu Bai. I was flying copilot for Captain Arch Ratliff.

Khe Sanh airport from the air, fall of 1966.
At that time, the Khe Sanh area was very peaceful.
Elephants grazed off the end of the runway.

We had heard rumors that enemy helicopters might be operating in the area. Since Khe Sanh was very close to the borders with both

Laos and North Vietnam, this was the most likely area to encounter them. On a break between flights, hanging around operations, a message flashed to us that our Marines in the field were being strafed by an enemy helicopter. Ratliff and I and the second crew dashed to our helicopters, leapt into the air in record time and sped to the area where grunts reported the enemy helicopter.

We were excited because this was a big chance for fame and glory, the chance to do a little air-to-air combat between helicopters and maybe even shoot down an enemy helicopter. We had all been weaned on stories of World War II dogfights. Pappy Boyington and his Marine Corps VMF-214 Black Sheep Squadron were our heroes. Primarily, we were driven to get out there to protect our Marines in the field. No filthy "gomer" helicopter pilot was going to strafe our Marines and get away with it. We were out for revenge, to kill! But when we arrived in the area, there was no enemy helicopter in sight.

We saw only a Vietnamese Air Force (VNAF) H-34 "Butterfly" (the same type machine that we were flying). We contacted the Marines on the ground and confirmed with them that this indeed was the aircraft that had strafed them. The VNAF H-34 was casually flying around the area above the Marine positions. We added maximum power to our engines and caught up with it. We tried to contact it by radio, but we had no common frequency. No joy.

We weren't sure what we were getting into. Was this an enemy helicopter posing as a VNAF? Perhaps it was a renegade VNAF, shooting our Marines on purpose. We didn't know how its crew would react to our presence. We approached from both sides, drew closer and closer to the chopper, anticipating that it might shoot at us. We instructed our crews to bring their machine guns from the outer sides of the helicopters to the inner side of the formation, so that each of our two helicopters now had two M-60 machine guns trained on the VNAF aircraft. Then we slid our formation position tighter and tighter to the VNAF helicopter. We instructed our gunners to be alert and, in the event of any hostile fire from that helicopter, they were cleared to fire at will. We could blast the VNAF helicopter out of the sky in an instant.

Once they noticed us, it only took a few seconds for the pilots of the enveloped H-34 to realize that we were very serious in our actions. Since we were unable to contact them on the radio, we made hand signals for them to return to Khe Sanh airport. They acknowledged and began a very careful, slow and deliberate turn back to the airport. All three helicopters flew back to Khe Sanh airport, landed and shut down.

Captain Ratliff and I were very surprised to see, climbing out of the VNAF helicopter, a United States Air Force lieutenant colonel and a United States Army major. The two pilots climbed down from their machine, got into the back of a six-by truck and ordered their driver to return them to operations. Even though we had just forced them to land, they acted as if we were not even there. Captain Ratliff hailed to the driver of the truck to stop. He then yelled up to the two senior officers. "What the hell do you guys think you were doing out there? Don't you know there were troops below you? You just shot up a bunch of our Marines!" Instead of acting surprised and apologetic, the two got very defensive and arrogant. They acted as if it was their right to go out and shoot up a bunch of our Marines if they wanted to.

Wrong attitude!

Captain Ratliff and I started up the side of the stake bed truck, intent on tearing these two assholes into dog meat. Neither of us gave a thought to the consequences of our actions. Thoughts of courts-martial and years in prison for the very serious offense of assaulting a superior officer were simply pushed to the backs of our minds. For an instant, the thought of any punishment meant nothing to us. No assholes were going to shoot up our Marines and get away with it. Ratliff headed for the throat of lieutenant colonel, and I was headed for the major. Superior rank was going to be no protection for these two flaming assholes from the wrath of two livid Marine Corps helicopter pilots We felt it was our duty to thump these two guys, hang the consequences. Just as we got to the rails and were about to tear into these two jerk-offs, cooler heads prevailed. A few of our comrades grabbed us by our arms and restrained us from climbing further up the truck. By then quite a crowd had gathered, including our commanding officer.

Our CO ordered us to back off and told us to return to operations and write up a report on what had happened, which we did. We learned later that these two were the liaison officers to the to the Vietnamese Army unit at Khe Sanh and they had been out for a familiarization flight of the area. They had not bothered to consult any troop deployment maps, had not talked to any officers in charge of the troops in the field, and, consequently, they had no idea where any troops were deployed. If anybody should have known where the troops were deployed, these two morons should have known. They just happen to be over our Marines when they decided to test their machine guns. Fortunately no Marines on the ground were killed. One required a medevac for a wound to his thigh. It probably saved his life in the long run. I doubt seriously that any reprimand was given to the two jerk-offs. The wounded Marines were surely given Purple Hearts for their injuries due to "direct enemy action."

A South Vietnamese Air Force H-34 "Butterfly,"
similar to the one that shot up our Marines.

Rocket Attack

8 May 1967, Dong Ha.

I was awakened by several loud explosions. From a deep sleep
I leapt up, throwing aside my mosquito netting and running for the
hootch door, shouting at the top of my voice, "Incoming! Incoming!"
There was no doubt about the sound of it. I knew the sound of
"outgoing" from my experience at Tam Ky. This was decidedly different.

I hit the back door of the hootch, turned hard left, rushing for
the bunker opening as another 130mm rocket came screaming close
overhead. The sound was at once a loud hissing scream, a loud whistle
and a loud hum. It sounded too close for me to take the additional
half dozen steps to the bunker, so I dove onto my belly and tried to
become one with the sand. One of my hootch mates right behind me
was braver (or more scared). He ran right over me, stepping on my
foot as he continued his dash to safety. When my buddy stepped on
my heel, he pushed my bare toes into the rice-paddy dirt, forcing a
small stone about the size of a half grain of rice under the toenail of
my right big toe.

After that barrage, I slithered into the bunker with about 20
other guys, and we spent a very uncomfortable couple of hours there
until all-clear was announced. At one point Captain Paul Courtney,
suffering from a bad case of diarrhea, had to move his bowels. He
was too much of a gentleman to let loose there in the bunker, where
the smell would have made the rest of us very uncomfortable, if not
sick. Perhaps the smell might have driven us out into the fresh but
shrapnel-filled air. Finally, in severe discomfort, Paul excused himself
and left the bunker in the middle of the bombardment. "Tell Mom I
love her," were his last words as he ascended the steps of the bunker.
He somehow sat through the remainder of the bombardment in the
nearby outhouse without injury.

Lieutenant Dan Smithson, while scrambling to the bunker from his
hootch, had the presence of mind to grab a small tape recorder and carry
it into the bunker. He recorded some of the most graphic and honest

thoughts of this bunch of young Marine Corps officers that could have ever been recorded. There was a war going on right above our heads, and we did not feel safe to even peek out and see what was going on. Also, there was the threat of one of the big missiles falling directly onto our bunker.

We had to take for granted that the Marines defending our base and fighting the enemy off were doing their job. But ... what if they weren't? What if they were failing? What if an enemy soldier came to the door of the bunker shooting full bursts of automatic fire? A spray of bullets would get us all! We felt extremely vulnerable.

There is no way I could ever begin to duplicate the honest, earthy, genuine remarks of this bunch of young Marine officers facing possible death. Much of the conversation revolved around how very disconcerting it felt to be sitting in the bunker feeling helpless and not knowing what was going on in the world above us. We felt very naked. No one had a weapon, most of us wearing only boxer shorts. What if the attack were successful and the enemy was able to penetrate to our defenses? We could all be shot to death down here in this dark, dank hole in the ground. How embarrassing it would be to have no chance to defend ourselves.

We also wondered what would happen should the bunker take a direct hit. Many of us would be killed, maimed and badly wounded. We represented probably half the pilots of the squadron. What a disaster either of these possible events could be.

The Smithson tape would have been the basis for a great movie or novel all by itself. Everybody wanted a copy of the tape. Dan promised to duplicate it and send a copy to each of us.

Unfortunately, after his tour in Vietnam, Dan loaned the mini-recorder to his very religious mother-in-law. She took it to her church and recorded a sermon over the top of our great adventure. Much to his mother in-law's great embarrassment, there was only one word left over of our adventure in the bunker. At the end of the sermon, the single word "FUCK!"

Leftover rockets from the rocket attack on our base.

Rocket shrapnel fragments gathered after the attack.

One of our pilots never made it to his bunker. Lieutenant Rob Lancaster had decided, based on the rumors of a possible attack, that he wanted quicker access to his bunker than the rest of us had to ours. He did not want to have to run the length of his tent to get to the door, then have to run the same distance back between tents to get to his bunker (as we had done from our hootch). He cleverly loosened the piece of corrugated sheet metal that formed the bottom half of the tent wall next to his bed, and placed it back into its position, hanging loosely on its nails. His idea was a good one; in case of attack he would simply roll out of bed onto the floor, push the sheet of metal out of the way, and slide down into his bunker.

This clever idea almost worked for him. Came the attack, he woke up abruptly, rolled onto the floor and charged the metal with his head, intending to head-butt it out of the way. He slammed into the metal, knocking himself unconscious, and fell to the floor, where he spent the remainder of the attack exposed to the barrage. In the excitement of the barrage, he forgot that he had changed hootches that same day, and had not yet gotten around to loosening the piece of sheet metal on his new hootch. Except for a headache, he also was unharmed.

Early the next morning we saw that 130mm rockets and 81mm mortars had peppered the base, blasting craters out of the earth large enough to hide VW Beetles. All through this, our helicopters sat out in the open, unprotected by revetments or even by the guards who hunkered down in their trenches. When all was tallied up, very few troops were hurt, all wounds were minor, and there was very little damage to our machines.

The Marines found many dead Viet Cong on our perimeter fence. One of them was our base barber, who, in weeks prior, had given me several haircuts. At the end of each haircut, he had trimmed my neck with an old-time straight razor.

When I returned to my hootch, I found a hole in my locker door about navel height. Embedded into it was a piece of shrapnel about the size of a quarter, but shaped like a thumbnail, flat on one side, round on the other, about a quarter inch thick.

I drew a bull's-eye around the hole in my locker, just for fun.

I point to the shrapnel hole in my locker.
Note my sleeping cot right behind my knees.

Standing in rocket blast hole about 50 feet from my hootch door. This is probably the blast that caused me to get the Purple Heart and made the hole in my locker.

Strangely enough, the accuracy of the attack was somehow connected to the team of Vietnamese surveyors who had "surveyed" their way up the road to and through our security gate just few days prior to the attack. They looked so official that no one ever thought to question them about what they were doing. They surveyed right through our front gate and down the main street of our camp, taking notes all the way.

May 1967, the pilots of HMM-363 flew 1,640 hours, carried 3,345 passengers, hauled 567 tons of cargo, and rescued 1,583 medevacs. I personally flew 58 hours.

The Summer of Love

The summer of 1967 was the "Summer of Love." I spent most of the summer of love trying to avoid being murdered by my fellow man.

I have often wondered what path my life might have taken had I not been recruited by Captain Thatcher into the MARCAD program. Sometimes I think I might have been right in the middle of the hippie phenomenon. Living very near San Francisco, I could have very easily have been seduced into becoming a long-haired, pot-smoking, draft-dodging, love-in attending war protester.

While I was based at Tustin after my tour in Vietnam, the war protests started breaking out all over the country. At USMC Lighter-Than-Air Facility Tustin I was assigned to be the Riot Control officer for the base. Should those filthy hippies try to enter our base, I was in charge of the squad of riot control Marines especially trained to repel them at our gate.

In Berkeley the students were rioting and the Hell's Angels Motorcycle group volunteered to help the California National Guard to quell the riots. Governor Reagan declined their offer. The National Guard used helicopters to spray tear gas on the rioters. At the time I wished I could be one of those National Guard helicopter pilots. In my later years, I have decided that I wish I had been one of the protesters.

I am awarded a Purple Heart

Later that morning, after the rocket attack, my toe was throbbing. I knew I could get a bad infection from this dirty small stone under my toenail, so I went to the flight surgeon, Doc Houts, to get the stone removed. He took a simple tool and flicked the stone out from under my toenail and painted my toe tip purple with Mercurochrome. He then picked up a clip board and wrote my name down on a list. I said, "Doc, if that is a Purple Heart list, forget it; take my name off it." This was not a wound to speak of, and it was not inflicted by the enemy. The blood I lost would not dampen one-tenth of a Q-tip. I figured there was at least one honest Purple Heart in my immediate future anyway, if not a posthumous one.

I forgot all about that until mid-August 1967 when I was checking out of the squadron to rotate to CONUS.[8] The admin clerks did not have my orders ready, so while I was waiting for them to finish, I flipped through my file. On the awards page I saw that I had

---

8 CONUS: Short for Continental United States, otherwise known as the land of the big PX, and the land of "round-eyed" women.

been awarded a list of medals, mostly air medals. I also saw I had been awarded the Navy Commendation Medal, with a combat "V" for valor, for my FAC experience in Quang Ngai. Then I noticed in the middle of the list, between air medals, the award, "PH." *What the hell is PH?* I wondered. Then I realized that I had been awarded the Purple Heart for that minor wound ("avulsion great right toe") in the Dong Ha rocket barrage. Oh, well. I couldn't refuse it now; it was a done deal.

Another friend dies

"As a pilot only two bad things can happen to you, and one of them will:
a. One day you will walk out to the aircraft, knowing it is your last flight.
b. One day you will walk out to the aircraft, not knowing it is your last flight."

–Author unknown

12 May, 1967, north of Dong Ha.
A good friend, Dick Basinger, was killed. Dick and his copilot, George Hadzewycz, while departing a hot zone just south of Con Thien, in support of the 1st Battalion, 4th Marines were struck by a rocket propelled grenade (RPG) or mortar fire at about one hundred feet of altitude. The helicopter crashed on its right side and burst into flames.

George and the gunner, both on the left side of the helicopter, scrambled out, badly injured. Dick and his crew chief, Corporal John Wendell Jackson, did not get out.

Dick and I had spent hours drinking beer at the Dong Ha officer's club, discussing what we were going to do with our lives once we returned home from the war.

Now he was dead. He left a young widow.

I visited George on a trip through Pensacola in early 1968, where he was still recovering from his extensive wounds, but I never heard from him or about him again.

Sometimes the B-52 bombers bombed the area between Dong Ha and the DMZ, which was about eight miles away. When one of these "Arc-Light" strikes happened, we could feel the earth shake at Dong Ha. If we were flying, we could see huge clouds of dust flying. At least the B-52 bombing runs were announced ahead of time, so we knew what areas to stay away from. I wonder if the enemy was privy to those same notices. Probably. I am sure these bomb strikes had to be devastating for the enemy underneath them and beneficial for the Marines up at the front. The aftermath of one of these strikes left neat rows of holes about 20-30 feet in diameter and 10-12 feet deep. Later when it rained, they became rows of ponds.

I heard years later that the Vietnamese now use these ponds as fish farms.

29 May 1967, north of Dong Ha.
Helicopter YZ-74 crashed while landing in an LZ as the port strut rolled into a deep pit and the aircraft partially turned onto its side. The medevacs and crew were returned to Dong Ha unharmed in their wingman's helicopter. YZ-74 was recovered the next day by an H-53.

An F-4 Phantom drops in on us

At Dong Ha, one afternoon in July 1967, several of us were approaching our helicopters in the rice paddy, preparing to take off on a mission, when suddenly the roaring sound of an F-4 Phantom jet fighter passing very low and very close nearly struck us dumb. We could tell from the markings that it was an U.S. Air Force F-4, and we just thought that the idiot Air Force pilot was having some fun by buzzing our base at low altitude and high speed. Cheap thrills for him, we thought, but at his speed he could have easily run into one of our helicopters taking off or landing. As we flinched from the sudden aural assault, one of the fellows, pointing east toward the sea, said, "Look there!"

About half a mile out, on short final approach, was a second F-4, silently gliding into our short PSP (pierced steel planking) airstrip, engine out.

His wingman had buzzed our strip to get out attention because we had no common radio frequency, and he wanted us to know his buddy was coming in "dead stick" (without power). We watched as the Air Force pilot made a perfect Air Force landing on our 2,000 foot long runway. I call it a perfect Air Force landing because this pilot was used to landing at Air Force bases where he had a 6,000- to 8,000-foot runway to land on. He normally took much more room to touch down than the length of our entire short runway; he wasted half our 2,000 feet by landing in the middle of it. It was obvious that he was going to run off the west end of the runway.

As he departed the runway, still traveling about 50 mph, he failed to raise his landing gear. That oversight immediately rectified itself. Right off the end of our runway was a ditch about 20 feet wide and about eight feet deep. As he crossed that ditch, the embankment on the opposite side neatly removed everything from his aircraft that was extended or hanging down. Landing gear, flaps, bomb racks, whatever there was, flew up into the sky in a big cloud of debris and dust.

Fortunately, the Air Force pilot did a skillful job of sliding the heavy jet to a stop, and it did not roll over or flip end for end as it could easily have done. In that event, he probably would have died. He got out and walked away, abandoning the heap of scrap metal that had once been an expensive, powerful high-tech jet fighter-bomber.

The wreckage sat there for weeks. We all assumed it was a write-off, so whenever we needed a piece of tubing or a piece of scrap metal for something, we would go over to the disabled jet and help ourselves. Several of the fellows used fuel and hydraulic tubing to improvise a water heater so we could have hot showers. Some of the guys even went so far as to take out some of the flight instruments and cockpit controls.

Much to our surprise, weeks later an Air Force crew arrived and began to take the jet apart. They removed the wings and then, using a huge fork lift, placed the rest of the hulk on a big truck and hauled it away for repairs. I believe we did tens of thousands of dollars worth of damage to the aircraft as it sat there, but no one ever came around to ask for the parts back, or asked why we took them or what we did with them.

Another one for the taxpayers.

U.S. Marine Corps F-4 Phantom jet fighter-bomber – Wikipedia.

Another flight hazard was parachute flares. At night the troops in the field would have the orbiting C-130s or C-47s drop huge parachute flares. As these bright-burning stars descended slowly from the sky, they gave the troops on the ground light so they could see.

Sometimes the burned out flares still floated around in the sky, impossible to see. Occasionally we encountered dud flares that had never ignited that were a major hazard to our flying machines. I saw one flash by in a blur like a giant ghost jellyfish. Had it been in our direct path, these is no way we could have avoided hitting it. Running into a 50-pound flare hanging on a small parachute would have ruined our night.

Parachute flares light up an outpost. Source: Wikipedia

Call Smoke

To find the troops in the field we were supporting, we had a very high-tech navigating system. On the wall in our ready room hung a large tactical map of our operating area. In the center of the map, right where our base was located, there was a nail sticking out of the wall. Around the nail was fixed a cheap, circular plastic protractor with zero degrees oriented to north on the map. There were concentric circles penciled on the map at one-mile intervals from home base. Attached to the nail was a string. It was a simple matter to find on the map the coordinates of the unit we were to support. Then we pulled the string out to those coordinates. This showed us instantly what direction and distance we had to fly to find them. After that it was a simple task to use our TACAN navigation radio to duplicate these numbers.

Once overhead the general area, we established radio contact with the grunts on the ground. They marked their LZ with smoke grenades. Once activated, these spewed out a very dense cloud of red, green, yellow, purple or white smoke, the purpose of which was twofold. The primary reason for the smoke was simply to mark the LZ from the surrounding countryside and to tell us exactly where the grunts wanted us to land. The smoke made it much easier to find Marines dressed in camouflage in a landscape of green and brown rice paddies. The second reason for the smoke was to give us pilots a distinct and immediate picture of the wind conditions in the LZ. It was very important to know the wind direction and velocity so we could land into the wind whenever possible.

When I was first in Vietnam, it was easy enough to establish where to land. We would simply fly out to the general area where the unit was, call them on the radio, and ask them to, "Pop a smoke." In the early days, a pilot would just say "OK, I have your smoke," and he would spiral down to alight beside the smoke in the LZ.

As the war progressed and the enemy accrued some captured equipment, tactics became more challenging. As soon as the Marines radioed they had popped smoke, several smokes popped at the same time in the surrounding area. When we pilots contacted the ground unit, we had to ask them what color smoke they had popped. Any time a unit was unwise enough to tell us what color smoke they were going to smoke before they popped it, we might expect to see several smokes of the same color over an area of a quarter-mile square. To descend over the wrong smoke was to get shot at, probably get hit, and very possibly sustain damage to your machine and perhaps get someone wounded or killed.

We had to get trickier, and trickier. We asked the Marines to pop smoke and to then identify the color. Then the enemy countered with waiting until we had identified the color of the smoke, and threw out a similar one, hoping that in our confusion of the spiraling descent that we might pick up on the wrong smoke, and fall into their trap. To counter this, once we determined the correct smoke, we often called artillery or gunships to attack the site of the bogus smokes.

Sometimes we could not spiral down directly to the troops, and we had to take an indirect route. Our tactics evolved to the point that one helicopter would orbit over the LZ and talk to the grunts, while the second helicopter would go a half-mile away, make a plummeting descent, trade his vertical speed for horizontal speed, and then zoom toward the LZ at a very low altitude, so low that any enemy on the ground would not have time to aim and fire his weapon as the helicopter flashed over.

The H-34 handbook says the maximum airspeed for the H-34 is 129 knots. I routinely saw speeds of 148 knots (163 mph)!

The obvious problem with this was that the low-and-fast-flying helicopter pilot had some difficulty determining just where he was in relationship to the LZ. The rice-paddy countryside all looked similar, especially at low level and 140+ knots. Our counter to this was that the helicopter on high, orbiting above the LZ, would then guide the lower one in by radio, a radio-controlled approach, so to speak. "You are a quarter of a mile out; turn left ten degrees, 500 yards out now, doing OK, right five degrees, get ready to begin flare, FLARE NOW!" It was a little risky, and required absolute faith in your buddy to do this kind of an approach, but we made it work, and we made it work well. Those were our Marines in the field. We had to get their ammunition and supplies to them. We had to get our wounded Marines out.

A natural outcome of this kind of flying was what we called the "blade stall approach." Aerodynamically, the helicopter was flying at its maximum speed at about 148 knots, considering the temperature, humidity, air density, and altitude at the average LZ. To go any faster or to put any more load on the rotor system was to risk retreating blade stall, a condition in which the left half of the rotor disk ceases to produces lift, while the right half of the disk produces maximum lift. If blade stall is allowed to fully develop, the resultant imbalance in lift of the rotor disk is such that the helicopter will flop over very abruptly and violently onto its left side.

Fortunately, in the H-34 anyway, retreating blade stall gives good warning before full stall occurs. In the very beginning, the helicopter starts to waddle and shuffle; then the rotor system starts to make a distinctive, almost grunting, noise, and as it progresses, the helicopter starts to buck like a horse. We figured the bucking was the last stage before a violent roll-over. At this point, to add any more stress onto the rotor system was to go too far, and we knew it. It was time to back off a bit.

So it was: make a screaming 4,800 feet per minute rate of descent to tree-top level, pull enough power and back stick to get into level flight before smashing into the ground, translate that horrific rate of descent into maximum horizontal air speed of 148 knots, then fly at tree-top level for a half-mile or so, downwind relative to the LZ, then manipulate the helicopter into a maneuver which was basically a prolonged, hairy horizontal autorotation.

About Autorotations

Most people think that when the engine of a helicopter quits, the machine drops out of the sky like a rock. Nothing could be farther from the truth. When the engine quits, an automatic clutch mechanism in every helicopter disengages the engine from the rotor system, removing what would be a dead drag on it. The rotor system is then free-wheeling.

Yes, the helicopter does instantly drop into rapid descent, but the air flow through the rotor reverses and air begins to flow up through the rotor blades. (Think of putting a child's pinwheel into a stiff breeze.) This reverse air flow causes the blades to keep turning, and they keep producing lift. True, the helicopter is coming down a pretty good rate, but the pilot has absolute control. In most helicopters it is the turning rotor that powers the electrical generator and the primary hydraulic systems, so the helicopter usually loses none of these essential items.

It is then just a matter of having someplace to land. A skillful pilot can put his helicopter down in a space as small as a tennis court and walk away with no damage to the machine and of course no injuries. We practiced this maneuver hundreds of times during our flight school and routinely practiced many more times after flight school. Every training flight usually included a few practice "autos."

It is when there is no place to land that things get a bit dicey, but many helicopters have been crash landed in forest and jungle or ditched into water, and the occupants survived. Catastrophic failures of the H-34 rotor system were so rare as to be not worthy of mention.

At about that time, if we did it all correctly, all forces balanced out to a hover at zero airspeed and zero altitude. To achieve this we had to slowly bring in maximum power and simultaneously reduce collective lift, to not cause us to rise above the ground and give the enemy a target. As we slowly pulled in this maximum power we gave the left rudder pedal (anti-torque) just a little less pressure than what was needed to keep the nose straight on. This caused the nose of the H-34 to drift left, giving the pilot an unobstructed view of the terrain in front of him. This was corrected when he added landing power. The added torque brought the nose to the right and lined us perfectly for landing straight ahead. Sometimes as we pulled in maximum power, we used much less left pedal which would cause the helicopter to make an abrupt 180 degree turn to the left, to turn us into the LZ. It was a hairy maneuver and not for the faint of heart, but we got the point where we did it routinely. So far as I know, no one ever crashed while doing this.

To depart a hot LZ we then reversed the process. We added maximum power, dumped the nose over and stayed as close to the tree-top level as we safely could. We accelerated at low level, right down on the tree tops, until our speed was near the maximum, then we pulled back hard on the stick, putting the machine into an exhilarating zoom climb. At times I saw a momentary rate of climb of 4,800 feet per minute here. These procedures worked soundly to prevent us from taking hits from the enemy rifles and machine guns. The enemy soldiers on the ground did not have time to raise their rifles and shoot, we passed over them so quickly. The scariest part was the first few seconds immediately after take-off. We flew right over the enemy and we had not yet attained any great speed to avoid enemy bullets.

Adrenaline rush

To do one of these hairy, high-speed, high danger approaches, and to then come out of a hot LZ with bullets flying and both machine guns blazing, was an extreme adrenaline rush. I remember feeling omniscient, that I was at once aware of everything around me in both micro- and macro-perspectives. I knew what was being said on any one or all of three radios, I was aware of the grunt situation on the ground. I knew what my copilot was doing. I knew the status of my engine and all the readings on my instrument panel. I knew where and what my wingman was doing. I felt my thinking was clearer than ever before. I was simultaneously aware of the feelings in my body from the beating of my heart to the tingling in my fingertips, from the blood rushing through my arteries to my fingertips. At least once I was also aware that I simultaneously raised my left butt cheek and farted. Adrenaline gave me all this awareness at once.

I became addicted to this adrenaline rush, craving it, seeking it out time after time.

The H-34 was a tough machine. It could take a beating. Built for shipboard operations, it had massive oleo struts that could absorb a lot of energy on hard landings. The big balloon tires gave it even more cushion.

Whenever we approached into a contested LZ, we came in hot and fast. We quickly learned that if we stabbed our tail wheel into the ground while making a final high, nose-up flare into the LZ, it slowed us down. Then we let the machine fall through the translational lift, settling to the ground. The big tires and struts absorbed the extra momentum and brought us down gently. Sometimes, room permitting, we also rolled 20 to 30 feet to decelerate more gently. Our very effective disc brakes allowed us to control this final roll-out phase of the landing.

The collective control. The collective in a helicopter is a horizontal lever just below and parallel to the pilot's left forearm. By adjusting that lever up or down, the pilot collectively increases or decreases the angle of attack at which all the rotor blades bite the air. Overly simplified, if a pilot wishes to descend, he decreases the "pitch" or angle of attack of the blades to create less lift. If he wants to ascend, he increases the pitch of the blades to create more lift. If he is interested in rapidly departing a hot LZ, he can change the attitude of the helicopter by lowering the nose, turning that (relative to the vertical axis of the machine) vertical lift into forward thrust-airspeed. Conversely, in combat situations, coming hot and fast into a contested LZ, we threw the nose of the helicopter up and then added full power. To keep from climbing, we reduced the collective pitch to reduce upward lift. The combination made for a fast, powered deceleration.

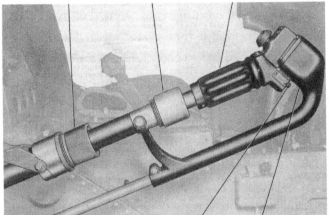

The collective control with throttle. NATOPS manual.

Throttle. The H-34 was the last major helicopter built that used a reciprocating (piston) engine. Subsequently, most helicopters have turbine engines. The advantage of the turbine is that it allows for a governor that keeps the RPM at a steady rate, usually called one hundred percent. The pilot then does not have to worry about maintaining his RPM manually. With a recip engine, the throttle had to be regulated manually by the pilot.

In the H-34, as in most recip helicopters, the throttle is on the collective lever and is rigged much like the throttle on a motorcycle – a rotating sleeve surrounding the end of the collective stick that the pilot can twist with an easy turn of his wrist. RPM had to be maintained within certain parameters. Too much RPM would be harmful to the engine which might cause it to fail. Too little RPM would not create enough lift. At very low RPM it was theoretically possible for the blades to stop providing lift altogether, which would have been disastrous. I never heard of this happening.

The tail rotor is simply a small rotor system mounted vertically; the tail rotor blades can be adjusted by the pilot using the airplane-like rudder pedals. Rudder pedals increased or reduced anti-torque as needed.

It took a few hours to learn to control the RPM with the manual throttle. Every time any power was added, corresponding left tail rudder had to be added to counter the torque and to keep the aircraft going straight. Conversely, any time power was reduced, right tail rudder pedal had to be added to compensate for the reduced torque.

We found that when using low power while coming into a short final approach into a landing zone, it was advantageous to use a little less right rudder than was required to keep the nose pointed straight ahead. This caused the nose to drift left, giving the command pilot in the right seat a totally unobstructed view of what lie in front of the helicopter. Adding power just at touchdown brought the nose right and lined the helicopter up for a perfect straight-ahead landing.

Cyclic is another word for "stick." It functioned just as the control stick (or wheel) in any aircraft. Usually as some change in RPM and torque cause a slight change in the attitude of the helicopter. The cyclic would require a small adjustment to keep the aircraft in the same attitude.

All of these compensations and changes became second nature to us. We got to the point where we could tell our RPM by ear and did not have to distract ourselves by looking frequently at the RPM gauge. We did not drive these H-34 helicopters. We did not fly them. We put them on. They became an extension of our bodies. We became one with them.

USS Repose

Many times when we picked up wounded Marines, we took them directly to the hospital ship USS *Repose*, which loitered offshore specifically for that purpose. I am sure that many Marines and soldiers are alive today because of the immediate care that was available just those few minutes away instead of in Da Nang or even farther away. There were times that we delivered wounded Marines from the LZ to the operating room in fewer than 15 minutes. We always felt good about being able to carry our wounded comrades to such a nice, clean place.

It was a nice break from our normal routine to fly out to the *Repose* and to land on the gleaming white ship with the Red Cross insignia. The thing that most made it a special treat was that whenever we went out there we could see "round-eye" nurses on deck. Sometimes if we were lucky, we might see the nurses sunning themselves on the topmost decks. That always got our young hormones going.

Often as we flew out to the ship with wounded Marines we would call ahead and ask someone to meet us at the helo with cigarettes for those members of the squadron who smoked. Usually the only cigarettes available were Raleigh's. These were the cigs that came with coupons that you could save up for premiums. One day Captain Rudy Nebel and I were flying out, and he asked specifically for a carton of Raleigh's. The ship's radioman asked Captain Nebel if he saved those coupons (thinking perhaps, if the captain did not, that he could keep the coupons for himself?). Captain Nebel's immediate and spontaneous response was, "Of course I collect those coupons; where do you think I got this nifty helicopter?"

One day the ship's crew brought us a large, round cardboard container of ice cream. We took that immediately back to base and shared it with our fellows. This very special treat was consumed instantly.

Hospital ship USS *Repose*.

If you look carefully, you can see an H-34 sitting on the aft deck of the USS *Repose*.

In early July 1967, I had occasion to spend a night aboard the USS *Repose*. I had orders for an R&R to Taiwan, but when I got to Da Nang to catch my plane, I was told that my orders were wrong. I was a day early reporting to Da Nang. I had a whole day to myself. Rather than return to Dong Ha simply to turn right around and go back to Da Nang again the next day, I chose to stay in Da Nang. When I learned one of our helicopters was going out to the USS *Repose*, I hitched a ride out to visit with my friend Jim Stroupe. Jim had taken a bullet to his left leg and was recovering from surgery on board. As I was visiting with Jim, he invited me to join him at the officer's mess for dinner with the ship's officers, including the nurses. I couldn't pass up this opportunity. The food was great. The company was better. I was wearing a khaki uniform for traveling on R&R, so I was dressed formally enough to join the junior officers' mess on this ship.

I enjoyed dinner so much that I missed the last helicopter back to shore because the helicopters rarely flew out to the USS *Repose* after dark. Darn! I was forced to spend the night aboard the ship. At dinner I met and had a lengthy conversation with one of the nurses, Dolly, from Aberdeen, Washington. She was brunette, blue-eyed, very well built, charming and very friendly. I was in love! When it was time to retire I was given a nice, quiet, clean air-conditioned stateroom all to myself. I slept well with dreams of sweet nurse Dolly in my head, dreaming that she might sneak into my room in the middle of the night. For a few weeks after that nurse Dolly and I passed notes to each other via the helicopters going and coming from the USS *Repose*, but I never got the chance to see her again. She eventually was transferred to Whidbey Island, Washington State. We corresponded for a while, but we never saw each other again.

June 1967, the pilots of HMM-363 flew 1,290 hours, carried 3,239 passengers, hauled 783 tons of cargo and rescued 726 medevacs. I personally flew 72 hours.

McNamara's Road

About late spring or early summer 1967 somebody in the higher echelons of the war machine came up with a sure-fire way to stop the North Vietnamese army from infiltrating troops into South Vietnam. It was decided to build what came to be known as "McNamara's Road." The idea was to sterilize a swath of ground about a thousand feet wide, to create a space that could be observed and controlled, an obstacle to keep the enemy from advancing into South Vietnam. Many bulldozers and huge brush clearing machines arrived and began scraping this path clean of all vegetation, and by default, any living thing, thereby denying the enemy a route into South Vietnam from the north.

No one seemed to take into consideration that the path would naturally have to end at the mountains to the west, that there was sea to the east or that it got dark every night. The destructive work went on. We supported the troops protecting the operators of the huge forest-eating machines. The major advantage of the road was that any time we had troubles with one of our helicopters, we had a huge, wide, long, clear place to land. I left two helicopters out there myself, one while flying with Major Eckman, as related elsewhere. The whole idea was insane to start with, and all it did was create enormous environmental destruction. Sometime later we described it as "McNamara's folly."

McNamara's Road

THE ADVENTURES OF A HELICOPTER PILOT

Yet another H-34 left for the recovery crews to rescue.

We always flew two helicopters together in case one of us went down, which was often. I left two or three helicopters in the field, but never under any great duress. I would get a warning light telling me something was coming apart. I would land safely, before it did.

Another time I had a chip light that had gathered large pieces of metal on the magnetic plug. That engine was finished. I left that one in McNamara's Road for the recovery crews, too. Sometimes the warning lights were false alarms. Bits of carbon or water could build up on the plugs to complete the warning circuit.

Our Wright 1820-84A engines were good for only 600 hours before they required changing. The dangerous periods of time on engines were the first 50 hours and the last 50 of those 600 hours. Defects in overhauls occasionally caused engines to fail within the first 50 hours. Sometimes we worked the engines so hard that they did not make the full 600 hours between overhauls. The maintenance crews kept busy.

6 June 1967, near Dong Ha

YZ-64 lost all engine power while attempting to depart an LZ. The crew abandoned the helicopter, which was later recovered, and returned to Dong Ha without damage.[9]

7 June, Hill 881, Khe Sanh

While waiting in the LZ to load wounded Marines, a mortar round exploded next to the helicopter, killing eight Marines instantly. The helicopter received only minor shrapnel damage and continued to fly.[10]

25 June Dong Ha

While approaching the fuel pits at Dong Ha after a night medevac mission, YZ-66 lost control due to some unknown mechanical failure, struck the ground in a nose-down attitude and overturned. The pilot and copilot escaped the now-burning machine and were able to rescue the injured gunner. The pilot tried to rescue the crew chief, but he was unable. The crew chief perished in the ensuing fire.[11]

Here is a picture of a helicopter I left behind after having engine trouble. I had an engine chip light. Investigation showed large pieces of metal on the magnetic oil sump plug. It was an engine failure about to happen.

9 Texas Tech Archives.
10 Texas Tech Archives.
11 Texas Tech Archives.

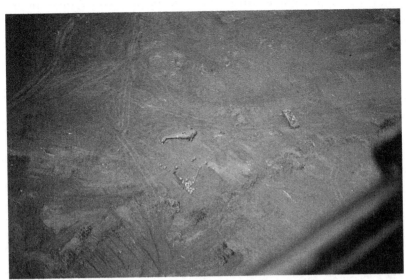

Another one of my buddies had an engine failure and crashed into the road. He must have hit a hole or a stump to cause him to roll over. No one was injured.

Sometimes a pilot would have a hard landing and knock off one of his struts. He would return to base and the helicopter mechanics would stack up a pile of sandbags so he could place his "lame foot" on the pile while the strut was repaired

Part of the road plan was to build tall towers so that troops could sit in the towers and observe the enemy crossing the road. The towers were built horizontally lying on the ground. A huge Army flying crane then came to lift them up into the vertical, take them to their emplacements. I watched an army Sky Crane lifting one of these pre-fabricated towers up and take it away.

A Marine runs from the dust cloud kicked up by the Sky Crane.

Somehow, no one could get Vietnamese soldiers to place themselves in such a vulnerable position, to be a grand target suspended well above the ground in a tower that might be blown over at any time. That road idea went by the wayside, leaving an enormous scar on the countryside, when it became obvious that the enemy could walk across the strip at night, make an end run around it in the mountains on the west end, and probably just ignore the whole thing anyway. From what I learned later about the tunneling capabilities of the enemy, they could have possibly tunneled under the road, too.

One day I was flying with Major Eckman near the east end of McNamara's Road. We got warning lights telling us that our engine was about to quit. For safety, we landed as close as we could to a Marine outpost on top of a small rise. The Marines at that redoubt got all excited and radioed us not to land where we were, but to move a hundred feet further out. Major Eckman was unknowingly landing us in the middle of the Marines' protective mine field. Fortunately our engine had enough power remaining to get us away, and we did not trigger any mines. We left that one for the recovery crews, too.

I kept a rough tally in my mind. By the time I left Vietnam, I had rescued four other pilots. I had been rescued five times. Never were any of these under any great duress. They were just a factor of how hard we worked our engines.

Later, while flying for Air America in Laos, I got ahead on that score.

Agent Orange

Another huge environmental impact was Agent Orange. I was flying out west of Quang tri with another pilot when we saw three U.S. Air Force C-123s flying along in formation, spraying out a cloud of spray behind them, like low level crop dusters. I asked my HAC, "What the hell is that?" He answered that the Air Force planes were spraying herbicide to kill the vegetation to deprive the enemy of cover.

He assured me that the spray was, "Only herbicide, and it is not harmful to people." We all learned much more about that in the years to come.

Air Force C-123s spray agent Orange over the countryside.
Photo Source: Wikipedia

July 1967, the pilots of HMM-363 flew 1,379 hours, carried 2,864 passengers, hauled 443 tons of cargo and rescued 1,137 medevacs. I personally flew 68 hours.

First R&R, Taipei, Taiwan

14 May 1967 to 25 May 1967

My first R&R was to Taipei, Taiwan. From my earlier time here, while visiting aboard the USS *Iwo Jima*, I knew the location the Military Assistance Command, Vietnam (MACV) Officer's Club. I thought it would be a good base of operations during my R&R. But my squadron buddies were not there to play silly drinking games with. I found it boring, so I decided to leave. As I walked out the door, I locked eyes with an attractive brunette who was entering. One of us said something which led to more conversation. Her name was Linda. She frequented the club to round up business for a tailor. Her main goal in going to the MACV club was to meet guys and entice them to his establishment so that she could make a commission.

While I was there I did a lot of shopping at the PX, and Linda also took me to a shop where I purchased a large teak inlaid foot locker for my younger sister Tanya's upcoming birthday. (As a Marine, I couldn't call it a hope chest.) I had read the regulations on the post office wall about the size limitations for mailing items, and I thought the chest was within them. When I got to the post office, the counter man scoffed. The trunk was way too large to mail home. So what to do with it?

I took it to the R&R center where we marshaled up to catch our flight back to RVN and asked the young Army officer in charge if I could take this thing back to RVN with me. He said he didn't think so; it was way too big. But he would see what he could do. He must have made a special effort for this fellow officer, as it was loaded onto the flight. I was told that it would be delivered to my squadron. Sure enough, about four to five days later I went to the club after a hard day's flying. Two guys were sitting on a huge cardboard carton that had my name on it. I now had the fanciest foot locker in Vietnam.

I also had bought a complete new wardrobe and a nice collection of monogrammed shirts, and a lot of wonderful memories.

Going to Da Nang for R&R, I had the dubious pleasure of riding in a Sikorsky H-37 "Mojave." It was going my way. On final approach it shook so hard that I thought the fillings in my teeth were going to shake out.

The front clam-shell doors opened out. The troops could drive a jeep into one of these.

The H-37s were slow, cumbersome Sikorskys, used only for hauling cargo and passengers between bases.

Aptly, their call sign was, "Junkman."

Their external-load capability was less than that of the H-34.

Vietnamese Women

Except for the occasional hootch maid, we never had any contact with Vietnamese females. It was just too scary to contemplate, for most of us. The Viet Cong owned the night ... to go off base at night to the local village was to ask to be killed; at least so we thought. Picture a base full of macho, masculine, horny men, all afraid to go off base in search of women.

We were told that the women who were out there were, in addition to being Viet Cong sympathizers, also dosed up with all sorts of heinous venereal diseases that would cause our penises to fall off. Even worse, some were said to have diseases so awful that if we caught one we would be packed off to a secret VD ward for the rest of our short lives, until we died. These diseases were said to have no cure, we would simply just be listed as MIA, and never see our loved ones and home again.

We even heard stories of women who rigged razor blades in their vaginas to cut a fellow's penis to shreds. I heard this story repeated as truth as late as January 2012. We didn't actually believe that shit, but ... why take a chance? I never went off base at night to a village. I went off base only once during the daytime and then briefly and very nervously outside the gate at Ky Ha.

One of the pilots at Phu Bai had a larger ration of hormones than most of us. He would grab a clipboard and make a tour of the local village whorehouses, "inspecting" the girls. He always returned to base alive and intact with a grin on his face. He invited others to go along, but no one ever took him up on the offer.

I don't know how he got away with that without being killed - or dis-membered.

My "Girl Back Home"

Sandy was my girl back home. I can't relate about Sandy without telling the magical way in which we met and the wonderful time we had on our very first date. I was based in New River, the Marine Corps Air Station (MCAS) adjacent to Camp Lejeune, in North

Carolina. We hated the place as it was very isolated. There was a definite shortage of eligible females there, and NO night life. NONE. ZERO. ZED. ZILCH. We could go to downtown Jacksonville any time night or day, and all we would see was Marines in uniform.

As pilots we had the perfect escape, because we were required to fly many hours of cross-country flying as part of our training. As frequently as possible, we put together a trip away from base. Unfortunately, or perhaps fortunately, we were limited in our range and the places we could go to, so we often ended up going to Washington, D.C. We flew into either the Marine base at Quantico or Andrews AFB.

One weekend Mike Kennett, Al Cizmesia and I flew up to Andrews. After securing our machines, we went to the base officer's club for dinner. As we were seated, it just happened that I sat facing a saucy, petite redhead with great big brown eyes. She was with a couple and seemed to be the "odd man out." Over dinner her eyes and mine met many times. My buddies and I discussed the captivating beauty of the spicy little woman, but none of us could figure a suave way to meet her without risking embarrassment or, even worse, rejection. We finished our dinner and retired to the bar to work on lubricating our personalities.

While having a drink or two at the end of the busy bar, lamenting the fact that that Air Force guy had two beautiful women and we had none, a strange man walked up and said to me, "Did you like the looks of that little redhead?" To be honest, I at first did not know who he was talking about. I did not recognize him. I had not looked at him enough to recognize him as the man who sat the next table with the two young women with his back to me. My buddies helped me out of my confusion, introductions were made all around, and I had a date for the night. I bid my buddies a hasty adieu and met Sandra.

Sandra was a college speech teacher, traveling with her best friend, Dorothy. They had come down from Boston so that Dorothy could meet up with her boyfriend, the Air Force officer who recruited me to be Sandy's date. Sandy was from a much different culture than I was. I was a basically an uneducated technically minded person from

California; she was a college teacher, Jewish, raised on the East Coast.

Sandy became the love of my life. I called her from New River frequently. I flew commercially to DC and saw her once again, and then before Vietnam I drove to Boston and spent a week with her prior to driving across the country to Travis Air Force Base in northern California, where I departed to the war. She showed me the sights of Boston. We took a long weekend and drove to Montreal where I met her parents, and we spent time with close friends of hers in Connecticut. We stayed later than we should have. Racing back to Boston late on a Sunday night, she wrote a pop quiz for her students on the back of an envelope because she had done no preparation for her speech class at Emerson University the next day. A gust of wind sucked her pop quiz out the window of my car, and she had to start over.

Sandy and I corresponded the whole time I was in Vietnam. Upon my return, I visited her in Bloomington, Illinois, where she was then teaching. She visited me on the West Coast for a few days. We went to Disneyland. After that, we drifted apart. After a couple of years, I called some mutual friends. They told me she had gotten married.

Captain Hill hits an ambulance

Captain Tom Hill and I brought in a load of wounded to Dong Ha airstrip. We idled on the loading apron beside the runway while the wounded were off-loaded into a military ambulance.

Captain Hill was eager to get back out to the field and rescue some more wounded Marines. He got a little over-eager. Without clearing himself, and faster than I could stop him, he hurriedly started the helicopter rolling forward, then kicked left rudder to turn the helicopter onto the runway. Too fast! The tips of the tail rotor blades walked across the top back right corner of the ambulance, cutting huge gashes into the metal frame and making one hell of a loud noise. The tail rotor blades were destroyed. We had no choice but to shut down and have the helicopter towed off for repair. That was called "sudden stoppage." This, too, was also written off to "enemy action," I am sure.

THE ADVENTURES OF A HELICOPTER PILOT

The Seabee bar

One day we flew to Marble Mountain on a routine administrative flight. One of the fellows somehow bought an entire pallet of beer. A pallet of beer was way too much to carry on a single H-34 with a full fuel load that we needed to get home, but we loaded it into my aircraft anyway. Too heavy to hover, I taxied it out to the runway at Marble Mountain, tilted the rotor forward and used the wheels to roll the helicopter down the runway. Without a doubt this was the longest take off roll I have ever done out of necessity. It probably took a good quarter of a mile to get that hog airborne, and then the rate of climb was dismal. Fortunately we took off north, over the bay where there was no danger of ground fire. I took the entire width of the Da Nang harbor to climb high enough to clear Hai Van Pass to the north, and then just barely. By the time we got to Dong Ha, we had burned enough fuel to make a safe landing.

We took the entire pallet of beer to our hootch and piled it in the middle of the floor. We sold shares to our hootch mates and then got down to some serious drinking. We decided we needed a bar, so we traded a couple of cases to our local Seabees to build us a bar. We got a beautiful five-foot long bar made out of one-inch thick plywood for only two cases of beer. Love those Seabees. They loved our beer.

Dan Smithson and I enjoy a cool one after a hard day's flying at our new bar built by the Seabees in exchange for two cases of beer.

Major Dog, team leader

One day in Dong Ha we received an assignment to carry a Marine recon team out into the bush. Recon's job is to sneak around amidst the enemy and report their findings. They were not supposed to engage the enemy but to spy on them, behind enemy lines. Part of the team was a large German shepherd dog. He was the ears and nose of their team. His good hearing and keen sense of smell had alerted the team members to nearby enemy several times. The team members were very attached to the dog. The dog had been trained so well that it growled any time even a friendly Vietnamese came nearby. A couple of times it had to be restrained from attacking our camp workers and hootch maids. I have to assume that the dog was quiet and did not attack the enemy while the team was out on "sneak and peek" patrol.

All the members of the recon team were enlisted and the highest rank among them was perhaps staff sergeant. The dog, however, as a token of love and respect from his team mates, was wearing the golden leaf of a major on his collar, and his name was "Major." The dog was the highest-ranking member of the team.

Major Dog and his Recon team.

Major Dog and handler. The dog's stripes are camouflage paint.

On another day I was riding copilot with a certain major, who shall remain nameless for obvious reasons. A former jet jockey, he thought himself both a natural-born pilot and God's gift to women. He despised the fact that he had been "downgraded" to be a mere helicopter pilot. We had carried a load of military nurses up from Da Nang to Dong Ha. As the young ladies climbed off the helicopter, he tried to blow up their skirts by increasing the RPM instead of pulling up on the collective, which would have had the desired results. Instead of blowing up their skirts, he oversped the engine, making it necessary for us to hop the helicopter over to the shops for an engine inspection.

Taking off to go to the repair shops and still intent on impressing the nurses, he made a hurried take off with the brakes locked. Instead of rolling forward and flying off, the helicopter pivoted on its wheels, rocking forward. The blades came so close to the ground that they scooped up a 4x4-inch post that was lying at the edge of the helipad. The rotor blades hit it, chopping the board to bits and ruining a set of rotor blade tips.

We got an engine overspeed and a blade strike all in one minute without leaving the ground! More "direct enemy action."

I did my share of damaging helicopters. Trying to do a hoist pick-up from a high hover one day out just south of the Rockpile, I got too close to some pine trees and chopped a few feet off the tops. I pretty well ruined a set of blades, but I was able to fly the helicopter home. It had been one of the smoothest helicopters in the squadron, capable of flying normally without automatic stabilization equipment, until I chopped those trees. Fortunately, the wounded Marine below who was supposed to be loaded into the basket was not yet in it. He would have experienced one wild and crazy ride.

Hitting the trees caused a drastic loss of RPM, and we were about to crash onto the Marines below. I had to take immediate and abrupt corrective action to stay airborne. I instantly kicked hard right rudder to reduce the torque on the system to give me more RPM, and simultaneously pumped up the collective, trading that extra RPM for lift. This maneuver hopped us up and over the nearby tree-tops. Clear of the trees, I jammed the stick forward, dropped collective, and dove down the canyon to get forward airspeed so that we could attain translational lift for better aerodynamics, requiring less power, to attain normal flight. We just barely made it. That was another of the battlefield maneuvers I had learned at the bar over drinks.

A time or two we had to pick up wounded Marines who were in deep elephant grass on the side of a steep hill. The giant grass was as big around as a finger and grew to be as high as 13 feet. When we tried to get down to the Marines on the steep hillside, we had no choice but to mow our way into the hillside with our rotor blades. The outer eight inches of the blades were replaceable, so it was no big deal to use them up if necessary. We sounded just like a big lawn mower as we slowly cut into the large weeds. That facilitated us getting down low enough so that the Marines could load a wounded fellow and not have us hover over them for the extended period that a hoist pick-up would take. Usually this was in a place where the enemy was nearby and we did not wish to linger.

I landed my H-34 at the base of the Rockpile to pick up some wounded Marines. They had wandered into an enemy land mine field and had encountered the evil anti-personnel mine called a "Bouncing Betty." This mine is designed to spring up to waist height before exploding. Here such a mine had done its job well. The Marines had several badly wounded.

As I watched, the Marines loaded a wounded, black Marine. One of his legs was blown off above the knee, the other leg missing below the knee. I was impressed by the fact that his skin had changed color to the point where he looked like a spotted gray whale; his skin, in contrast to its natural dark black, was mottled in various shades of gray and brown. *Shock*, I thought. *He must be in a bad way.*

It was then that I noticed that there were some strange, long white things on the stretcher with him. They looked a lot like large, long scissor blades, but very white. What in the world could that be, and why were these strange objects so important that they were being loaded into the helicopter with this badly wounded Marine?

I almost vomited at the instant I realized that the large, white scissor-blade looking objects were the remnants of the Marine's leg bones.

A Long-Dead Marine

We flew out on a mission near the heavy battle area between Cam lo and Gia Lihn, in the area later named "Leatherneck Square." A tank detachment had a KIA (killed in action) they wanted us to take off their hands. We found the tankers and landed at their smoke. The dead Marine had been rolled up in a poncho and strapped to the outside of a tank in the hot, humid weather for several days. He reeked of the rotten, putrefying-meat death stench. It was all we could to keep from vomiting from the smell. The handful of maggots that fell out of the poncho as he was loaded did nothing to alleviate our sick reaction.

A good friend dies

Shortly after 8 May 1967, I flew an admin run to Marble Mountain Marine Air Field just east of Da Nang. I went alone to the officer's mess for lunch. It was always a treat going there for lunch as we were able to get fresh milk, ice cream and salads. These fresh foods were never available at the outlying bases.

First Lieutenant Tom Knowles joined me. This was the same Tom Knowles who had inspired me to join HMM-161 months before. Tom asked me, "Bill, did you hear about Bake?" Whenever somebody asked that question, you knew the answer; you just had to fill in the details. "Bake" was Captain Jon Baker from Chicago. He and I had started flight school together. We were the only two cadets from our class to finish flight school and get our shiny new golden Navy wings and our second lieutenant bars together on the same day in mid-December of 1965.

18 months later, Baker was dead, killed in a mid-air collision with another H-34 on 8 May 1967. He left a wife and toddler son, whom he never met, in Birmingham, Alabama. Killed with him was Captain Jeff Chessnut, another flight school chum, also married, and the two crew members, Michael Gukich and Philip Vanasse.

Before he was killed, Jon used to joke that he had a great idea to protect himself should he ever become a prisoner of war. He said, "I am learning to speak Vietnamese so that I can communicate with my captors. If I can communicate with them, perhaps they will not torture me too much."

He elaborated, "I am learning three phrases of Vietnamese. I think that is all I will need. I am learning:

'Why, yes, I am an American pilot;'

'No, I can't stand pain;' and

'What would you like to know?' "

In reality, knowing Jon, true-blue Marine that he was, he would have never divulged a thing beyond the basic information required by the Geneva Convention: name, rank and serial number.

Four aviation cadets as we passed through VT-5 at Saufley Field near Pensacola in September 1965. We practiced at Bronson Field, and then landed our T-28C airplanes on the aircraft carrier USS *Lexington*. From left to right, NAVCAD Curt Huffman, MARCAD Bill Collier, MARCAD Jon D. Baker ("Bake"), and NAVCAD Marty Drexler. We earned our Navy Wings of Gold 7 September, 1965.

11.
Khe Sanh

The Snake and the Ducks

The recon Marines patrolling out of Khe Sanh, in the summer of 1967 encountered a nine-foot long snake of the boa constrictor variety. They decided it would make a great mascot, so they captured it and brought it back to Khe Sanh. They cleaned the debris out of a fox hole, covered the hole with wire mesh and placed sandbags on the wire around the hole to keep the snake contained.

They put up a sign: BEWARE OF THE SNAKE

After a few days, they realized that the snake would have to eat, so they went to the nearby Montagnard village at Lang Vei and bought two ducks. The Marines lifted the wire, threw the ducks in, expecting to see the snake immediately pounce upon the ducks and devour one or both. Apparently the snake was not hungry just then so it lay still;

nothing happened. Later that night, after all the Marines had turned in, there arose a great ruckus from the snake pit – lots of hissing, quacking and thrashing about. Everybody assumed that the snake had fed.

The next morning, they went out to see the well-fed snake. It was dead. The ducks had pecked out its eyes, killing it. Later that day the Marines erected a new sign: "Beware of the ducks."

Hill 950

We flew to Hill 950, just north of Khe Sanh, to resupply the Observation Post (OP) on top. It was a challenge to land at this hilltop. At 950 meters above sea level, the air starts to thin out pretty seriously, rotors lose lift and piston engines lose power. We calculated our load carefully to make sure we did not have too much weight aboard, and made our approach into the LZ with caution. It was not good to come in with too little power or to let the airspeed get too low which would be a recipe for landing short and crashing down the hillside into the mine field. Fortunately, there was lots of airspace around the hilltop to go around if need be.

A few weeks after our squadron left the area, this hilltop outpost was overrun by the enemy. The enemy had to scramble up an incredibly steep, jungle-covered mountainside carrying all their equipment to accomplish this.

Hill 950 from afar.

The Observation Post on Hill 950.

The Observation Post up close. LZ on far side of open ground.

View from the cockpit of the H-34 while sitting in the Hill 950 LZ, waiting for the cargo to be off-loaded.

THE ADVENTURES OF A HELICOPTER PILOT

The H-34 that crashed while approaching Hill 950 (in background) sits without its tail after being lifted down the hill, awaiting a trip to the shops to be rebuilt.

One of my squadron mates, Tex Crutcher, leans on the tail of the H-34 that crashed going into Hill 950. Tex was not the pilot. This broken H-34 was rescued and brought back to Khe Sanh by an H-53. No one was badly injured in this crash. Note C-130 landing in the background.

The Battles for Hills 881N and 881S

Another mission we flew at Khe Sanh was to support the troops on Hills 881 North and 881 South. This was during the build up to siege of Khe Sanh. The NVA had encroached upon these hills, which were a ring of outposts on the high ground around the air field. The Marines on these hills lived under an unrelenting artillery and mortar barrage. For protection they lived underground in bunkers. The tall teak trees and jungle vegetation had been blown all to hell, and all that was left was a spooky forest of ragged snags, devoid of any foliage whatsoever.

Picture of Hill 881N devastation. What had once been lush, triple-canopy jungle is now a few broken snags.

Our job was to sneak in under threat of mortars and artillery to bring these guys food, water, mail, ammunition and rotate the troops as needed. We brought in fresh Marines and took out broken bodies. The enemy had a spotter somewhere nearby, so he knew whenever a helicopter landed on the LZ. As soon as any helicopter touched down, the spotter called for mortars. We soon learned that we could not make any kind of normal approach, for to do so was to give the spotter too much time to work with. We knew it would be only seconds after touchdown that exploding mortars would threaten our machines, our crews and our very lives.

We developed an adrenaline-filled procedure to negate this threat. We would fly up the valley on the friendly side of the hills, below the level of the hills so that the enemy spotter on the west side could not see us. We then would make a quick, decelerating, climbing-right button-hook turn and flop over into the LZ. The enemy observer really did not know until we landed that we were there. Once he saw us, he then had to radio his mortar squad somewhere to the west of his position. The mortar crew would then drop mortars into their tubes. It would take maybe 25 seconds for the mortars to reach the LZ. This whole procedure took a total of about 40 seconds. We got it down to a science. We knew exactly how long we had before we had to be off the ground and away from the LZ.

We would scream up the valley as fast as we could go, make the quick button-hook, climbing-right turn into the LZ, using the climbing turn to decelerate. As we touched down, the crew chief and gunner would dump out whatever cargo we carried. The Marines in the LZ knew we were coming; they would quickly load one or two wounded into the helicopter. Then it was full power and blast the hell out of there! Mortars often impacted the LZ right after we lifted off. By then the Marines on the ground had scurried back into their underground safety. Our squadron never lost a helicopter doing this maneuver, but other squadrons lost many helicopters in those hills.

Mortared at Gia Linh

"Courage is being scared to death … and saddling up anyway."

–*John Wayne*

I was flying with Tim O'Toole, going into a hot LZ somewhere southwest of Gia Linh. The LZ was really hot. Everybody going in and out had been shot at; some helicopters had taken hits. Incoming mortars were common and frequent. That is exactly why we were going into the LZ. There were several badly wounded Marines who needed evacuation.

We made a hot approach, landed in the LZ, and sat exposed on the ground, waiting for the crew to unload the supplies that we had brought in with us. Unloading really took but a few seconds, if that. It often seemed much longer. The crew never tied any cargo down, and when they loaded it, they stacked it right by the door. The crew loaded the boxes of ammunition in first, and placed other supplies on top of them. All the crew chief had to do was pull up on the rope handles of the ammo boxes and dump all the cargo out onto the ground. What took time was loading the wounded Marines.

Sitting on the ground, heavily exposed to enemy fire, I heard a muffled explosion – a mortar fell probably a hundred yards from us. The grunt radio operator reported the obvious to us: we were under mortar attack, and we should depart the LZ as soon as possible. Not too scary, but it told me that the enemy knew we were in the LZ and that they were gunning for us.

During the next 30 or so seconds, which seemed like an eternity, four more mortar rounds landed nearby, each one closer than the last. Each one sounded loud enough to be right next to us, but each explosion was progressively louder and scarier. I began to fear that the very next round would be right on top of our rotor system, blowing us to bits, or at least causing the helicopter to burst into a fireball, crispy-frying us all to death.

I put my left hand on the throttle and brought the engine up to full RPM, and raised the collective up to the point where the helicopter was lightly dancing on its tires, eager to leap into the sky in an instant – to safety.

Tim very calmly rolled the engine back to normal RPM and reduced the collective control to the bottom stop. Once again I rolled it up to full throttle and gave a little tug on the collective to begin an ascent. I was not trying to take control of the helicopter from Tim; I was simply communicating to him that it was time for us to be getting the hell out of there! I again had the helicopter as ready as it could be without actually lifting it off the ground. Tim once more gently pushed down on the collective and rolled the throttle back to ground idle. I thought I was going to mess myself. The next mortar round sounded like it landed right next to us behind the helo. In my mind I saw the explosion and could see the dirt from the blast being thrown against the helicopter. I imagined pieces of hot shrapnel ripping through the helicopter toward me.

The enemy had our range. The next round would be right on top of us.

It reminded me of a time in flight school at Whiting Field when I was "home" in my room because I was sick with a cold. Normally we could never be in our rooms during the day because we were always supposed to be at class or flying. The cadet officer of the day came down the long hallway, inspecting rooms to make sure no one was malingering. As he came down the hallway looking into each room, he slammed each door behind him. The sound of the mortars reminded me of those barracks doors slamming, except these slams were deadly mortar explosions meant to harm us, to kill us. Each slam was closer and louder than the previous one; each slam more threatening, more ominous. I just knew the next door to slam would be mine. When I had been sleeping in the barracks during working hours it was because I was sick; now I felt with the next slam I was about to be dead!

After what seemed to be forever, the wounded Marines were finally on board. Tim coolly added power to our engine, and we leapt off to safety, somehow avoiding ground fire on the way out as we had done on the way in. We escaped without a scratch on any person or any part of the helo. I am sure to this day that the enemy had walked the mortars in on us until they had our exact range, and the next round would have been right on top of us, but I think they must have run out of mortar rounds at that very time, allowing us to escape.

Some poor bastard in an NVA supply regiment spent several months humping a load of mortars all the way down the Ho Chi Minh Trail just to have them expended getting our range. I'd bet if he were watching, he said to himself, "Shit! If only I had carried one more round!"

Gia Linh was the site of a major artillery duel with the NVA across the border in North Vietnam. We hauled many medevacs out of this area and nearby Cam Lo. Hyne's and Stroupe's dual crash occurred very near here.

One of my favorite cartoons in the Army Times was the "Sergeant Mike" series; one depicted two soldiers in a fox hole looking up at a helicopter. One says to the other, "I wish I was up there, wishing I was down here."

Another famous cartoon of the era was the Pogo cartoon in which Pogo says, "We have met the enemy and he is us."

For money we used MPC, "Military Payment Certificates." This was to keep U.S. dollars off the black market. They came in all denominations, down to five cents.

6 July, 1967

At 22:45H, pilots of helicopter YZ-82 observed two missiles from North Vietnam headed directly at his flight of four helicopters orbiting over YD 134645. The flight took evasive action and dove for the ground. YZ-82 levelled off at 150 feet and observed one missile explode directly over-head at 2500 feet. No damage or injuries were reported.[12]

[YIKES! I have no recollection of ever hearing about this while I was there. I flew 3.5 hours in the same area that day with David Laviolette, and did not know about this until reading the archives in early 2014.]

Air America

A hot summer day in Dong Ha, we were sitting in the fuel dumps hot refueling (refueling without shutting down). A Huey helicopter hover-taxied into the turbine engine refueling area nearby. This was not a drab green U.S. Army Huey. It was the civilian version of the Huey called the Bell 205. It was silver on its lower two-thirds and had a purple top.

"What the hell is that?" I asked the pilot I was flying with that day.

"Oh, that's Air America – the CIA," he replied.

Then I noticed the small, discrete lettering on the side of the aircraft, *AIR AMERICA.*

"Too spooky for me," I said. "I don't want anything to do with that spying business."

Little did I know at the time, but in less than three years, I would be flying for the company in Laos.

---

12 Texas Tech. University archives, Command Chronology of HMM-363, 6 July, 1967

12.
A Borrowed Story

Paul Gregoire's story

At a POPASMOKE reunion in Las Vegas 1988 I heard this story from Paul Gregoire. I had to include it, with his permission.

Paul was tooling along, fat, dumb and happy one day at 2,200 feet, just south of Chu Lai somewhere, when his aircraft was laced by tracer bullets, hitting the fuel tanks.

"Sir, we've been hit!" said the crew chief over the intercom.

Before Paul could respond, the Sergeant said, "Sir, we have FIRE in the cabin!"

"Use the fire extinguisher!" Paul yelled over the intercom.

"Already have sir, it's all used up, and the fire is getting worse!"

Paul had already started an autorotation instantly upon hearing the word "FIRE!" and the aircraft was plummeting out of the sky, approaching at the rate of 4,000 feet a minute. The helicopter was only seconds from the ground, but Paul did not want to waste any time in getting down. A high-octane gasoline-fed fire was bad enough, but he knew it was only a matter of seconds before the gasoline fire, whipped by the slipstream of the plunging helicopter, would ignite the magnesium body of the helicopter; then it would only be 15 seconds until the entire helicopter and its crew would be consumed in a white hot, star-bright incandescent flare!

Under normal conditions, in a controlled descent, in balanced flight, it was difficult to get the old H-34 to descend at a rate greater than 2,800 to 3,000 feet per minute. But we Vietnam pilots, seasoned veterans of combat by now, had learned a lot about the machine and how to get the most from old beastie. We had learned how to coax more out of her than the handbook said was possible, and how to get her to respond to demands never imagined by the engineers who designed her. This was a case where the absolute limits were demanded, with no margin for error, and no forgiveness for hesitation or ignorance.

Paul knew his machine well. He pushed it well beyond limits. He threw it over on its side as far as he dared to reduce the vector of lift in the vertical direction; the effect of this was to increase the rate of descent. He stomped on the right rudder pedal to get the aircraft out of balanced flight as much as possible in order to further reduce the efficiency of the helicopter's rotor systems and to further increase the rate of decent. Right rudder was the choice here because that choice also tended to increase RPM.

Paul also allowed the RPM to increase well past the limits for normal flight. It didn't matter anymore for this helicopter if the rotor system was over sped beyond limits; it would never fly again – there was no doubt about that in anybody's mind – had anybody taken time to think about it. Paul's mission was to keep the crew alive so they could fly again. And breathe, and eat, and laugh, run, make love, and simply live to see another day.

Most importantly, though, high RPM was important at the bottom of this ride, if it were to end happily for all involved. Only by having high RPM at the flare-out would there be enough momentum in the spinning rotor system to allow Paul maintain complete control of the aircraft to effect a safe landing.

But the most important action he took, and the one that happened instantaneously and automatically, was the reduction of collective pitch to the bottom. By shoving the collective pitch full down, he caused the usual air flow around the blades to reverse, decreasing lift to the minimum, and initiating a tremendous rate of descent. These combined techniques created the desired maximum highest rate of descent approaching 5,000 feet per minute.

A few seconds were all they had. They expected to die any

second as the magnesium of the airframe ignited and burned them all to death, literally in a flash.

Meanwhile, down in the cabin, the fire was raging out of control. The crew chief was driven out of the cabin. To escape the flames, he climbed out onto the main horizontal landing gear strut, hanging onto the vertical strut for his life in the slipstream of the falling helicopter. The poor gunner, in the rear of the cabin had no such option. The rapidly growing flames blocked his way to the cabin door. Out of sheer survival instinct, he began grabbing boxes of live ammunition, stacking these boxes of high explosives between him and the fire to keep the flames at bay. This was a desperate move, should they even be so lucky as to make it to the ground, because after the helicopter landed, there would be no way for him to escape. There was an emergency window to his left, large enough to jump out of, could he get to it once on the ground, but he was rapidly being forced by the flames to retreat farther and farther into the tail cone of the helicopter, farther and farther away from the windows. Farther and farther from escape.

Throughout this wild ride, Paul maintained control of the machine. No vital flight control cables parted. No part of the magnesium body ignited to create a stupendous Fourth of July display.

Rapidly approaching the ground, Paul flared the helicopter into a hairy nose up attitude to arrest their incredible rate of descent and to slow their mighty forward airspeed. Paul kicked the nose left to clear the now smoke-filled cockpit and to get a good view of the landing area in a rice paddy.

It wasn't one of Paul's better landings, and it was very good thing that it wasn't. The helicopter hit hard and bounced. The crew chief was catapulted a dozen yards forward from his precarious perch on the strut, tumbling into a rice paddy, landing without serious injury. In the meantime, the slightly-less-than-soft landing, combined with the weakening of the airframe by the fire, caused the tail pylon to break away from the body of the helicopter. The gunner, trapped in the tail pylon by the flames, was dumped out like the yolk from a cracked egg and was thrown clear, also without injury.

In Paul's words from here on: "There I sat, in complete shock. I had gotten the aircraft down. It was on fire and burning all around me, and all I could do was sit there. Somehow, before I could even start to move, the copilot got out of his side of the helicopter, climbed down and ran around to my side, climbed up to me and began pulling me out. Then I came to and began helping myself."

As they ran to the awaiting wingman's helicopter for rescue, they had to stop to return fire to the Viet Cong who were shooting at them. Seconds after they fled the helicopter, the magnesium of Paul's helicopter ignited, and it flared to a pile of ashes in the usual 15 seconds.

13.
Da Nang

Marble Mountain Air Facility

After our long, hot (in more ways than one) summer at Dong Ha, our squadron relocated to the Marine Corps Air Facility Marble Mountain, on the beach just east of Da Nang airport. This base would later become known as "China Beach."

Looking north at MCAF Marble Mountain, Da Nang, Vietnam. You can plainly see the air base at top-middle, Da Nang harbor to the top left of the picture, South China Sea to the right. In the lower left is the actual Marble Mountain. If you look carefully you can see the small white spot on top, the LZ for the observation post atop it.

Years later I read in an article in *National Geographic Magazine* that this sacred mountain was a honeycomb. Marines living on top reported hearing music at night but could never determine the source of that music. Because the mountain contained a sacred Buddhist temple, it was "off limits" to our troops. The Marines were not allowed to enter the temple to search it. The temple sheltered an enemy regimental hospital and an enemy regimental headquarters.

Looking south. An H-34 from HMM-363 approaches Marble Mountain to resupply the troops on top of it. You can see the left-over wisps of smoke from a smoke grenade the troops popped to show the pilot the wind direction.

While moving around with HMM-363, wherever we went, Steve Howell would always write on the wall: "The new home of Steve Wilkins and his magical and mechanical band." He refused to explain the significance of that phrase to anyone, just that it was important to him that this be written on each wall in every new hootch we occupied.

We also always wrote on the wall the following quotation, which was one of our heartfelt credos:

"A LETTER OF REPRIMAND IS BETTER THAN NO MAIL AT ALL!"

This was not just a slogan, nor just a funny saying to write on the wall. It reflected our whole attitude. By the time we had been in Vietnam for a while, we began to get pretty cynical, and most of us were pretty pessimistic about surviving the war as we saw people dying violently around us every day. We hauled hundreds of dead Marines, Vietnamese civilians, ARVN (Army of the Republic of Vietnam) and "enemy." Somehow the enemy ceased being the enemy when they were dead. Mostly we were glad it was them, not us.

We developed a feeling of supreme self-confidence. We knew what we were doing a better job than our leaders. Most of the majors and above whom we dealt with directly had not seen combat as helicopter pilots, and they generally made it a point to try to avoid flying into hot situations and to avoid flying in combat at all, if possible. We youngsters had better reactions and less fear as we had less to lose. The majors usually had wives and families.

I personally observed senior officers getting overly concerned about their careers once they were promoted to major. It seems that it suddenly occurred to them they were too old for the airlines, but did not yet have their Marine Corps retirement secured. They had to prove themselves fit for further promotion, lest they be discharged before they made retirement. Some of them became real jerks for a while during this period of their lives.

We used to joke behind their backs that once an officer was promoted to major, he would get orders to go to the hospital for a frontal lobotomy, where one-third of his brain would be removed. After making lieutenant colonel, he again reported to the hospital, where the docs would re-install a bit of that missing brain. This rebuilding of the brain continued with each promotion until the officer made general, then he would be a normal human again.

With the combination of feeling invincible and supremely confident, we developed an attitude that only we could do it properly. Judging by results, that was generally true. We knew we were the best, and we didn't care if we offended anybody too much. After all, what could they do to us? Make us helicopter pilots and send us to Vietnam? In our minds they couldn't do much worse to us, except perhaps make us grunts and send us out into the field, as FACs.

With the contradictory attitudes of "It don't matter because I'm going to die soon anyway" and "You can't do anything to hurt me," we developed the overall basic credo of a Marine we called the "Give a Shit" attitude of permeating indifference. The only thing that really mattered to us was to be there for our Marines out in the field. We would bust our tails to get out the wounded, or to get ammunition or supplies to those Marines in the field, regardless of the conditions.

Our attitude became "Accomplish the mission or die trying."

Even though I had not attended boot camp and had not been to OCS at Quantico, I became thoroughly imbued with the "gung ho," and "Semper Fi" attitude of all Marines. I bonded with my fellow pilots and put my life on the line to assist my Marines in the field.

A good example of this attitude was Captain Courtney. I heard that he was directly ordered to not fly out to a very hot LZ after dark in very low visibility. He did so anyway and successfully rescued severely wounded Marines. He did this by having Puff[13] throw out a large parachute flare and he then spiraled down through the soup (clouds) circling down around the descending flare to the outpost. For this brave action he was awarded a Silver Star. Rumor was he also got a letter of reprimand for the same flight for disobeying orders.

---

13 Puff was short for "Puff the Magic Dragon," a World War II C-47 transport, converted into a gunship. Also known as "Spooky," it had three 7.62mm machine guns mounted in the cargo bay. Each gun could fire 6,000 rounds per minute. (100 rounds per second or 18,000 rounds a minute) out the left cabin window. As the pilot flew left circles around a target area at 3,000 feet altitude, this combination could put a bullet into every square foot of a football field in 20 seconds. To watch Puff working from afar, because every third or fourth round was a tracer round, was like watching a huge, fire-breathing dragon, licking the ground with a fiery tongue.

Here is what a hilltop outpost looked like from above. This is a round hilltop with steep slopes down in every direction, surrounded by trenches full of booby traps and mines and Marines with machine guns. The triangular shape allowed for machine guns to fire on any approaching enemy from any two corners of the triangle. Still, these outposts got overrun at times.

The rescue of Lieutenant Barr

I was flying formation on the wing of First Lieutenant James Barr on one of the safest missions in our repertoire, a simple administrative shuttle. We departed MMAF, headed south west. Barr carried a colonel and his assistant to several outposts so he could visit each place to inspect that his troops were battle-ready and to give them a morale boost. Several of these outposts were up river valleys. For safety's sake, after flying up these river valleys, we normally flew back out toward the coast, then along the coast for a few miles to then enter and proceed up the next river valley.

We knew the enemy usually held the terrain between river valleys, making it a bit risky to fly over that forested high ground directly between outposts. This day Barr must have been feeling confident and cocky. He decided to fly directly from one outpost to another, cutting right over the precarious high ground possibly occupied by the enemy. He made it over the hills okay – by about 10 seconds. Just after passing out of the danger zone, his engine quit. He fluttered down, executing a perfect autorotation and made a beautiful landing in a large rice paddy. It was a very routine thing for me to fly down and rescue him, his crew and passengers. The present-day Lieutenant Colonel James Barr, USMC Retired swears that we were taking heavy fire as his crew ran from his downed helicopter to mine. I have no recollection of any enemy fire. We took no hits.

(This was a bonding moment for Jim Barr and me. We reconnected at a reunion in Washington, D.C. about 1988, and have been best of friends ever since. He was the best man at my marriage to my second wife, Carla, in 2003. We continue to get together occasionally, even though we live a thousand miles apart.)

The Marine Corps had a whole separate department dedicated to the rescue downed helicopters called "Sparrow Hawk." As soon as any helicopter went down, the sparrow hawk crew launched and brought a small unit to protect the helicopter. A second helicopter carried maintenance personnel to prepare the helicopter for lifting. These Marines quickly folded the blades and the tail and fitted a heavy cable to the rotor system of the disabled machine. Then a huge CH-53 or a Sikorsky Sky Crane would lift the helicopter away to home base for rebuild and repair. Thousands of helicopters were rescued from the field in this manner during the Vietnam War.

Barr's helo was rescued, repaired by our very proficient mechanics and was returned to service with our squadron at Marble Mountain. My good friend Tim O'Toole was the post-maintenance test pilot. Before actually flying the machine, part of the normal ground check with the engine and rotor blades turning was for Tim to individually shut off each of the two hydraulic pumps to make sure the other was working. Somehow the mechanics, several inspectors and test flight pilot Tim all missed that the hydraulic lines were crossed during the rebuild.

Because of the crossed lines, when one system was turned off to test it, the other took absolute control. When Tim flipped off the primary system, the aircraft rolled violently over in the abutments and beat itself to death. This is called this a "hard-over." Fortunately, there was no fire, and no one was hurt, except perhaps Tim's pride. The aircraft was totaled. After these two bad incidents, thinking of it as a jinxed helicopter, the maintenance officer had it stripped of all usable parts and had the smashed, broken hulk fork-lifted out to the bone yard, to be abandoned there forever.

Night TAOR

My good friend and ally Eddie "Odd Job" Allen and I were getting drunk every evening at Marble Mountain Officer's Club. At the bar we happened to make friends with "Red," the tall, thin, bespectacled, red-haired chief warrant officer in charge of the administration department of our squadron. One night he told us that the powers-that-be had come up with a new scheme to protect the city of Da Nang and the local bases from mortar and rocket attack. They had decided that two helicopters would be assigned to orbit the Da Nang area all night long, every night, weather permitting, to watch for the flashes of rocket or mortar attacks. This was to be called night Tactical Aerial Observation Reconnaissance, or Night TAOR.

One helicopter would be an H-34 from our squadron; the other would be a Huey gun ship loaded with machine guns and rockets, prepared to counter-attack instantly should any missile or mortar launches be observed. Since Eddy and I were down to our last three weeks or so in Vietnam, this seemed like a good thing to volunteer for, as it would keep us off the daily schedule of going into potentially hot landing zones.

We could now easily get in our required night flying for months in advance, get our quota of instrument approaches for at least the next six months, and all the while be safe from bullets and mortars in hot landing zones. We would also always be flying over or close to one of the airfields around Da Nang, so if we had any mechanical problems, we could land immediately. No one else wanted this job because of the long nights and the boredom involved.

Again we overcame our aversion to volunteering, and stepped up to do this boring mission.

Hooray! No more combat flying for us. No more hot LZs, no more bullets, no more mortars! We felt relieved. We also liked it because this gave us every other night off from work to go to the club. We could sleep in every other morning with impunity from being called upon to go combat flying with a hangover. This was perfect! For the next three weeks I flew about 22 hours, boring holes in the dark sky around Da Nang.

Captain Eddy Allen and I became fast friends during this time of night TAOR flying. We got drunk on the alternate nights and attended every party held on our nights off. During one of these parties, a guitar player, John (JR) Watts, taught us the "Robin Song." Occasionally Eddie and I would perform a duet of this song for the other pilots:

> As I awoke one morning, as all young things are born,
> A robin perched upon my sill to sing of coming morn.
> She sang a lovely lullaby, so sweetly did she sing,
> That thoughts of joy and happiness into my heart did spring.
> As she sweetly singing perched, she paused a moment's lull,
> I gently closed the window ... and crushed her fucking skull.

Fear Strikes!

About a week short of my rotation date (my day to depart the war zone back to the United States – to go home) Bill Elmore and I were flying night TAOR droning circles around Da Nang. The air controller called us and asked if we could participate in a medevac. An LZ nearby had badly wounded Marines and the regular medevac helicopters were fully engaged and unavailable. What could I say? No? Not. We took down the LZ information and turned toward it.

I instantly became extremely apprehensive and nervous. I thought that it was fateful that I should be called into a hot LZ just a week before my rotation date. If I were going to be killed, this would be the time and place! My fear affected me physically. My hands began to tremble and flutter around uncontrollably. I felt very afraid.

I was having a panic attack.

I didn't feel confident that I could do the approach. But I couldn't allow myself to show fear, so I mustered up my calmest, most controlled voice and told my copilot, Bill, "You got it, you do this one." I had confidence that this new guy could probably get us down, and I hoped that if I really had to, I could take the aircraft away from him and fly it. Elmore took the controls and flew us toward the LZ in a competent and skillful manner. Before we arrived over the LZ, the regular medevac chopper returned to duty. Our participation was cancelled; we flew back to our orbiting boredom. I never knew if Bill detected my fear.

I never have had that same fear reaction to any event, before or since, ever.

On 2 September 1967, three weeks after I left Vietnam, Bill Elmore was doing this "safe" job when he had a mid-air collision with the Huey gunship. The collision destroyed Bill's rotor system. Bill and his entire crew perished as his aircraft plummeted to earth. The Huey lost its skids and its tail rotor drive, but a skillful pilot was able to get it down and slide it onto a runway without rolling it over. No one was injured in the Huey.

Falling asleep on final approach

One of my very last flights in Vietnam early August 1966, I flew copilot for night TAOR with good friend and hootch-mate Captain Gary Connolly. We had been taking turns flying all night long. The sun was rising, the threat of mortar or rocket attack was over. We could RTB (return to base), get some breakfast, and sleep until we awoke. We then had another night off to once again get drunk.

I was flying our H-34 on final approach, I was fatigued and nodding-off-sleepy, when Connolly said those welcomed words, "I've got it." I was glad to relinquish control of the aircraft. As I did, I happened to look at the clock in front of me and notice the time, saying to myself, *Great, only a few more seconds and I can relax and go to sleep.* As I said this to myself, it must have been the power of suggestion, because I instantly fell asleep. My head falling down woke me up. I looked at the clock and realized that I had only been asleep for a couple of seconds because the second hand had moved only a few ticks.

We were still on short final approach, a flight sequence that only lasts for half a minute at most. During the next 20 seconds, while I watched the second hand of the clock move through those 20 seconds, I fell asleep and woke up six times.

Captain Gary Connolly, former fellow MARCAD.
Connolly had a plaque on his wall after the war:
"If ever there was an event that blew your mind, getting shot at was it."

Connolly and I became best of friends. After our Vietnam experience, we both went over to Air America to fly for the air arm of the CIA, on the other side (not *for* the other side) of the Ho Chi

Minh Trail. We shared a lifetime of adventures. In 1972 he pulled my backside out of a tight spot in Laos. That is a story for another time. I was never able to return the favor as he died in a crop dusting accident on 2 July, 1975, near Napa, California, at age 32.

Judging by results, it seems that the night TAOR must have worked, because once we began to do it there were no mortar or rocket attacks during our watch. The enemy probably knew what we were doing.

A Second R&R, Hong Kong

Another benefit of hanging out with Red from admin was that we picked up a second R&R, this time to Hong Kong. It seems that a couple of our buddies in another squadron had gotten themselves into a bit of legal trouble by acting out at the officer's club at the USAF base in Da Nang. They were in trouble enough that they could not take their scheduled R&R trip to Hong Kong. Even though we had only two weeks left in Vietnam, Red arranged for Eddie and me to substitute for them. Again we volunteered.

Off we went to Hong Kong for another grand adventure. Red joined us.

There was a disco night club in the basement of the Ambassador (Later the Hyatt) hotel where we were staying. Descending the stairs, I encountered an attractive young woman with her parents. They seemed to be departing. I acted quickly and asked her to dance. She briefly conferred with her parents, and they agreed to stay for short while so we could dance a few. Her father seemed to be impressed with the fact that I was a "helicopter leftenant" as he put it with his most proper British accent. Evelyn and I danced and danced, and had a great time. Her parents waited patiently.

When it was time for them to go home, I was pleased to receive an invitation to go boating with them the next day on their yacht, an elegant replica of a small Chinese junk. Evelyn's father was the owner of one of the most famous restaurants in the colony, if not the entire world. The next day we motored the yacht around the island to a quiet cove and had a nice potluck picnic lunch. There were three other older couples on board, friends of the family. Evelyn and I had a great day getting acquainted, eating lots of great food and just lazing about in the sun. Mrs. D. loved me because I had a voracious appetite, would eat anything, and was not shy about going for seconds. Many of Mrs. D.'s older friends were unable to eat this or that due to some dietary restriction or another. I could tell she loved playing Jewish mother.

At one point, Evelyn and I were sitting on the fantail of the yacht talking, our feet hanging over the edge of the boat where none of the "oldies" (to borrow an Australian phrase) could see. Our feet brushed together, accidentally at first, then deliberately, then aggressively. Soon Evelyn was pushing her big toe in between my toes, and gently stroking it in and out, and then in and out again. That was very exciting. There was no mistake in that invitation.

We adjourned to my hotel room for an afternoon tryst. It came to an end when she happened to phone home to check in with her mother. He mother had found birth control pills among Evelyn's things, and she was incensed that her innocent little daughter would have them. Evelyn had to go right home. We managed to get together again. Evelyn had, the day I met her, just returned from Switzerland where she had been sequestered in an all-girls school for many months. (Not too sequestered, I'm thinking.) I enjoyed her delightful company for several days. I left Hong Kong with wonderful memories, unlike those of any of my buddies.

As the Pan American Clipper took off from Kai Tak airport to return me to Vietnam, I had a great view of Hong Kong out the window of the Boeing 707. As we climbed away I said to myself, knowing somehow with full certainty, *I'll be back.* I was very, very right. Less than three years later, Hong Kong became a frequent stop for me while I flew for Air America out of Udorn, Thailand.

Six months after leaving HKG, I was sitting at my desk at the Marine Corps Air Facility Tustin California. My sergeant handed me a piece of personal mail. It was a letter from Evelyn. But how did she find my address? I had not bothered to exchange addresses with her, knowing full well that our little fling was not going to lead to anything serious. I certainly was not ever going to fly to Hong Kong to see her, and I wasn't going to telephone her long-distance clear across the Pacific Ocean just to chat.

She did not have my address either, so she had simply addressed the envelope:

Monsieur Lt. William Collier
United States Marine Corps
Vietnam

That letter arrived in Vietnam after I returned to CONUS. It bounced around to several addresses in Vietnam, then went to Headquarters Marine Corps, Quantico, Virginia and then found its way around bases on the West coast for a while. When it finally found me, it was covered with forwarding stamps and messages from many postmasters. There is little space left on the envelope that is not stamped with some forwarding information.

I feel a little sad that I never took the time to answer a letter that worked so hard to get to me. A few years later, passing through HKG while flying for Air America, I phoned her parents. Her father informed me she had gotten married.

Press people

While we flew all around I Corps, we often carried reporters and photographers. We disliked carrying these people because for every press person we carried, we felt it was one fewer Marine we could carry, or that much precious cargo needed by our Marines that we could not carry. This was especially important to us when we were carrying wounded Marines out of the field. It got to the point that whenever we saw someone pointing a camera at us, we flipped off the photographer. Somewhere, buried deep in the Marine Corps archives, there are hundreds, perhaps thousands, of pictures of Marine Corps helicopter pilots flipping off the photographers of those pictures.

It is hard to see, but in this picture approaching Phu Bai from the north, pilot John App is flipping off the camera.

Even though my upgrade to HAC had been delayed for weeks, I eventually made "section leader," which meant I could lead two aircraft on flights making our rounds to various LZs.

Just before leaving Vietnam, I was further promoted to "division Leader," which meant I could now lead four aircraft. I never made "strike flight leader" which means I could have led the entire squadron into an assault somewhere.

30 July, 1967. "At approximately 0330H, YZ-80 crashed in the vicinity of AT 902518 [near Da Nang] after hitting obstacles and trees on take-off while attempting an emergency medevac. Both aircraft received small arms fire from 3 positions during approach and take-off. (Texas Tech archives, Command Chronology, HMM-363 this date.) Since there was no mention of deaths or injuries, we can safely assume no one was hurt.

During July 1967, helicopters of HMM-363 flew 1,379.1 hours, carried 2,864 passengers, hauled 443 tons of cargo, and rescued 1137 wounded Marines from the field. I flew 68.2 hours.

Only One Hit

It seems to me that after my two most horrifying missions, I had a lucky charm in my pocket. I had scary experiences, but I always somehow managed to avoid getting hit by enemy fire. Our command chronology states that almost every day that at least one of our machines took fire. As often as not, at least one of our aircraft took hits.

With all this danger and harrowing trips into dangerous places, I am amazed that I took only one hit in my helicopters during my nearly 13 months in Vietnam. There were a few times that I flew into and out of hot landing zones with both machine guns blazing.

That single hit is really a misnomer, as rather than the bullet hitting me, I hit the bullet. I was flying Search and Rescue chase on an H-46 carrying a very high official (was it McNamara?) south of Khe Sanh. My job was simply to be there to rescue the official should his helicopter go down. We flew at an altitude of least 4,000 feet above the ground to keep the VIP safe from ground fire.

When we returned to Khe Sanh, my crew chief, pointing up at one of my rotor blades, said, "Look, sir, we took a hit!" The bullet had penetrated the bottom of the thin honeycomb section of the blade but did not go all the way through it, making a small bump in the skin on the top surface of the blade. The path of the bullet was almost horizontal. It was obvious that the bullet had reached the peak of its trajectory and was floating up there in the sky when my blade ran into it. The crew chief offered to dig out the bullet for me, but I declined the offer, knowing full well there would be many more. I was wrong in this. Somehow I never took another hit on my aircraft while was in Vietnam.

I made up for that later while flying for Air America.

12 August, 1967. I flew my last flight in Vietnam without incident.

14 August, 1967. My good friend Gary Connolly flew his last flight in Vietnam.

A few statistics

I started my helicopter combat flying experience in Vietnam with a total of 360.6 hours of flight time, of which exactly 187.5 hours were in helicopters; the rest was in airplanes during flight school.

In Vietnam I flew a total of 764.6 hours of combat helicopter flight hours. I averaged 58.8 hours of combat flying per month for almost 13 months.

Doing some very rough statistics, simply dividing my flight time into overall squadron flight times, and multiplying that small decimal by the total number of medevacs we carried during my time in Vietnam,

I calculate that *I personally carried approximately 375 medevacs* aboard my machines while in Vietnam – an average of better than one per day, one for every two hours I flew. I feel really good about that.

I did have at least one Marine die aboard my helicopter before I could get him to help.

Every time we flew from one point to another that flight was called a "sortie." It took 20 sorties to constitute a mission, and 20 missions to earn an air medal. I earned 23 air medals while in Vietnam.

20 sorties x 20 missions x 23 medals = 9,200 sorties in 764.6 hours.

I lost eight friends in Vietnam. Only one of these was lost to "direct enemy action." Patrick Ott, a former NJC fraternity brother, was lost in Vietnam due to a shipboard "operational incident" while flying F-8U fighter-bombers off a carrier. I saw him very briefly in flight school and never saw him again.

I am pleased to report that for my entire career of 7,000 hours and 32 years of helicopter flying, I have an equal number of takeoffs and landings.

USMC helicopter losses Vietnam

1962-1973

1 to SAMS	(surface to air missiles)*
31 enemy attacks on air bases	(mortars, rockets)
161 operational losses	(non-combat losses.)
248 to AAA & small arms	(bullets of all sizes)
441 helicopters lost total[14]	
150 of these were H-34s	
844 Marine Corps pilots and air crew died	

*"... A CH53 carrying troops in the assault became the first Marine helo known to be shot down by a guided missile. Its starboard engine was blown off by a heat-seeking SA-7. It continued in flight on the port engine until it reached the LZ where it crash landed, with its final mission accomplished and its aircrew becoming reinforcements for the assault troops." [No date found for this incident.] [15]

A short pre-Vietnam anecdote

After finishing Navy flight school in mid-December 1965, I took a month's leave. I then reported to the Marine Corps Air Station New River in North Carolina, adjacent to the famous Marine Corps Base, Camp Lejeune. I had hoped to be assigned to training in the latest new turbine-powered helicopter, the modern tandem rotor Boeing H-46A. I was quite disappointed to be assigned to an H-34 squadron.

At first I was assigned to HMM-365, but several of us bachelors were soon traded off to HMM-162. The CO of HMM-365, Lieutenant Colonel "Pop" Korn, wanted to have more married men in his squadron. It seems it was better for his squadron bowling team to have couples instead of bachelors.

Here we prepared ourselves for combat in Vietnam. We

---

14 (No mention is made of losses to "Friendly Fire.")
15 Statistics and above quote this page from www.popasmoke.com web site

practiced formation flying, formation landings, landing in confined areas, pinnacle approaches and every other maneuver a combat helicopter pilot must know to operate effectively. Our squadron had a couple of guys who had already been to Vietnam, and they gave us the benefit of their experience.

The basic credo of the Marine Corps is that "every Marine is first and foremost a rifleman," so we all had to learn to shoot the M-14 rifle. I missed shooting "expert" by a hair. I shot expert with the .45-caliber pistol. In our times off, we drank a lot. The officer's club was perhaps our first home, ahead of our places to sleep, shower and change clothes, whichever that place was. It could have been in the BOQ or an apartment off base. I actually did both, but found eventually that living in the BOQ was much more to my liking than living off base. I could walk to the O'club.

During these many trips to officer's clubs, we discovered the bachelor bar at Camp Lejeune. The main bar required "Class A" uniforms and stuffy manners. Around to the right side, the bachelor bar was very informal; one could go there in his underwear if he wanted; no one cared. It was a good place to be free and loose.

One night, about mid-May, 1966, several of us were there drinking. On the TV news we watched a report about college kids burning their draft cards. We all compared draft card stories. One fellow said his was taken away when he arrived at Pensacola for flight school. Another said he had returned his to his local draft board when he signed up, and so forth. I realized I had mine still in my wallet. I produced it.

David Golding said, "Let's burn it!" Someone struck a match. Right there in the officer's club at Camp Lejeune we burned my draft card. A grunt major sat at the end of the bar watching the antics of this bunch of crazy young aviators as we burned my draft card. I thought he was going to have a heart attack!

So far as I know, there were no repercussions for this action. It might have looked bad for me had anybody reported that prank to my CO.

14.
Postscript

Returning to the United States, I was assigned to the Marine Corps Air Facility at Tustin, California.

I decided I had had enough combat flying and decided I would terminate my USMC career. I was a reserve on active duty with a contractual end to my commitment. I decided to not extend that commitment past the three required years. At the end of my three years, in mid-December of 1968, I bailed.

Another factor was that when I arrived at my new base in Southern California from Vietnam, I had an audience with a major who placed me in the Marine Aircraft Group 56 group headquarters. I found out right away the meaning of the word officer that I had never contemplated before. "Officer: one who works in an office." I considered myself a professional pilot. I wanted nothing to do with a career of pushing papers. When my time came, I departed to civilian life.

I flew helicopters commercially for 27 years after leaving the Marine Corps, but except for my 30 months with Air America, I never seemed to get financially ahead doing it. I was always on the road to this job or that, this country or that. I never seemed to make a lot of money. I tended to specialize in small "Ma and Pa" type companies where, more often than not, I was laid off during the winter or just got fired when it was expedient for the company. Several times I quit jobs abruptly, usually citing safety reasons.

I spent a lot of winters unemployed, scraping by. I spent the better part of one year all but living in a VW van. I spent one long winter in an older motor home. I drove big rigs for North American Van Lines a few months and lived in the coffin-like compartment behind the driver's seat. I was a lost soul.

A life-changing event

In October 1993, after a summer of helicopter logging near Ketchikan, Alaska, I returned to my home area of Santa Rosa, California. Soon I met a beautiful woman four years younger than I. We began to get very close. As I regaled her with tales of my many travels and adventures, she began to worry that I would once again fly away, deserting her. She very gently, very carefully and very lovingly asked me questions about my feelings [Feelings? I don't got to show you no stinking feelings!] and thoughts and motivations concerning my varied actions in the past, none to which I had ever given any deep thought. She opened me up to think about why I had made so many changes in my life.

Finally one evening, in a warm, cozy snuggle, she quietly asked me if I had ever thought of having psychological counseling. Up 'til then, if a woman had said to me, "Bill, you are all fucked up, and I think you need counseling." I would have thrown all my stuff into my car and been in the next state by sunrise, without so much as saying goodbye. But she did it in such a kind, gentle, loving manner that I instead reflected on the conversations we had been having.

I realized that I just might need a little help here.

I had actually tried counseling three times before on my own. At first it was as marriage counseling as my first marriage disintegrated, but later I tried it again for myself. I knew something was not exactly right with me, but I could not define it. As the computer age dawned, I made a joke to myself that somewhere deep inside me I had a silicon chip installed backwards.

I failed at my first attempts at counseling for two reasons. The first was money. It was very expensive and I had always kept myself quite broke with all my periods of unemployment and moving around. The second reason is that most counselors had no idea about Post Traumatic Stress Disorder, and had no basis to start from even if I had stuck with it. One counselor even sent me to AA. I gave up.

When my new love, Carla, suggested counseling, my first

objection was the cost. I was broke – again – and barely getting by – again. Carla had a degree in psychology and worked in human resources for a major high tech company in Santa Rosa. She was very much a people person and saw something in me that warranted rescuing. She suggested that perhaps I could find a student or intern who might work for half price. For her I was willing to check into it. I made a few phone calls looking such cheap help. About my third call, someone informed me that the Department of Veterans Affairs had free counseling for Veterans.

Free! Yay, free! I could do free.

Many Vietnam veterans got seriously hooked on drugs and or alcohol to self-medicate their symptoms of PTSD. I drank a lot while in Vietnam and while I was with Air America in Thailand and Laos, but I don't think I was a seriously addicted. As soon as I got away from the rough and tumble environment and got a little wiser with age, my drinking diminished to very moderate amounts. But alcohol was a big factor in the early years.

My drug of choice to handle my PTSD was adrenaline. Flying helicopters gave me that adrenaline rush I needed on a regular basis.

Adrenaline was my addiction!

I made an appointment with my local county veteran's service officer, Randy Fowler. Randy was a Vietnam vet, a former Marine Corps sergeant who had been badly wounded about the same time I served in the war. It is possible that I was the pilot who carried him to Delta Med. We hit it off nicely. We talked for an hour. It was painless.

At the end of our session, Randy gave me a simple homework assignment. He said, "Bill, go home and make a list of all the changes in your life since Vietnam." Easy, I could do that. No mind fucking here, just a simple writing exercise, so I went home, grabbed a spiral binder and wrote down all those changes.

I pushed myself back from that writing and said to myself, *This may not be normal.* What I wrote down amazed me ... and this is no shit ... in the 27 years since leaving Vietnam in August of 1967 until the (then) present date of February 1994, I had worked about 80 jobs. I had moved about 50 times. I had gone through women like most guys change the oil in their cars.

I had made some major change in my life on average about every sixth week for 27 years.

I realized that perhaps I was suffering from something a little more serious than an over-developed sense of adventure. I realized that I could use some help. I immediately immersed myself in group counseling with a great bunch of guys. I did some one-on-one counseling with Randy from time to time. I eventually spent six months at the VA Hospital, National Center for PTSD in Menlo Park, California, near Palo Alto. That helped even more. It has taken me almost 20 years as of this writing to finally get myself under control and become somewhat of a centered, grounded person.

I could not have done all this without the support and love of wonderful Carla, who is now my wife and life partner in our retirement in the cozy small northern Idaho town of Sandpoint.

Carla helped me to find my way out of the abyss of confusion and anger that clouded my thoughts and directed my actions in self-sabotaging ways. Sometimes she used a little hard love, but mostly she loved me and very carefully, lovingly and tenderly manipulated my dumb ass until I was able to look at my own shit without being afraid and trying to run away from myself – again!

Like the song says, "I sold my soul, you bought it back for me."

I gave up helicopter flying for good in early 1996.
No more adrenaline rushes for me.

I cheated death many times that I know of. God only knows how many times I came close to dying and did not even know it.

The thing is, helicopters are different from planes. An airplane by its nature wants to fly, and if not interfered with too strongly by unusual events or by a deliberately incompetent pilot, it will fly.

A helicopter does not want to fly. It is maintained in the air by a variety of forces and controls working in opposition to each other, and if there is any disturbance in this delicate balance the helicopter stops flying immediately and disastrously.

There is no such thing as a gliding helicopter. [Wrong!] This is why being a helicopter pilot is so different from being an airplane pilot and why, in general, airplane pilots are open, clear eyed, buoyant extroverts, and helicopter pilots are brooders, introspective anticipators of trouble.

They know that if something bad has not happened, it is about to.

–Harry Reasoner, February 16, 1971
ABC Evening News, during the Vietnam War

15.
Post-Postscript

After leaving the Marine Corps, I become a dashing, devil-may-care, hot-shot helicopter pilot for Air America, the air arm of the Central Intelligence Agency (CIA), in the secret, dirty little war against Communism in the small Kingdom of Laos. Here I once again flew H-34s and then Hueys for another 30 months, for a total of 43 months of combat flying in Southeast Asia.

Airline benefits from Air America allowed me the opportunity to travel extensively on my down times at reduced airline rates. I traveled completely around the world twice, and halfway around and back probably 10 to 12 times. I have visited 45 countries and 47 of the United States.

My experience working for Air America will be the subject of a future book.

For a preview of that adventure-filled experience, look on www.youtube.com for "The Rescue of Raven 1-1."

From Asia, I proceeded to a career as a civilian helicopter pilot for an additional 23 years, for a total of 32 years flying, accumulating more than 7,000 flight hours. This civilian flying will be the subject of another "Adventures of a Helicopter Pilot" book.

LT. W. F. COLLIER
Over 400 Missions

Copter Pilot Hero Home From War

A 24-year-old Marine Corps helicopter pilot has returned home here after serving more than 13 months of duty in Vietnam, with more than 400 aerial combat missions logged.

He is First Lt. William F. Collier, who is a Purple Heart veteran. He has been awarded the Air Medal 18 times and has the presentation of three more Air Medals coming. He has been nominated for the Distinguished Flying Cross.

Lt. Collier was a member of the First Marine Aircraft Wing that helped form the air element of the Marine Corps air-ground team and provided close air support for ground forces c o n d u c t i n g search and destroy missions.

The son of the late William C. Collier of Sonoma, he is the brother of Calvin F. Collier, of 3605 Coronado.

Lt. Collier was commissioned in 1965. Following completion helicopter flight training, the lieutenant was sent overseas.

He now is serving with the Helicopter Medium Squadron 56 at the Marine Corps Air Base, Santa Ana. He received an associate of arts degree from Napa Junior College before being accepted for the officers' training school program.

This article appeared in the Stockton Record, Stockton, California, in the fall of 1967, right after I returned from Vietnam.

The Marine Corps has a very active PR section and it likes to get as much press for itself as possible. Almost everyone had some kind of press release sent to his hometown newspaper regularly.

There were probably other articles about my reporting to and graduating from Navy flight school, going to Vietnam and receiving my first Air Medal.

What is sad for me is that these articles never appeared in my home town newspaper, the *Sonoma Index Tribune*. Just before I left to flight school, I had a bit of a falling out with my stepmother, so during my military career I used my brother Cal's address in Stockton as my home of record. Therefore all press releases were sent to the *Stockton Record*.

No one, save my brother and his family, knew me in Stockton.

There was one small exception to this. The night before I departed for Vietnam, my brother took me to an office party with his coworkers. One of his coworkers, an attractive, charming lady a bit older than I, did me the favor of taking me to a motel and seducing me, giving me a great send-off to the war. We didn't exchange phone numbers or addresses, and I don't remember her name.

Thanks for the great send-off, nice lady, whoever you were.

APPENDIX

GENERAL DESCRIPTION of the H-34D HELICOPTER

(From USN NATOPS manual)

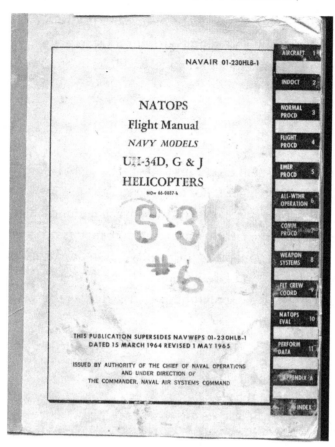

Model UH-34D helicopters are manufactured by Sikorsky Aircraft, Division of United Aircraft Corporation, Stratford, Connecticut. The helicopter is designed for transportation of cargo and personnel (including aeromedical evacuations). Configuration is single engine; a four-bladed main lifting rotor, a four-bladed anti-torque tail rotor, and conventional fixed landing gear. The fuselage is all-metal, semi-monocoque construction and is comprised of three sections: the forward fuselage section, the tail cone (aft fuselage section), and the aft pylon. The forward fuselage section consists of the engine compartment, pilot's compartment, main transmission compartment, cabin, electronics compartment, and fuel tanks. The engine compartment is located in the forward portion of the forward fuselage section. The engine is installed with the drive shaft pointed aft and upward. A hydro-mechanical clutch is installed at the end of the engine shaft. Large clam-shell-type doors which form the nose of the fuselage permit access to the engine for maintenance purposes. Above and aft of the engine compartment is the pilot's compartment which may be entered from the outside of the helicopter or from the cabin. Dual controls are installed in the pilot's compartment. Directly aft of the pilot's compartment is the transmission compartment housing the main gear box. The main drive shaft extends forward and downward from the main gear box and is connected to the hydro-mechanical clutch. The main rotor hub assembly, to which the four main rotor blades are attached, is splined to the top of the drive shaft. Shafting extends aft from the main gear box lower housing to drive the tail rotor. Directly aft of the engine compartment and below the pilot's compartment and transmission compartment is the cabin. The cabin is 11 feet long, 5-1/2 feet wide, and 6 feet high. Entrance to the cabin is through a sliding door on the right side of the fuselage. Provisions are made for the installation of 12 troop seats or eight pole-type litters.

Three multi-cell fuel tanks are installed below the cabin floor in the lower structure of the fuselage. Aft of the cabin is the electronics compartment containing radio, electrical, and electronic equipment. The electronics compartment is accessible in flight through an opening in the aft bulkhead of the cabin. The tail cone extends aft from the electronics compartment. The only equipment installed in the tail cone is the cabin heater unit and the gyro compass transmitter. The tail pylon is attached to the rear of the tail cone. A ground adjustable horizontal stabilizer is installed on the pylon.

The intermediate gear box is installed on the lower portion of the pylon and a shaft extends upward to the tail gear box at the top of the pylon. The four-bladed tail rotor is splined to the tail gear box. To permit moving on an [ship's] elevator 39 by 17 feet; the four main rotor blades are folded parallel to the fuselage, and the pylon is folded forward along the left side of the tail cone.

Length: 65 feet, 10 inches at maximum blade extension
Height: 15 feet, 10 inches
Width: 56 feet with blades extended
With blades and tail folded:
Length: 37 feet long
Height: 14 feet, 10 inches
Width: 12-14feet wide
   (varies according to landing gear configuration)

The H-34 can further be defined as 347 moving parts
flying in loose formation
put together by the lowest bidder
held together by grease.

Seen on helmets and flak jackets of Marines in the field:

"Yea, though I walk through the valley of the shadow of death, I fear no evil, for I am the meanest mother fucker in the Valley."

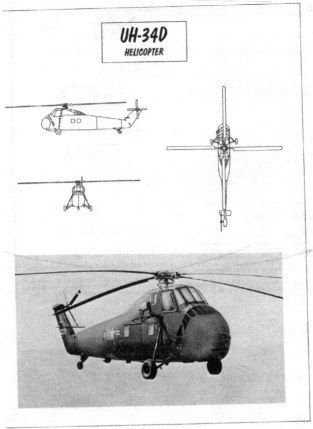

Figure 1-1. The Helicopter

BIBLIOGRAPHY

*Books with an asterisk were written by contemporaries.

1369, H. Lee Bell.*

1500 Feet over Vietnam, Bruce R. Lake*

The Assault on Khe Sanh: An Oral History, Eric Hammel

Author's personal Flight Log Book

Baa Baa Black Sheep, Colonel "Pappy" Boyington

The Best and the Brightest, David Halberstam

Distant War, Marc Phillip Yablonka

Bonnie Sue, A Marine Helicopter Squadron in Vietnam, Marion F. Sturkey*

A Bright and Shining Lie, by Neil Sheehan

Catch-22, by Joseph Heller

Chicken Hawk, by Robert Mason*

"Helicopter Heroes" video about Marine Corps Helicopter Flying in Vietnam, TV History Channel

Illusions, Richard Bach

The Making of a Quagmire, David Halberstam

Masters of the Art: A Fighting Marine's Memoir of Vietnam, Ronald Winter*

NATOPS, (Naval Aviation Training and Operations Procedures) *H-34 Manual*, U.S. Navy.

U.S. Naval Aviation, Naval Aviation Museum Foundation.

popasmoke, Vietnam Helicopter Pilots and Aircrew Association, www.popasmoke.com archives as cited

A Rumor of War, by Philip Caputo

The Siege of Khe Sanh, by Eric Hammel

Sikorsky Helicopter Flight Theory for Pilots and Mechanics, Sikorsky Aircraft Company

The Street Without Joy, by Bernard B. Fall

"Vietnam Center and Archives," Texas Tech. University, Command Chronologies, HMM-161 July 1966 to Dec. 1966, and HMM-363,

December 1966 to August 1967, various pages, as cited in text
http://www.recordsofwar.com/vietnam/usmc/USMC_Rvn.htm
VIETNAM, The Helicopter War, Philip D. Chinnery
"Wartime Vietnam," map by Vietnam Veterans of America

GLOSSARY

AAA. Anti-aircraft artillery.

AO. Artillery Observer.

BOQ. Bachelor Officer's Quarters.

Ceiling. Height of clouds above the ground.

CP. Command Post.

C-Rations, also **C-rats.** Packaged, pre-prepared meals for troops to eat in the field.

Charlie. The Viet Cong, cong, VC, gomer, gook and so on.

Collective. Pilot's lever for changing helicopter blade angle.

Command Chronology. Unit diary of military unit in war.

CO. Commanding Officer.

CONUS. Continental United States. Land of the big PX.

Delta Med. Field hospital.

DFC. Distinguished Flying Cross.

DMZ. De-militarized Zone between So. and No. Vietnam.

External load. Cargo carried under a helicopter on the cargo hook; a.k.a. sling load.

FAC. Forward Air Controller. Pilot who served in the field with the ground troops to coordinate their aviation needs.

Flight Ops/Flight Quarters. When an aircraft carrier is ready to launch or receive aircraft.

Friendly Fire. When our guns or explosive kill our troops.

Grunts. Military term for ground or infantry Marines.

HAC. Helicopter Aircraft Commander.

HMM-XXX. Helicopter Marine Medium No. XXX.

Hootch. Cheap, quickly constructed plywood housing.

I Corps. Northern-most of four military regions in Vietnam.

KIA. Killed In Action.

LSO. Landing Signals Officer. Signals aircraft landing on an aircraft carrier to help them land safely.

"Landshark Charlie." Artillery control center.

LZ. Landing Zone.

MACV. Military Assistance Command, Vietnam.

MARCAD. Marine Corps Aviation cadet going through U.S. Navy Flight School in Pensacola, Florida.

Medevac. Medical evacuation, usually by helicopter.

MIA. Missing in action.

MPC. Military Pay Certificate – used instead of greenbacks.

Mutter Ridge. Highly contested battle area northwest of Dong Ha.

NATOPS. Naval Aviators Training and Operational Procedures manual

NVA. North Vietnamese Army. The enemy. Supporting the Viet Cong.

OD. Officer of the Day.

Ontos. Tank-like tracked vehicle with six 106mm recoilless rifles on top of it.

OP. Observation Post.

Overboost. Too much manifold pressure added to engine.

Overspeed. Too many revolutions added to engine.

Popasmoke. Organization of USMC Helicopter pilots and aircrew. www.popasmoke.org.

POW. Prisoner of War.

PSP. Pierced Steel Planking. Used for creating a runway quickly and cheaply.

PTSD. Post-Traumatic Stress Disorder; Psychological damage caused by traumatic stress. "Shell Shock."

PUFF. Puff the Magic Dragon. A C-47 gunship that could be called upon to rain down hell from the sky.

REMFs. Rear Echelon Mother Fuckers.

RPG. Rocket propelled grenade.

RVN. Republic of Vietnam.

SAMS. Surface-to-air-missiles.

SAR. Search and Rescue.

TACAN. Navigation radio in aircraft.

TAOR. Tactical Area of Recon.

Viet Cong. Indigenous Communist insurgents.

VNAF. Vietnamese Air Force.

XO. Executive officer.

EPILOGUE

After surviving the Vietnam War, Captain Bill Collier continued to have many adventures flying helicopters commercially all around the world. He flew almost every size and shape helicopter produced in the U.S. from the smallest "whirlybird" to the largest CH-53 "Jolly Green." His last position was flying the UH-1 "Super Huey" for the Orange County Fire Department in Southern California. He also flew the French-built Alouette III.

Photo by Mike Satren, Coeur d'Alene, Idaho

In 2008, Captain Bill retired to the small, quiet, peaceful town of Sandpoint, in the Idaho panhandle. He keeps himself busy writing about his 32 years of helicopter flying. Watch for two more "Adventures of a Helicopter Pilot" books, "Flying for the CIA, Air America" and the collection of world-roving civilian flying stories.

He is a life member of several veterans organizations. Sandpoint Chapter 890 of the Vietnam Veterans of America recently rescued a derelict H-34 from the scrapyard. He and his veteran friends have refurbished it enough to make it towable for Fourth of July parades and other veterans' activities. He blogs about it at:
http://dawgdriverforever.blogspot.com/.

Made in the USA
Columbia, SC
19 July 2019